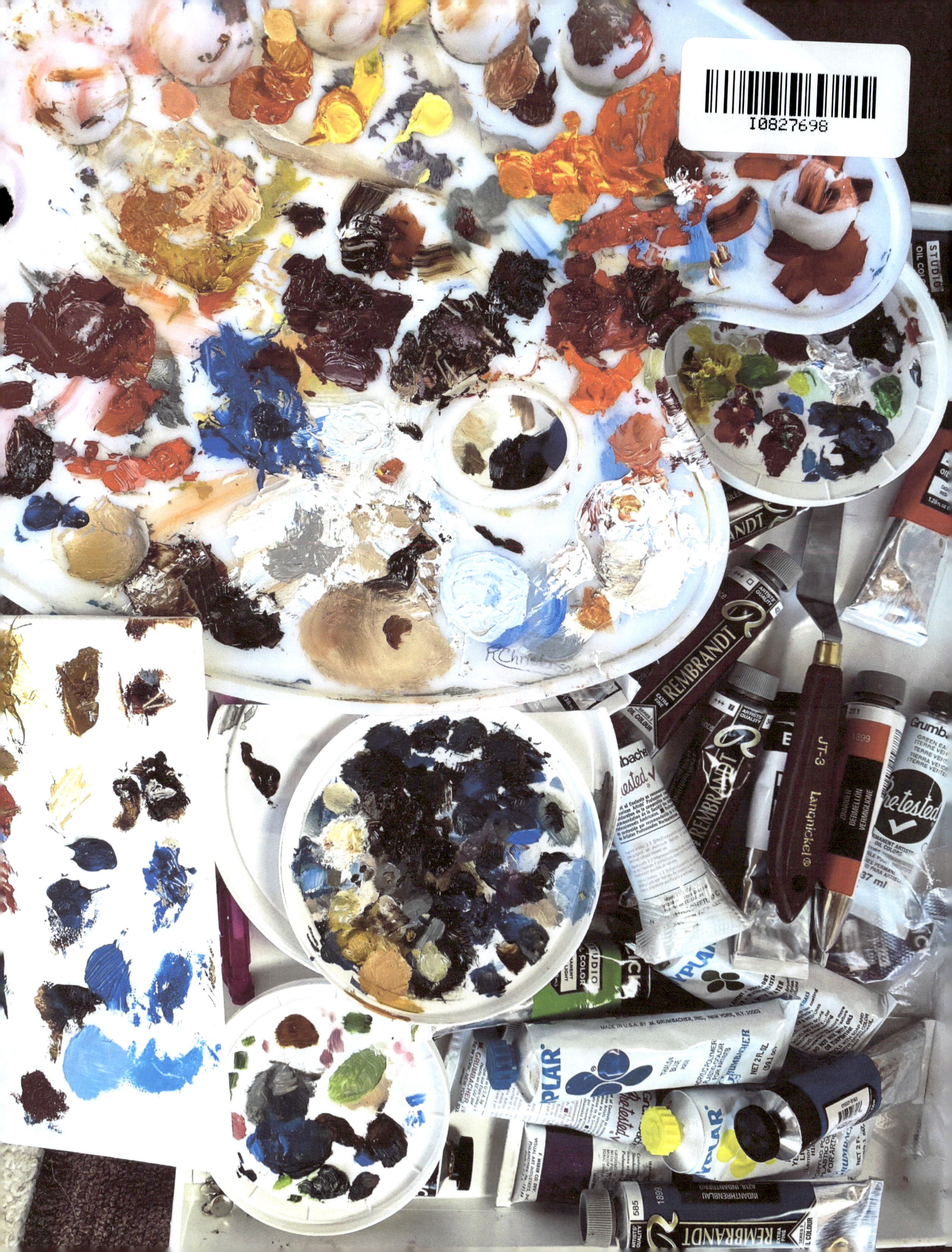
I0827698
REMBRANDT
REMBRANDT
JT-3
Langnickel
REMBRANDT

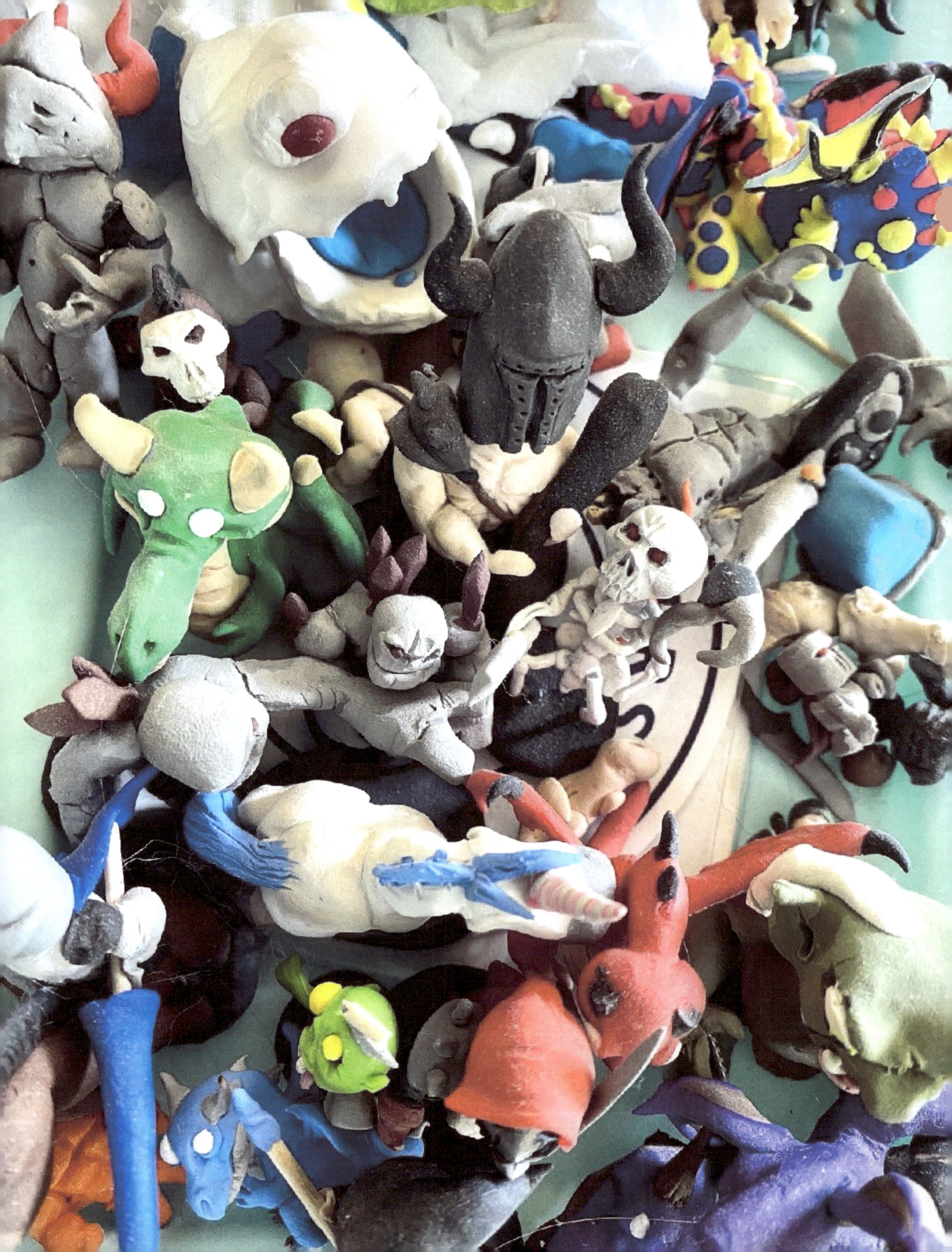

Effervescent Road Trip

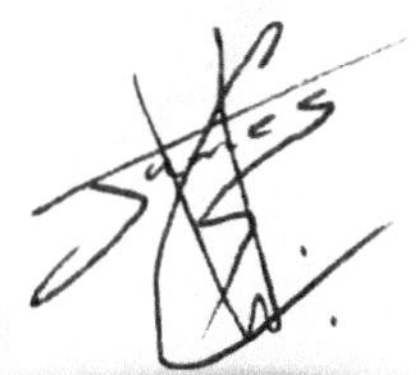

The Art of

James William Christenson

~ Volume 2 ~

Kayto & Co. Publishing
Minneapolis | Minnesota | USA

Effervescent Road Trip
The Art of James William Christenson Volume 2

Copyright © 2020
Authored & Illustrated by James William Christenson
ALL RIGHTS RESERVED.

8860 154th St W
Prior Lake, Minnesota, 55372, USA
jim@jamesartstudio.com
www.jamesartstudio.com

ISBN-13: 978-1-7327129-3-5

Library of Congress Control Number: 2020912395

Kayto & Co. Publishing
Minneapolis, Minnesota, USA
Editor: Jason J. Christenson
Introduction: Dr. Carl R. Christenson, MD

All Scripture quotations, unless otherwise indicated, are taken from the Holy Bible, New International Version®, NIV®. Copyright ©1973, 1978, 1984, 2011 by Biblica, Inc.® Used by permission of Zondervan. All rights reserved worldwide. www.zondervan.com. The "NIV" and "New International Version" are trademarks registered in the United States Patent and Trademark Office by Biblica, Inc.®

This publication is protected under federal copyright laws. Reproduction or distribution of this or any other publication or of the artwork included within, including publications and editions which are out of print, is prohibited unless specifically authorized by writing. This includes, but is not limited to, any form of reproduction or distribution on or through print or the internet, including posting, scanning, or e-mail transmission. For permission to reproduce or display artwork, to commission a work, or to contact the artist, email jim@jamesartstudio.com or visit www.jamesartstudio.com.

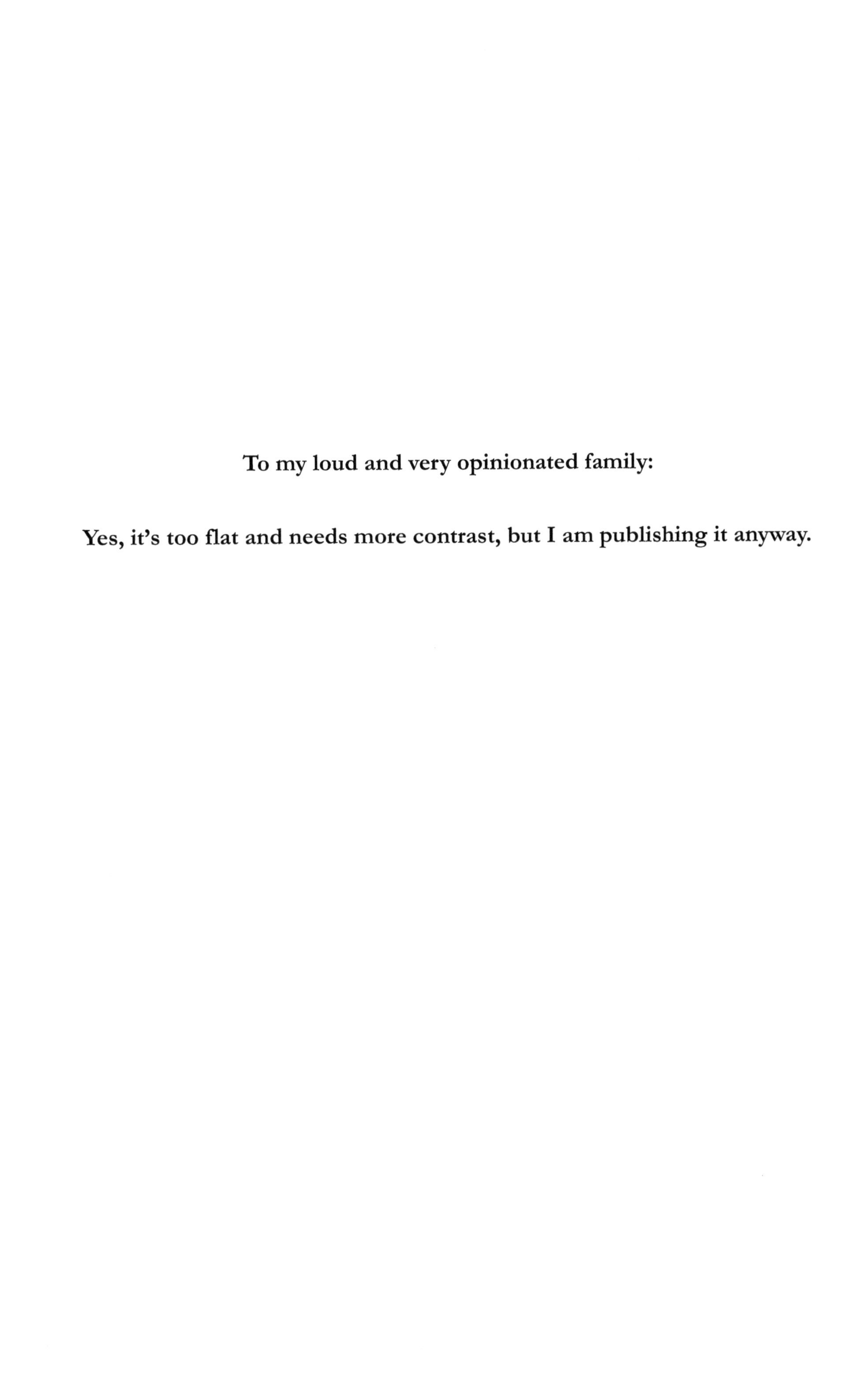

To my loud and very opinionated family:

Yes, it's too flat and needs more contrast, but I am publishing it anyway.

Artist Note

A small group of art students formed a circle around the long, thin man with the large nose whom they called "professor." His eyes were closed and his brow furrowed just slightly as he inhaled deeply through his sizable nostrils. For a moment he remained still, heightening the sense of anticipation and gravity with his held breath and closed eyes. He then released a heavy sigh, opened his eyes, and scanned the students.

"Before we get started, I want to ask," he paused and searched the faces of his students once more before continuing, "How is everyone…" another pause, "… feeling?" He put particular emphasis on the word *feeling.*

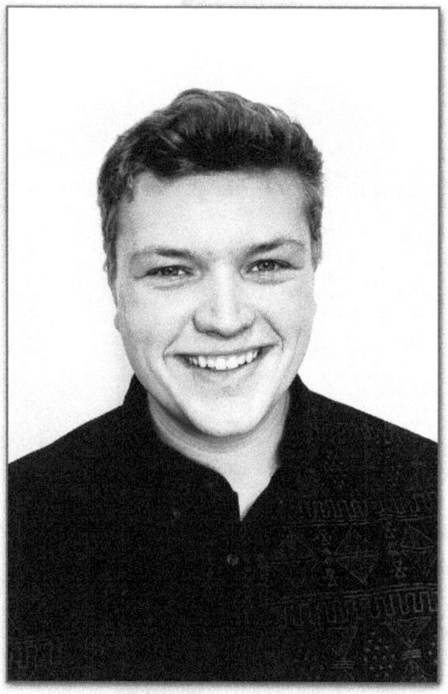

I began to formulate an answer in my head that consisted of words like "excited" and "happy" but, being the prospective student, I decided to observe how one was supposed to answer the question before offering my humble contribution. A student with his face contorted in angst stepped forward, head down, and with his hands clasped tightly to his bosom, began to spill his emotion for the entire class to see.

"I just…," he stopped to assemble his words then began again. "I just feel like I'm not, like, being true to myself. Like, you know? Like, I just feel like I'm wearing this mask, like, trying to be happy for everyone and I'm, like, not. You know?"

This sudden gush of anguish threw me off. It was not what I expected — and the depth of the feeling being expressed certainly seemed socially unacceptable given the very public audience for such an intimate answer. Much to my surprise, another student stepped forward and also slopped forth the baggage of his self-loathing and unhappiness into the classroom. After the third or fourth student followed suit and spoke of their deep, dark emotions, I began to feel my answer would be a little out of place. I imagined that if I gave my answer, the professor would pat me on the head, look at me condescendingly, and say to the real artists, "Ah, untainted innocence… impressionable youth. Isn't that cute? Don't worry, you'll get there soon enough." Needless to say, I remained in incredulous silence!

The joy of creating art no longer entered the minds of those afflicted souls. Expressing misery was the truest form of art for them. Unfortunately, I have since realized this attitude is a rather commonplace thread between artists today. Art can become an outlet for those who cannot voice their troubles but sadly, expressing depression, pain, shock, ugliness, and anguish seems to be the only art form taken seriously.

Throughout history artists have suffered greatly to pursue their craft, often going days without food and weeks without money. This suffering came as the cost for pursuing art as a vocation. They became artists, and with it, incurred suffering, but nowadays the roles are reversed. The "Starving Artist" attitude has become an end, viewed as the only appropriate and authentic source for the inspiration of so-called "High Art", not simply an unfortunate consequence of the journey in pursuit of a calling. Particularly in the United States, artists rarely starve, yet many modern artists assume that the attitude of suffering is required to sculpt a true artist.

I believe art can carry people out of the depths of despair to make them chuckle, bring a smile to their face, or observe the remarkable in everyday life. My art is based primarily on my joy and happiness and I strive for it to contain intrigue and storytelling elements. God has given me the talent; I feel joy when I exercise it. Art can bring others joy and serious art can reflect joy, too, just as it can reflect the darker side of life. And, until such a time as happiness can come back into vogue or I can encounter some vile unhappiness or tragic circumstances in order to be considered truly serious about my craft, I hope you can take an *Effervescent Road Trip* with me.

All the best,

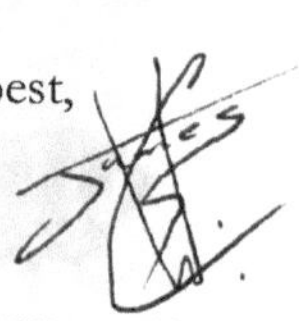

James William Christenson

Introduction

Effervescent Road Trip is the second compilation by James William Christenson. This set of works, compiled from various collections across the nation, is a reflection of the remarkable talent and breadth of stylistic techniques and media that Christenson commands. Unlike many artistic composers, Christenson does not often sit down to create a particular work of art. Rather, he often leaves behind a wake of artwork and projects in various styles, media, and stages of creation.

Bill Watterson's Calvin, of *Calvin and Hobbes*, once exclaimed "Look! A trickle of water running through some dirt! I'd say our afternoon just got booked solid!" Similarly, Christenson possesses this type of creativity and imagination. He is unhindered by what may seem mundane or devoid of possibility. He notices situations otherwise unnoticed by others.

Perhaps some of his creativity and imagination was born of necessity. He was the youngest sibling in a set of six in rural Indiana where the television, with its metallic telescoping antennae unceremoniously garbed in tinfoil to help receive the two available fuzzy channels, sat ignored. His mother's favorite mantra was, "If you're bored *I'll find* something for you to do!" Rather than experiencing ennui, Christenson has been creating since childhood.

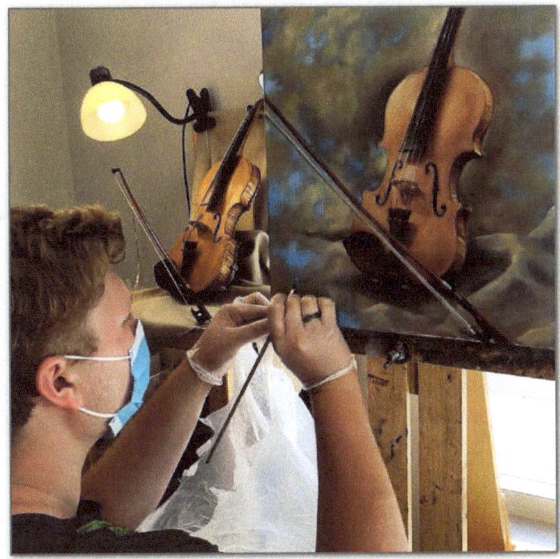

James William Christenson working on a still life oil painting.

On one occasion he asked me, "Carl, do you have tinfoil and a toothpick"? Once in his possession, he also took some clay, returning moments later to ask, "May I also use your oven?" Within a half hour he had fashioned a scaled replica ostrich egg, one which could fool even the most avid ornithologist upon first inspection. At another point, he took a single potato and a knife, only to return with a carved rendition of the "Sword in the Stone". If one were to walk along a beach where Christenson has been, you might find a rock etched with a beautiful seascape or what appears to be a half-buried pirate skeleton emerging from the depths formed from sand, pebbles, and shell fragments.

Sigmund Freud stated "What a distressing contrast there is between the radiant intelligence of the child and the feeble mentality of the average adult." This radiant intelligence has not been lost in Christenson's artwork. There is a brilliance in ability, creativity, and humor in his creations that reflect an unrepressed childlike creativity paired with the complex maturity of an adult. This results in artwork that is approachable; not because it is simple, but because it evokes an emotion, memory, or story in the mind of the viewer and reignites, in that viewer, that childlike imagination. Put simply, Christenson's works do not necessitate an explanatory placard or complex analysis, elucidation, or preface by an art connoisseur.

Look carefully as you peruse this book. You will note allusion to various historical and modern artists, references to the comic and absurd, stories, and experimental techniques. The more straightforward the piece may seem, the more the viewer should investigate. Enjoy your own road trip through the pages of this book!

Respectfully submitted,

Dr. Carl R. Christenson, MD

But, is it Good Art?

A Study on Good in the Art World

Fecal matter, urine, ripped carpet squares, piles of used condoms, broken urinals, soiled diapers, and mounds of melted rubber: If you saw a man in a garbage dump just staring in total rapture at a sight much like the aforementioned list, scrutinizing every detail, you might think him a bit mad. However if this same man and situation were set in a museum, you would think everything to be quite all right with the man, and you might even join the fellow. One might wonder if this were even a realistic scenario. Why would an artist "create" such nonsense and who would pay for it, much less wish to view it?

Andres Serrano, a world-renowned artist and photographer, created an image entitled "Piss Christ," which displayed the Christ on a crucifix submerged in a small glass tank of the artist's urine. This was funded in part by the National Endowment of the Arts, which uses tax dollars to promote art and has hung in many galleries across America including the Stux Gallery in New York. Serrano is well known for his works displaying bodily fluids of every kind.

Gedi Sibony, a well known sculpture artist, is probably best known for his work entitled "Carpet Tape," which features a piece of carpet hung backwards on a wall allowing the viewer to see the underside of the carpet. Sibony has exhibited in New York, Las Vegas, Canada, Vienna, and Paris.

Marcel Duchamp entered an up-turned urinal as an art piece in the Society of Independent Artists. He was known for his "ready made" sculptures where he would use or combine already formed objects to make his art. One of his more famous sculptures is the top half of a bike on a stool.

Niki Johnson created a giant seven-foot tall portrait of the Pope out of condoms. It hangs in the Milwaukee Art Museum.

Mary Kelly presented her son's dirty diapers to the Institute of Contemporary Art in London.

Chakaia Booker, a sculptor, created sculptures of masses of melted rubber tires.

Maurizio Cattelan became one of the world's most famous artists in just a week in 2019 when he taped a banana to the gallery wall at the Art Basil Miami Art Fair and sold it for $120,000. This created such an uproar that a different artist ate the work right off the wall. This simple act exploded in

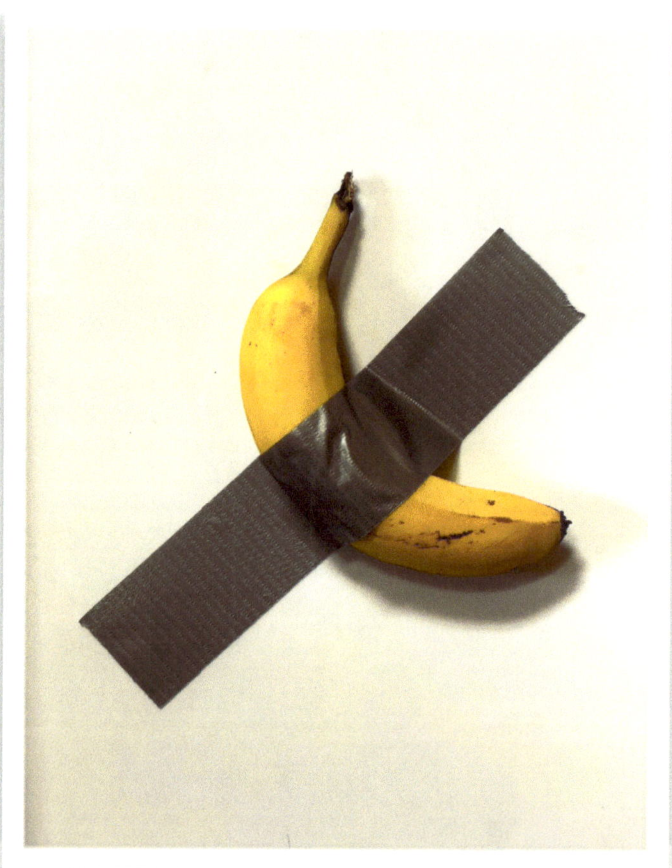

A photograph recreating Italian artist Maurizio Cattelan's "Comedian".

The work consisted of a fresh banana purchased at a local grocer and taped to a wall with a single piece of duct tape. Two editions of the piece sold for $120,000 USD at Art Basel Miami Beach.

the media and made Cattelan's work one of the most well known works of the 21st century.

The list goes on and on, with each work more shocking than the last. Is this freedom in the arts revolutionary and praise worthy or should art be confined to some definition? Who should decide whether a work is good or not?

What is Art?

For hundreds of years artists have attempted to push the limits on what is considered art. Impressionism, for example, broke away from the rigid artistic standards and expectations of the day. Impressionism was light, happy and carefree.

Manufactured paint tubes made artistry more accessible to the public and what was once viewed as a profession could now be a hobby in the hands of laymen. Impressionists used copious amounts of paint, much to the distress of the "professionals" and, much like the name suggests, only gave an impression of the scene they were painting. All the colors were bright and saturated. Most of the subject matter concerned landscapes and everyday life. Impressionism was a sort of breaking away from art's clearly defined terms of the day.

To be true art, there were standards one had to meet, but with the rise of impressionism those standards were tested and broken. The impressionistic artists didn't strive for deep meaning or to capture heroic scenes. Their art was merely a simple, beautiful, morally ambiguous thought, or so it endeavored to be. Impressionistic subject matter and mood gave off an optimistic and lively feel. The artists didn't concern themselves with political statements or noble ideas. Frances Schaefer stated in his book, *How Should We Then Live?,* that Impressionists strayed so far from rules that the reality they were attempting to portray became a dream. "As reality tended to become a dream, Impressionism as a movement fell apart."

Postimpressionism spring boarded off of Impressionism's newfound freedom but attempted to capture the loss of meaning that Impressionism had forced out. While Impressionists were making the statement that there didn't need to be a statement in art and that art could be free from morals, Postimpressionists took a different approach to bend the meaning and definition of art. Void of ultimate truth, namely the Bible, the great leaders of this movement couldn't find absolute meaning, and so Postimpressionism gave way to the modern idea of individual reality and truth with no ultimate truth or authority. Thus relative truth stepped out onto the stage with Fauvism, Surrealism, Dadaism, Cubism, and modern art. Each of these movements, in their own way, were attempting to search for meaning by actively running from it. They had the freedom to define art as they wished.

When everyone defined art as he liked, art lost its definition. In the words of Disney super villain, Syndrome, from *The Incredibles,* "When everyone's super… no one will be!" Likewise, when every definition is acceptable, there is no definition. With the loss of a definition, postmodern ideals thrived. Instead of grieving the loss of meaning, Postmodernists embraced this and praised it as the epitome of relevancy. Art had opened its arms to anything and everything. To the Postmodernist this looked like the beginning of the peak of progress in art.

The postmodern ideals have ravaged the universities such that some professors no longer have a concept of what art is. When asked to give his definition of art, the dean of the art department at a particular university answered, "It's whatever you want it to be. I guess you can't really define it."

At another school the professor of drawing, when asked the same question, responded, "There are a lot of different opinions on the definition… I guess I don't really have one." How are these professors grading their students? What criteria or standard do their students have to meet? Without a definition of what good art is, all grading becomes subjective and meaningless.

One might argue that beauty is in the eye of the beholder and, therefore, each should employ his or her own definition to assess a work. Therefore the question remains:

Why do we need a Definition?

What are the ramifications of not having a definition or a scale by which to judge whether a work is good art?

Right after the fall of Rome, people had no government ruling over them, which gave them complete freedom. No rules governed how they spent their money. No rules inhibited their business transactions. No one punished them for wearing purple (wearing purple in ancient Rome was for the emperor alone and was illegal for anyone unworthy of the color). In addition to these freedoms, no one stopped anyone from stealing from, murdering, or enslaving anyone they wanted. Unfortunately, even though people gained a few good outcomes with the fall of the government, many more dangerous "freedoms" came with it. Within a generation or two people couldn't read or write because they were too occupied with protecting their property and families. The fall of the constricting rules of government gave way to so much freedom that people lost it all trying to protect their own freedom from someone else's freedom. In the end, people had less freedom than before the laws were abolished. With this the world entered the period known as the Dark Ages.

We are in the Dark Ages or entering the Dark Ages of art in a sense. There was some beauty that coincided with the abandonment of rules in art, but more hideousness than beauty resulted from this loss.

While less apparent than in medieval times, artists are now forced to protect their own freedoms from everyone else's. Since there is no measurement or scale by which one can judge good from bad, an artist can be subject to the scrutiny or praise of anyone. Likewise, because there are no standards, schools have no fair way to grade their students. Professors can create rubrics, but in the end they are little more than arbitrary measurement schemes. Still another dean of an art department from yet another school, when asked what good art was, said, "It's like, whatever. You can't really limit it to a definition 'cuz there's too much of it."

The French people worked tirelessly to overthrow the corrupt government in the 1700's, but their efforts were rewarded with terror. In order to keep the terror at bay those same people allowed an emperor to fill the empty throne, a symbol which had, at one point, given hope of freedom to the people. Napoleon was able to take the throne so easily only because the pain of having a ruler paled when compared to the pain of the reign of terror. A ruler will rise to fill the lack of order. A natural definition of art will rise to fill the void of standards, but the new, natural definition has the potential to be far more dangerous than the old standard artists worked so hard to get rid of. The definition will reflect the culture and ideals of the day. If those ideas are wrong or malevolent, this could have devastating consequences.

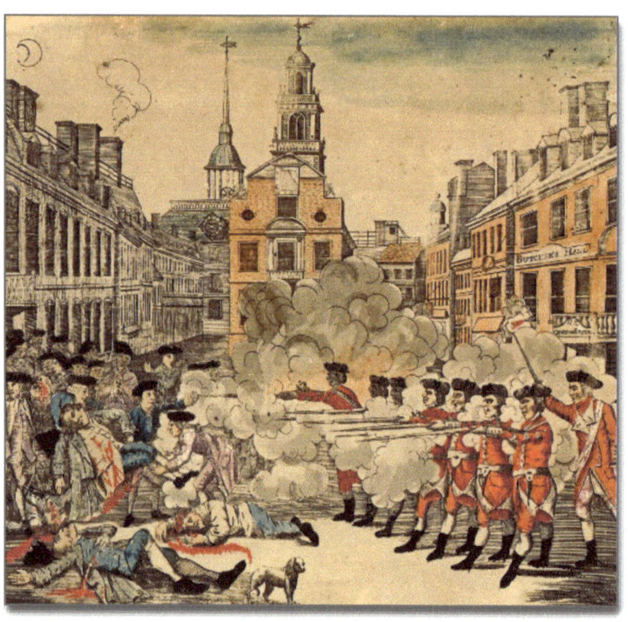

Most Revolutionary War era Americans pictured the Boston massacre in their heads based upon of a piece of art made by Paul Revere depicting a line of British soldiers mowing down dozens of defenseless townsmen and women.

In actuality only five men were killed in the event, but the piece was instrumental in promoting the cause of the Revolutionary War

Art is a back door into the minds of people. Art plays on people's subconscious minds and becomes like a subliminal advertisement. Even the United States used art propaganda to promote the cause of the people in Boston. Most Revolutionary War era Americans pictured the Boston massacre based upon of a piece created by Paul Revere depicting a line of British soldiers mowing down dozens of defenseless townsmen and women.

In actuality only five men were killed in the event. However, the art had a far more potent effect on the colonists than the facts, and soon there was a revolt against King George and his men.

Art can be used to sway a population, so leaving the definition of good art floating for anyone to catch can have a devastating effect. This has been demonstrated in history several times. One of the most shocking examples comes from Germany just two years before World War II. Hitler defined good and bad art and used this to help his drive for genocide. He created two museums. The first he called the Degenerate Art Exhibition and the second The House of German Art. The first was a shabby building filled with art Hitler considered bad. He displayed the collection to elicit in the viewers a sense of superiority of the German race over other races and to create a sense of rage towards the inferior artists who were polluting Germany with their weak ideas. The second museum was a grand building filled with beautiful displays of German art.

Hitler gave a commencement speech at the opening of the Exhibition of German Art and he began his speech by depicting the degeneration of Germany and asking why this had occurred. He then answered by blaming those with the weak and destructive degenerate ideas. The sense of patriotism this pair of museums created and the rage it provoked towards those who were "destroying" the greatness of Germany and her people gave rise to a justification for the death of many innocent people. Hitler wrote:

"...The collapse and overall decline of Germany was – as we know – not only academic or political, but rather, and perhaps to a far greater extent, cultural. Moreover, this process was also not solely attributable to the fact of the lost war. Such catastrophes have often afflicted peoples and states, and these events have not infrequently provided an impetus for their cleansing and, with it, their inner elevation. But that flood of slime and refuse, which the year 1918 spewed onto the surface of our lives, was not produced by the loss of the war, but instead only released by it. It was only through the defeat that such a thoroughly rotten body first experienced the full extent of its inner decay. After the collapse of those earlier social, political, and cultural forms that were only seemingly in order, the baseness that was underlying them for so long began to triumph, and in all areas of life at that....

The question has often been asked: what does "to be German" actually mean? Of all the definitions that have been put forth over the past centuries by so many men, one appears to me as the worthiest; it attempts less to provide an explanation than to establish a law. The most beautiful law that I could wish to imagine for my people as their life task on this earth was already declared long ago by a great German: 'to be German means to be clear.' This implies, therefore, that to be German also means to be logical and above all to be true...

Art is in no way fashion. In the same way that little changes in the nature and blood of our people, art, too, must lose its character of transience; instead, in its continuously intensifying creations, it must be a worthy visual expression of the life's course of our people. Cubism, Dadaism, Futurism, Impressionism, and so on, have nothing to do with our German people. For all of these terms are neither old nor modern, but are simply the stilted stammering of people to whom God has denied real artistic talent and has given instead the gift of blather and deception. I therefore wish to affirm in this hour my immutable resolve to do for German artistic life what I have done in the area of political confusion: to purge it of empty phrases....

'Works of art' that cannot be understood on their own, but rather require a pompous user manual to justify their existence, in order to finally find that intimidated person who will patiently accept such foolish or impudent nonsense – such art works will no longer find their way to the German people!"

This propaganda worked well and soon anyone affiliated with the weak mindset, the "gifts of blather and deception," were persecuted or killed in concentration camps. In fact, the artist who produced the art used on the posters, advertisements, and the covers of the pamphlets for the Degenerate Art Exhibition was sent to a concentration camp and murdered because the effect of the museum on the people was so potent. The most terrifying

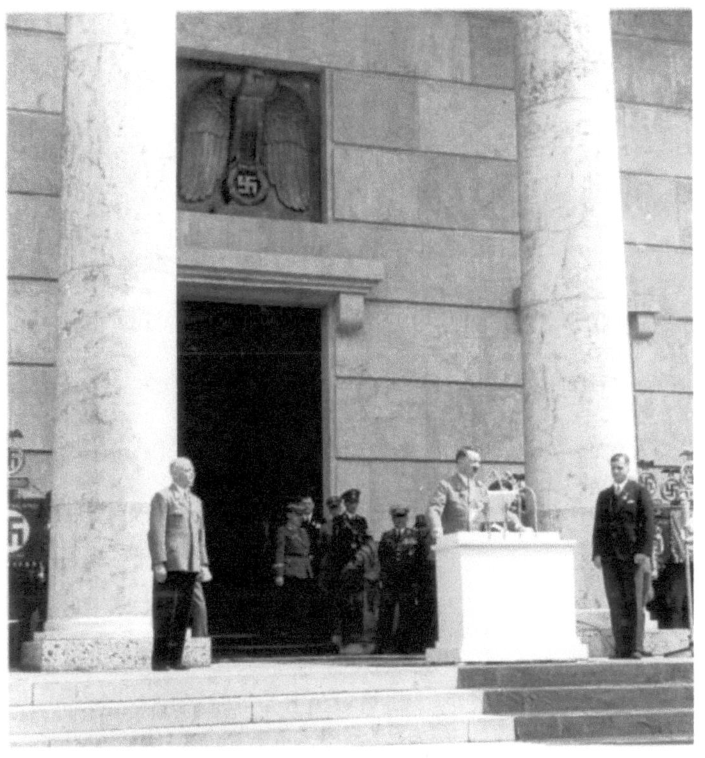

Even Adolf Hitler recognized the tremendous importance, message, and cultural significance of a culture's artwork. He, like so many others before and after, offered his own definition of art during his 1937 commencement speech at the opening of the Exhibition of German Art (Pictured Above).

His views on art darkly and ominously foreshadowed the coming holocaust and were leveraged effectively to evangelize, promote, and normalize his propaganda on the German people. The most terrifying and powerful of all people are those who can deceive others with the truth. While it may seem a bit far-fetched at first, a good definition of art is necessary, even to protect people's lives.

and powerful of all people are those who can deceive others with the truth. While it may seem a bit far-fetched at first, a good definition of art may be necessary even to protect people's lives.

Who has the Authority to Judge Good Art from Bad?

As stated previously, the Postmodernist believes that, free of morals, meaning, and rules, art can achieve its true beauty. That would be an impossible achievement, as every individual has a worldview, whether right or wrong, by and through which they judge all things. According to GK Chesterton,

> *"All denunciation implies a moral doctrine of some kind and the modern skeptic doubts not only the institution he denounces, but the doctrine by which he denounces it. Thus he writes one book complaining that imperial oppression insults the purity of women and then writes another book, a novel in which he insults it himself. As a politician he will cry out that war is a waste of life, and then as a philosopher that all of life is waste of time. A Russian pessimist will denounce a policeman for killing a peasant, and then prove by the highest philosophical principles that the peasant ought to have killed himself. A man denounces marriages a lie and then denounces aristocratic profligates for treating it as a lie.*
>
> *The man of this school goes first to a political meeting where he complains that savages are treated as if they were beasts. Then he takes his hat and umbrella and goes on to a scientific meeting where he proves that they practically are beasts. In short, the modern revolutionist, being an infinite skeptic, is forever engaged in undermining his own mines. In his book on politics, he attacks men for trampling on morality; in his book on ethics he attacks morality for trampling on men. Therefore the modern man in revolt becomes practically useless for all purposes of revolt. By rebelling against everything he has lost his right to rebel against anything."*

When artists rebel against definition and strive for meaninglessness, art becomes self-destructive. If a definition of good art can have such an effect on people, who has the authority to create a definition of good and bad? Since human standards of good are arbitrary or flawed, one must be grounded in truth in order to make such a claim. The only sure truth is the word of God.

While God does not directly specify the scale by which art can be judged, He does lay out principles to live by and declares what good is. Based on the following Scriptures, one can draw parallels to what characteristics or properties good art should contain. Colossians 3:23 "Whatever you do, work at it with all your heart, as working for the Lord, not for human masters."

Artists must put their all into their work. In the Book of Exodus, the people of Israel built a tabernacle for God. God gave instructions on how it should be built and designed it using artists. When God first created the universe He declared it good, so one can assume He would have held high standards for his dwelling place among his people. He didn't have just anyone aid in the construction of the tabernacle. He selected the skilled, the learned, the hard working, and those with an eye for design.

Exodus 35:25-26 "Every skilled woman spun with her hands and brought what she had spun—blue, purple or scarlet yarn or fine linen. And all the women who were willing and had the skill spun the goat hair."

God endowed a select few with the wisdom and craftsmanship to create good art.

Exodus 35:30-35 "Then Moses said to the Israelites, 'See, the LORD has chosen Bezalel son of Uri, the son of Hur, of the tribe of Judah, and he has filled him with the Spirit of God, with wisdom, with understanding, with knowledge and with all kinds of skills to make artistic designs for work in gold, silver and bronze, to cut and set stones, to work in wood and to engage in all kinds of artistic crafts. And he has given both him and Oholiab son of Ahisamak, of the tribe of Dan, the ability to teach others. He has filled them with skill to do all kinds of work as engravers, designers, embroiderers in blue, purple and scarlet yarn and fine linen, and weavers - all of them skilled workers and designers.'" God did not choose everyone to be artists for the tabernacle; Rather, He chose only those with skill.

God wants art to be virtuous. Philippians 4:8 defines what one's mind should be occupied with, and therefore, what one's art should contain. "Finally, brothers and sisters, whatever is true, whatever is noble, whatever is right, whatever is pure, whatever is lovely, whatever is admirable if anything is excellent or praiseworthy think about such things." Good art communicates a virtuous message. God wants art to be good. By applying the principles in the Bible to art, art will reflect God and therefore be good.

What is Good Art?

Good art is a creative visual expression demonstrated by its craftsmanship, communication, meaning and purpose. To this end, I have five claims for the reader to consider when evaluating a piece of art for its merits:

Claim 1: Craftsmanship is evident in good art through the artist's investment of his time, skill, and training.

Time is money. The value of almost anything increases with the amount of time one has spent on it. An athlete will only improve if he spends time honing his skill. By expending time and effort his value to his team increases as he becomes better at the sport. In the same way, an art piece's value and virtuosity increases with time spent.

There was a king who hired a portrait artist to paint his queen. The artist came to the palace and stayed with the royal family for several months, studying. When the time came to paint the portrait he produced it in a very short time. This angered the king. While the work was beautiful and perfect in likeness, the king felt cheated. The artist had stayed in the palace for months, yet it only took him a short while to actually paint the portrait. The artist explained to the king, "I could only do the painting so swiftly because I had spent months studying and sketching." He spent a short while painting the final work, but in actuality he had spent months in preparation, meticulously practicing his technique for the portrait. Thus, the portrait's value benefitted far more from months spent in study than the few hours' of brush strokes. It is interesting to note that the king didn't think the painting was worth what he had spent on the artist until he had the understanding that the work had truly taken time. Time, being the only parameter humans have control of, in a sense, to dedicate to a particular work, lends intrinsic worth to that work.

However, time alone, spent by an artist on a piece, is not what makes a work great. Expertise is a critical element of excellent art. There are two facets of expertise: skill and talent. Skill has to be learned. A person doesn't wake up one day and say, "Today I think I'll be a doctor," then march into a hospital and perform surgeries. The more a skill is developed the better the result. People have natural talent, which is often the catalyst in pushing them toward a career, but natural talent only goes so far. A boy may be very tall and this can help him in comparison to other boys his age at basketball, but unless he practices and acquires skill, his natural advantage can easily be surpassed. Likewise, someone can be naturally inclined to create art, but unless he works to acquire the necessary skill his art will never evolve much past his starting point.

Andy Warhol, a prolific artist and leading figure in the pop art movement, once said, "Don't think about making art, just get it done. Let everyone else decide if it's good or bad, whether they love it or hate it. While they are deciding, make even more art." This statement demonstrates many current beliefs about art. Many believe that all art is good in its own way; that everyone can create masterpieces; and that those who say it is not good are ignorant of the truth.

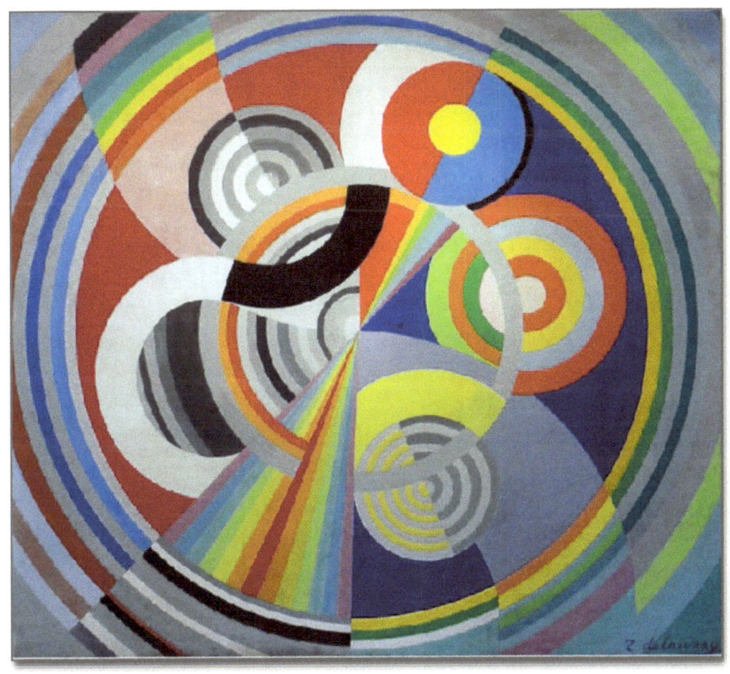

Robert Delaunay's
"Rythme n°1, décoration pour le Salon des Tuileries"
Oil on Canvas. Painted 1938. 208L x 233W Inch
Collection: Musée d'Art Moderne de la Ville de Paris

Even within abstract art, skill is evident in some work and not in others. If one compared Willem de Kooning's work [next page, left] to that of Robert Delaunay [above] - both are abstract expressionists - one can tell which piece took more skill and care to create. While both artists' works sell for millions of dollars, Delaunay's work shows that it required more skill.

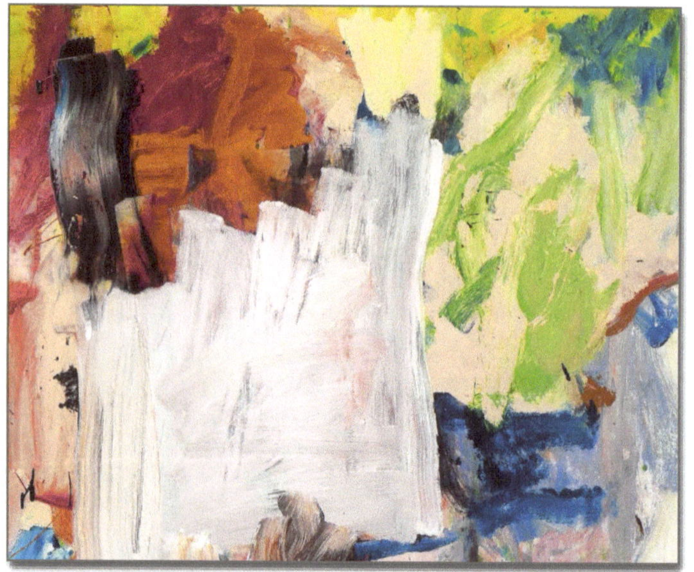

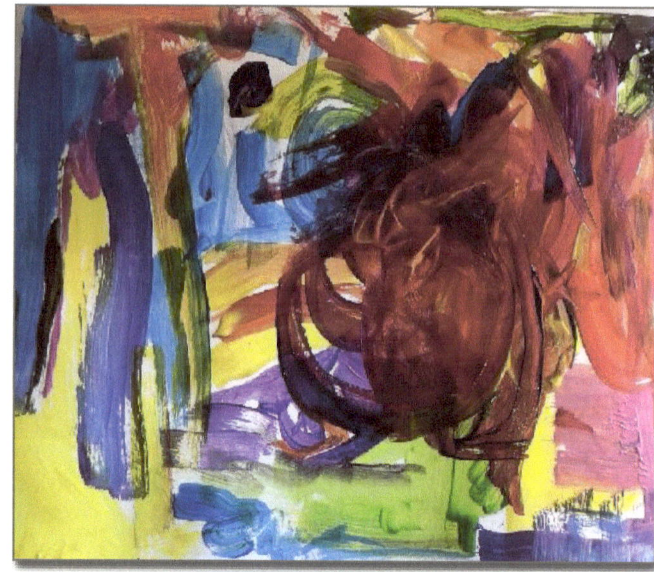

Detailed portion of Willem de Kooning's "Untitled XXV"
Oil on Canvas. Painted 1977. Original: 77L x 88W Inch
Private Collection
Sold for $66,327,500 USD in 2016

Eleanor Morton's "Untitled No. 1"
Finger Paint on Printer Paper. Painted 2020. 8.5L x 11W Inch
Posted on the Refrigerator
For Sale: One College Education for Eleanor in 2035

Kooning's work is virtually indistinguishable from the artwork of three-year-old Eleanor Morton's "Untitled No. 1". Most would not be able to discern the professional work from that of the three-year-old. When compared, the biggest differences between the two paintings are the quality of paint, a slightly more muted color palette, and dimensional size. Both paintings contain bold brushstrokes, similar smudges, paint splatters, and saturated colors. Cover this description with your hand and see if your friends can tell which was the professional painting worth tens of millions of dollars and which was the toddler's picture!

Some have said that "you can do anything you put your mind to" or that "if you just believe in yourself, you can do anything," but this is not quite right. The act of telling oneself that he or she will succeed does not bring about success. It is the acquired and well-practiced skill and hard work of the individual that produces results. This seems rather harsh but not everyone is made for certain jobs. A person who faints at the sight of blood would not make a very good doctor. A four-foot, nine-inch person would not make a very good professional basketball player. Since not everyone can become a pro basketball player, it would follow that not just anyone can be a good artist.

The old masters are masters because the skill in their work is evident. They were truly masters of their craft. They had mastered their talent. People have been imitating and gleaning from their skill for hundreds of years. Anyone can appreciate something done well. When the skill is evident in a work, the appreciation and value for that work increases. For most, possessing a talent is a natural motivation toward an interest in a subject because most people are drawn to things at which they excel. Skill has to be involved in making something exceptional.

Even within abstract art, skill is evident in some works and not in others. If one compares the art work of abstract impressionists Robert Delaunay [previous page] to that of Willem de Kooning [above, left], one can tell which piece took more skill and care to create. While both artists' works sell for millions of dollars, Delaunay's work shows that it required more skill. It looks as if not everyone could reproduce his work. By comparison, De Kooning's work could be mistaken for a child's drawing if it were taped to a fridge and not hung in a gallery.

Now look again at the detailed portion of De Kooning's *Untitled XXV* [above, left]. Immediately to the right of De Kooning's work is a three-year-olds' craft [above, right]. When compared, the biggest difference between the two paintings is the quality of paint. Both paintings contain bold brushstrokes, smudges, paint splatters, and saturated colors. The skill required to paint *Untitled XXV* was in fact matched by a three year old.

Skill must be developed, which takes training. Skill mandates an understanding of the subject at hand and knowledge of how to execute that understanding well. In other words, skill is attained through training and practice. Like all skills worth learning, training can be quite rigorous in art. This is another reason that skill adds value to a painting, because skill is yet another evidence and demonstration of time and hard work spent on a piece.

Claim 2: Good art is a creative visual expression that communicates clearly.

Daniel Schwabauer, an author and educator, suggests why people read, stating, "People read to live vicariously." I believe the same applies to art. People view art to see what others see, to seek new ideas, and to find a voice for something they can't articulate. Few would argue that communication wouldn't be necessary in art. However, many artists around the world lament, "You just don't understand me!" when critiqued. No one can understand someone who fails to communicate what he is attempting to express. One would think this statement as ludicrous as saying that things get wet in water, but it is necessary to say, as there appears to be a rise in persecuted artists whom no one seems to understand.

Gerard Way, a famous American singer, stated, "Anything can be art. Anything can be self-expression. Now you take the weapon and run with it." This statement encompasses the Postmodern ideals. If anything can be art, it follows that anything can be a correct interpretation of that art. If anything can be an interpretation then that interpretation stems from within the observer. Some would say this is the beauty of the art. However, if the message of the painting was already within the viewer, then nothing has been added to the viewer. If the work can represent anything, then it can represent nothing, because it may always have an equally valid opposing interpretation. A note on a door that said, "Clean room!" may be interpreted in many different ways. One could take it to mean that the room he was standing in was, in fact, clean and the note was to draw his attention to it. One could take it to mean that he was supposed to clean the room, or one could take it to mean he was suppose to clean the room behind the door on which the note had been posted. With so many differing meanings, the note becomes meaningless. The same goes for the "it can mean anything" art. Clarity is needed to pass the correct message along.

In neuropsychology, memorization is separated into three sections: visual, auditory, and semantic. Studies have shown that semantic memorization is the most effective form of memorization. Semantic memorization uses an understanding of the material one is trying to retain in order to solidify it in one's mind. If one is trying to memorize a new word, one will have better success if he knows the definition of that new word rather than if he just knows how to spell it. He can memorize it quicker with an understanding because he can appreciate the value of that word. The same goes for art. If a work has clear meaning it will be more memorable and appreciated for the value of its message. Communication in a work can range from subject matter identifiability to a clear message stated through the image. If one knows what he's looking at, he will most likely appreciate it more. If one understands a message through a work, the essence of the work is appreciated and not easily forgotten.

Claim 3: Good art is a creative visual expression demonstrating virtuous meaning and purpose.

When an artwork communicates well, value is added purely because it is understandable. That value can be stripped from the work if the message of the work is unwholesome. The art world has become gradually more grotesque in its messages. With the rise of Postmodern ideals morals have become "old fashioned" or "out of date." The idea of individual sovereignty has become very commonplace, particularly among artists. Our culture praises acts that go against cultural constraints and expectations. Usually these acts violate Biblical principles or social norms. So-called "artistic elements" like fecal matter, urine, ripped carpet squares, piles of used condoms, broken urinals, soiled diapers, and mounds of melted rubber clearly illustrate this.

Marcel Duchamp believed art should have no meaning, and that the beauty was in the meaninglessness. In his attempt to strip meaning from his work he created a message with meaning. Marcel Duchamp was a leader in the Modernism movement. He carved a new direction for the river of art to flow with his message in and through his work. Marcel challenged the very concept of art and even was so bold as to deride the work of the old masters as just "retinal pleasure." Marcel embodied the ideals of the modern

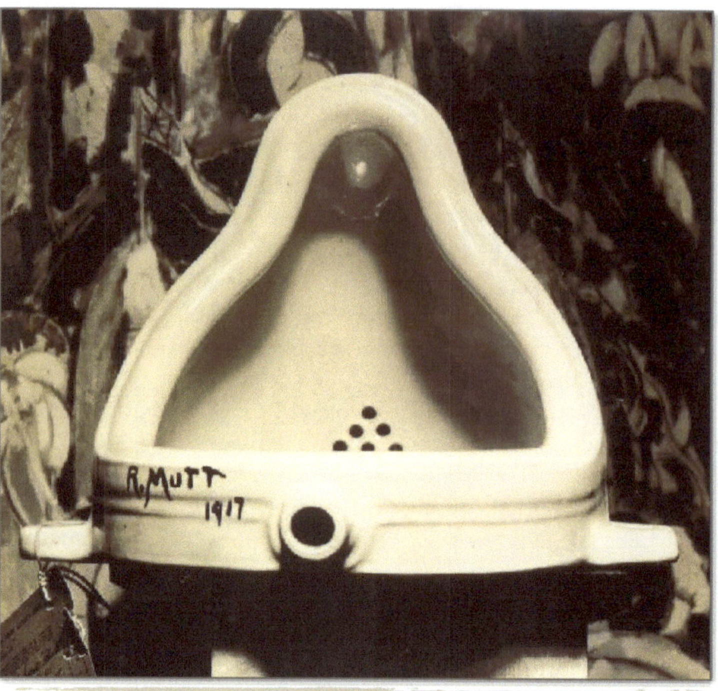

Marcel Duchamp's, "The Fountain"
Photograph by Alfred Stieglitz at the 291 (Art Gallery) following the 1917 Society of Independent Artists exhibit, with entry tag visible.
Upturned Urinal. 1917.
The Original work of Duchamp is Lost or Destroyed

Duchamp pushed the limits of art normality's when he entered an upturned, signed urinal to an "all inclusive art show." The show would not permit his entry in the exhibit saying that the piece was "immoral." The people who rejected this piece may not have fully understood how profoundly right they were in their excuse for denial. While a urinal in itself is not immoral, the violation of good standards is. There was no meaning other than that art should be meaningless.

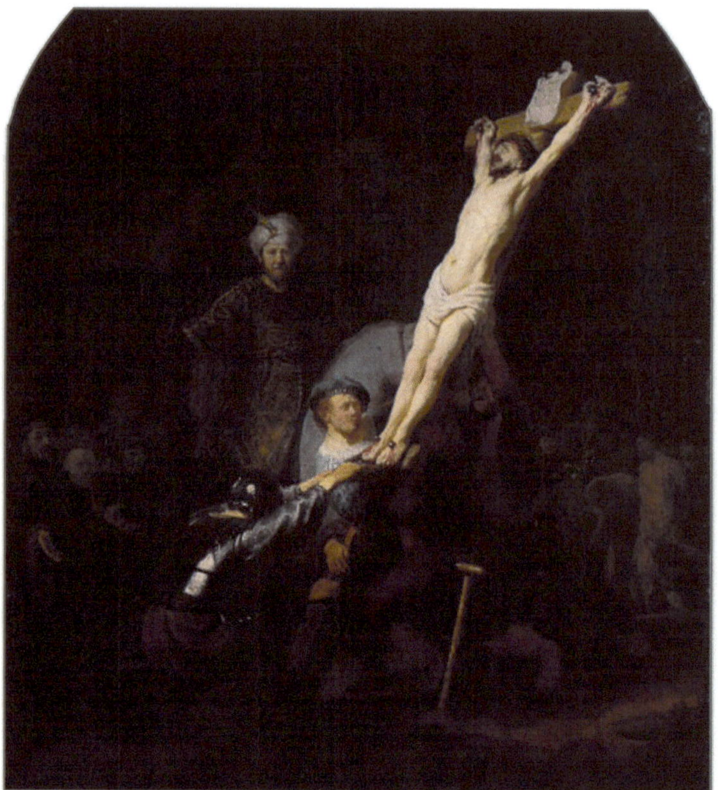

Rembrandt's, "The Raising of the Cross"
Oil on Canvas. Painted 1633. 38 L x 28 W Inch
Collection: Alte Pinakothek

In spite of the theater-esque setting, this painting demonstrates the sincerity of Rembrandt's beliefs within the boundaries and rules of art. He presents a shocking message in spite of the constricting regulations of the day. Rembrandt paints Jesus being lifted on the cross in Rembrandt's own time period. He painted his message by painting himself at the foot of the cross. Rembrandt bent the concepts and rules to help convey his message.

movement. He worked tirelessly to destroy meaning. The goals and thoughts of the modern movement were incredibly destructive. Dada's goal, like many of the other factions of modernism, was first to destroy, then to renew. Pablo Picasso stated it this way, "Every act of creation begins with an act of destruction." Marcel opened the world to a new concept of art by obliterating the former concepts, guidelines, and borders. Many thought this brought great progress to the art world, however, with the destruction of rules, borders, and expectations, they destroyed the very thing they thought they were achieving, namely, progress. If one has no finish line, how does one know if he has finished? Marcel's life was spent attempting to destroy the finish line so that anyone could be a finalist. Rather than elevating everyone to a more valued state, he ended up lowering the cultural expectations of art thereby devaluing art and artists. "When everyone's super… no one will be!" Marcel attempted to overcome what he thought to be segregation. He tried to bring equality by destroying the pedestals people created for the masters. Still, when everyone is an artist and anything is art, nothing is.

Marcel pushed the limits of art normality's when he entered an upturned, signed urinal [above, left] to an "all inclusive art show." The show would not permit his entry in the exhibit saying that the piece was "immoral." The people who rejected this piece may not have fully understood how profoundly right they were in their excuse for denial. While a urinal in itself is not immoral, the violation of good standards is. There was no meaning other than that art should be meaningless.

Marcel would consider Rembrandt [previous page, right] a "retinal pleaser." Rembrandt, a Baroque artist who lived from 1606 to 1669 and is considered one of the most famous and influential artists, had a more conservative view and approach to art. The Baroque period, stylistically, was very dramatic, and most of the paintings looked as if they were set in a theater.

In spite of the theater-esque setting, this painting demonstrates the sincerity of Rembrandt's beliefs within the boundaries and rules of art. He presents a shocking message in spite of the constricting regulations of the day. Rembrandt paints Jesus being lifted on the cross in Rembrandt's own time period. He demonstrated his message by painting himself at the foot of the cross.

Rembrandt bent the concepts and rules to help convey his message. Marcel Duchamp destroyed the rules to express his own. A virtuous message betters the viewer. An unwholesome one only robs the viewer of the virtue for which they unknowingly hunger. This is why the ideas behind the Postmodern movements are dangerous. Postmodernists want all the power art can offer without any of the responsibility or work. A message presented through art can be culture changing, so depriving the work of an upright message is voiding a culture of righteousness. Likewise, presenting a bad message is instilling depravity.

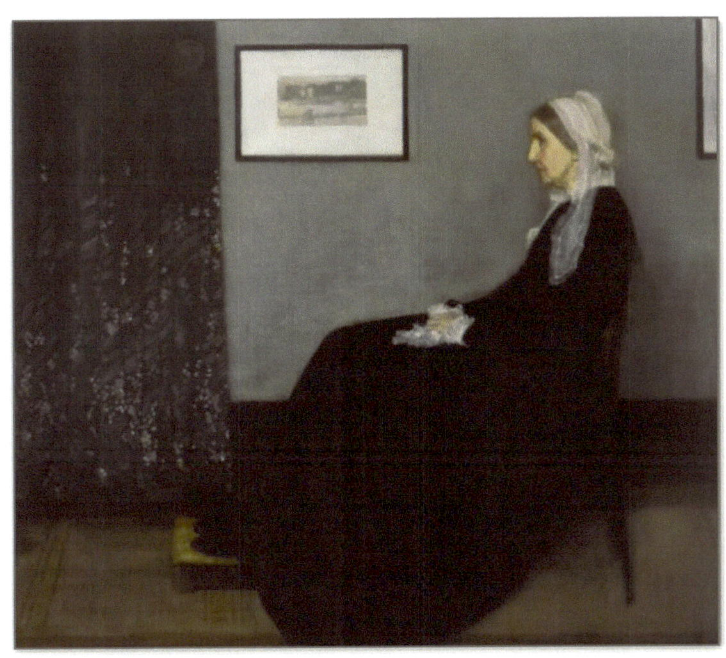

James Abbott McNeill Whistler's, "Arrangement in Grey and Black No. 1" also called, "Whistler's Mother"
Oil on Canvas. Painted 1871. 57L x 64W Inch
Collection: Musée d'Orsay

Whistler's Mother is yet another painting that doesn't seem very special at first, but became far more interesting once its backstory was revealed. Whistler painted his mother to spite a girl's impertinence. With this information, the image of the rather uninteresting and plain looking woman becomes somewhat comical and fun to view.

Claim 4: Context can make art great.

Perception of the value of art can be dramatically increased based on history of the piece, though rarely does anyone have control over the context. Everyone appreciates a story. Humans are creatures of sentiment. Some would attach more value to a five-dollar bracelet than a hundred-dollar necklace purely because of its association with the giver. If a piece has an interesting backstory, the appreciation for that work increases because viewers can understand the context, and have an emotional connection with, the art and its maker.

Take, for instance, a rather childish, simplistic painting of an elephant with what appears to be an extremely large flower. Little about the work would convince someone to hang this picture in a prominent place in his or her home, let alone spend $550 for it. It is a rather unremarkable picture; that is, until one knows the context for it. An elephant named Hong produced the painting (there are videos of elephants actually painting similar pictures on youtube.com - it is worth looking up!). Once the origin of the painting was known, the painting's value jumped in value. Indeed, when context is added to an image, value is added as well.

Whistler's Mother is yet another painting that doesn't seem very special at first, but became far more interesting once its backstory was revealed. James Whistler, an influential American painter who lived and worked in the UK, received a commission from a member of Parliament to paint a portrait of his daughter. After a few studies of the girl, which consisted of the girl sitting for hours, Whistler prepared to paint the real thing. When the appointed time came, the girl never showed. So, having already prepared his canvas, palette, and workspace, Whistler painted his mother to spite the girl's impertinence. With this information, the image of the rather uninteresting and plain looking woman becomes somewhat comical and fun to view.

Even fictional stories surrounding a piece of art can give a work extra value. *Whistler's Mother* was also featured in a *Mr. Bean* movie during which it was accidentally defaced by the comic character, Mr. Bean. The added fictional storyline has given the work more notoriety and, subsequently, increased value.

In addition to the story behind a piece, the historical significance of a piece also plays a role in the works' value. If the work is a historical artifact or a rarity from a time period, the work gains additional value simply for its historical significance. A story line gives us an appreciation beyond what the image alone has to offer.

Value can also be added if the work itself is a historical artifact. Some of the most shocking art pieces are so expensive, not because they are so skillfully executed, but rather because they mark a period in history. If one truly appreciated the beauty of Marcel Duchamp's *The Fountain,* one could purchase a urinal and turn it on its side for far less than purchasing the real work. If it still existed today, *The Fountain* would be expensive, not because it is an amazing piece of art, but rather a piece of history.

Claim 5: Good art is creative.

Clear communication, craftsmanship, and virtuous message all depend upon, and are the responsibility of, the artist. Creativity, on the other hand, relies to a great degree on the viewer's knowledge and even intellect. Assessment of the creativity of a piece might be rather difficult for a dullard. Conversely, the more genius a person possesses, the more creative the judge, the better he is at identifying creativity. When something is particularly clever it usually plays on the viewer's previous knowledge or experience. A joke is only funny if one understands the components, elements, or situation of the joke. A creative painting is then, in a way, the punch line. You wouldn't find a joke funny or clever if you didn't know the context.

Usually creative art communicates a story or idea, but sometimes the creativity is not in the image itself but in how that image was made or the story behind the picture. A fun example of creativity outside of the image itself was in the title of an abstract painting. The painting was nothing but a black background with a small red splotch in the middle. One feels the slightest bit underwhelmed viewing it. The most common thought people have when they see it is, "Even I could do that!" All those feelings of animosity dissolve and are replaced with a grin when one reads the title: "But you didn't!" While the painting is truly terrible, the very creativity is in the pairing of the clever title and the stark unremarkability of the piece. Without the title, the work would have little value. Some have mistaken newness or strangeness as creativity but this is usually not the case. Overcoming functional fixedness is an example of creativity. Assigning the title of art to an overturned urinal is not.

When the church defined art and music, it was rich, beautiful, and creative as evidenced by the architecture of the cathedrals in which it was displayed and performed. However, as art has drifted further and further away from God it has turned rather repugnant. Postmodern thinking asserts that boundaries destroy creativity, but without boundaries you have nothing but chaos and meaningless disorder. A Postmodernist would posit that language and music are just organized and orderly noise. Without organization you cannot understand language or music. Creativity comes when you color outside the lines, not when you get rid of the lines entirely.

Utilizing the Definition

Does the work demonstrate excellent craftsmanship? Does the work communicate a virtuous message? Does the work display creativity? Does the history of the piece add deeper appreciation to the work? Is the work clever or creative? To what degree have these criteria been met? One can judge the value of art based on these criteria. If only some of these criteria are met, the work one is assessing will be fair. If all requirements are met, the work will be outstanding.

One can apply this method of assessment to any art piece. Albrecht Dürer's *Praying Hands* provides an example of how to measure the value of a work of art.

Is excellent craftsmanship evident in this work through time, skill, or training? Yes, the craftsmanship is quite apparent. The quality of the drawing clearly demonstrates the skill and trained eye of the artist. The hands are proportional and the lighting and values are executed very well. One can clearly infer the hours spent on this drawing, as well as the time Dürer spent to train himself to get to this level of expertise.

Does the work communicate clearly? The artist displays a multifaceted communication. Dürer's subject is identifiable. He tells the viewer that they are hands, but his communication reaches far beyond a mere demonstration to his audience that he can draw hands. There is a clear message displayed through the work: The work communicates to the observer.

Does this work exhibit virtuous meaning and purpose? The *Praying Hands* demonstrate a simple act with immeasurable repercussions: Dürer shows the created communicating with the Creator. It testifies to accessibility: The weakest or simplest may speak directly to the Most Powerful and Omniscient One. Indeed, Dürer's message is holy and virtuous.

Is the work creative? A simple picture of hands folded in supplication and prayer is not, at first consideration, particularly creative. There's nothing exceptionally clever or imaginative about the subject of the image. The creativity is slightly hidden but is demonstrated in the style that Dürer decided to use to draw his subject. The etched appearance of the drawing adds an interesting element to the work as well as the selection of blue paper when paired with the composition of the image.

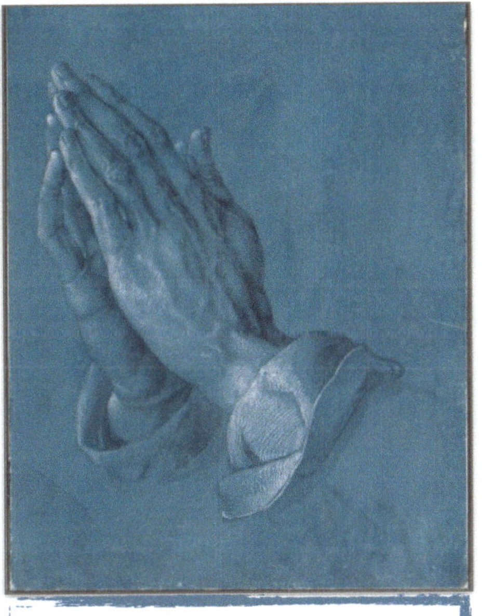

Albrecht Dürer's, "Praying Hands" Brush, gray and white ink, gray wash, on blue prepared paper. Painted 1508. 11L x 7W Inch Collection: Albertina

Dürer's, "Praying Hands" meets the definition of good art.

Does the history of the image add depth of appreciation? Yes, the history behind the piece adds another layer of virtuosity, once understood. Dürer and his brother both wanted to go to art school, so the story goes, but coming from a large family that already struggled to put enough food on the table made the very thought seem unattainable. So the two brothers devised a plan. One of them would work and pay for the other to attend school, then the other would work and trade places with his brother. On a coin toss they determined who would attend college first and who would work. Dürer won the toss and went off to school. His brother worked day after day and into the dark hours of the night to make enough money for the payments. Meanwhile, Dürer put his all into honing his craft and soon surpassed his educators in skill. When the time was completed Dürer had made a name for himself in the art world and was ready to repay the debt to his brother. His family held a feast in honor of Dürer's success. At the celebration, Dürer rose from his seat to honor his brother who had made his dream possible. He finished his toast by saying "And now, brother, it is time for me to work while you attend school."

His brother, with tears in his eyes, raised his hands to show the injury they had endured while working. "I cannot go, brother, for my hands are too damaged to hold even this spoon steady." His brother had worked so tirelessly that he sacrificed his well-being and dreams to help Dürer attain his. In a demonstration of gratitude to his brother Dürer drew his brothers hands.

Dürer portrayed his brother's gnarled hands in prayer, most likely portraying the two things he cared for the most: namely his brother's sacrificial love praying to the God who sacrificed his own life for Dürer. The history behind this piece gives the work a rich depth that one couldn't experience if he or she did not know it.

In addition to the historical and sentimental aspect, the piece is an historical artifact itself and somewhat of an icon, adding yet another layer of value. Because, to a degree, all of the criteria for good art was met, Dürer's *Praying Hands* may be classified as an example of good art.

These five elements should all be considered in judging a work of art but some elements will have a greater impact on the viewer. The greatest elements to consider are craftsmanship, communication, and virtuous message of a piece, as these affect all the other elements.

The best art is that which glorifies God. According to Ecclesiastes, man's duty is to fear God and keep his commandments. F. Schaefer once said, "In great art, technique is united with worldview." If our worldview stems from the Bible and God, art will truly be great, as it will reflect the original artist!

Fecal matter, urine, ripped carpet squares, piles of used condoms, broken urinals, soiled diapers, and mounds of melted rubber; good is not an all-inclusive term. One must sift through the copious rubbish to extract the rare gold.

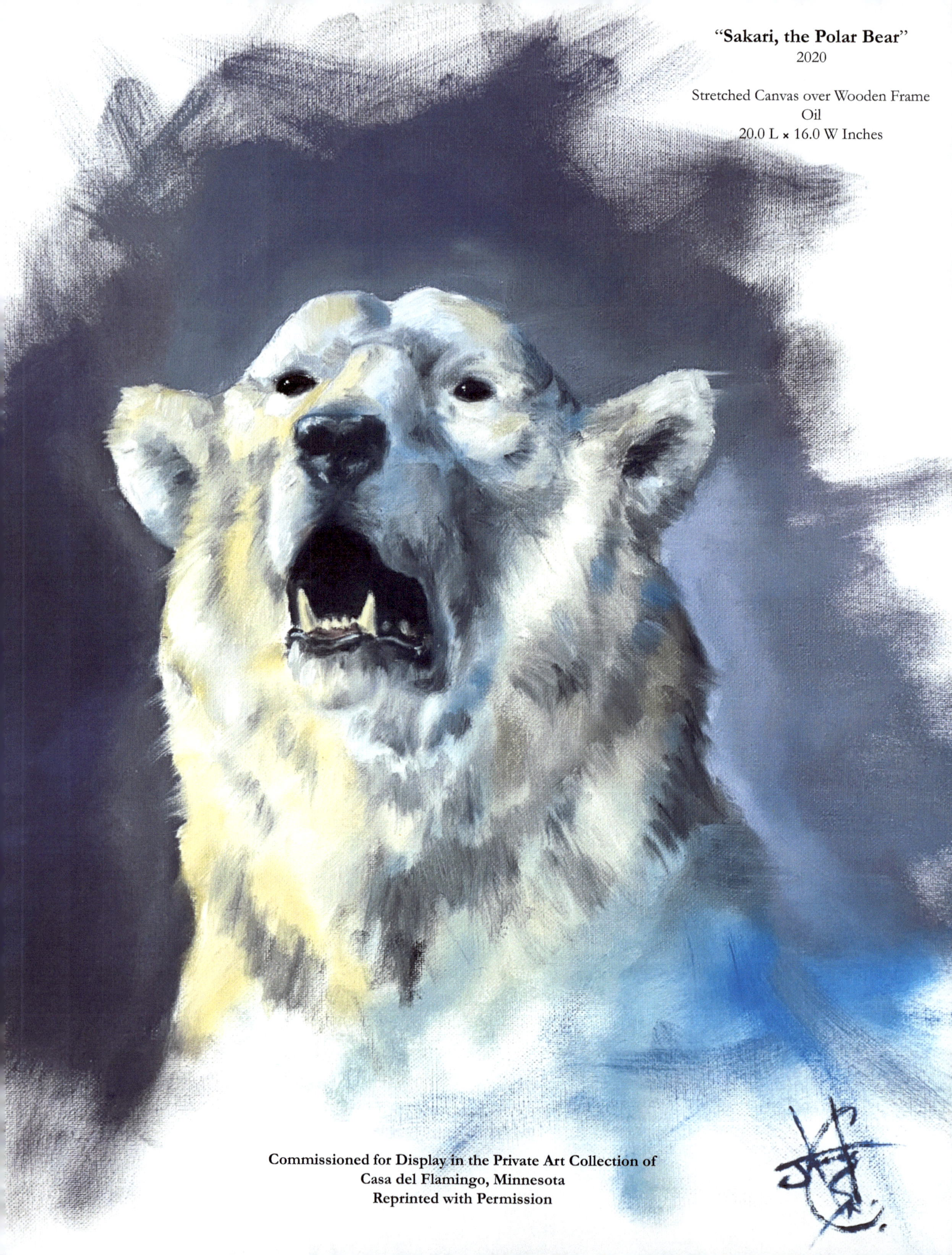

"Sakari, the Polar Bear"
2020

Stretched Canvas over Wooden Frame
Oil
20.0 L × 16.0 W Inches

Commissioned for Display in the Private Art Collection of
Casa del Flamingo, Minnesota
Reprinted with Permission

“Michael, King of Pop”
2020

Paper
Graphite
12.0 L × 9.0 W Inches

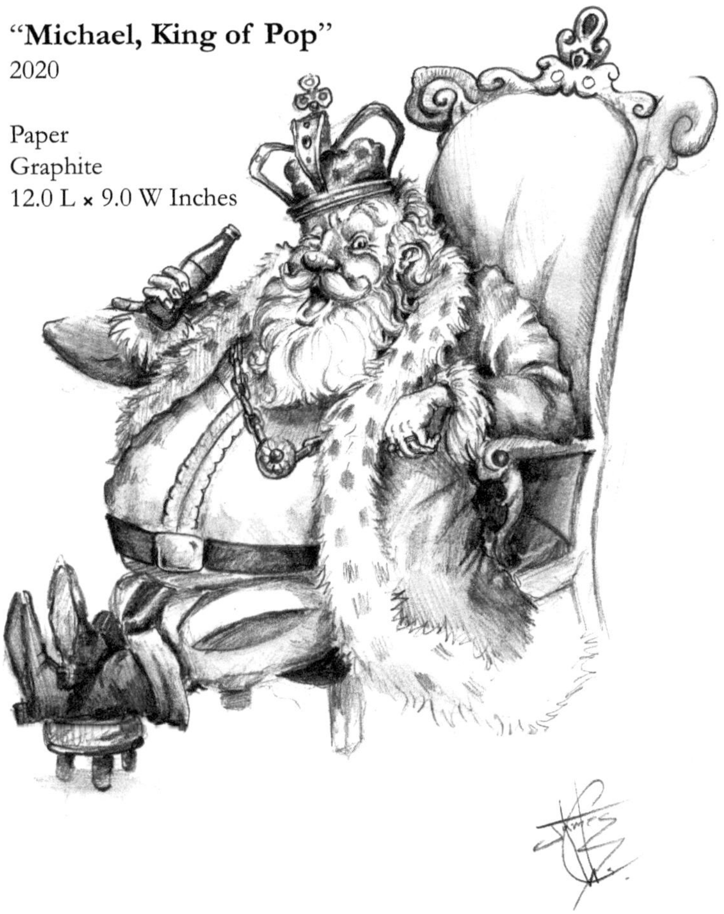

“Froward”
2020

Paper
Graphite
12.0 L × 9.0 W Inches

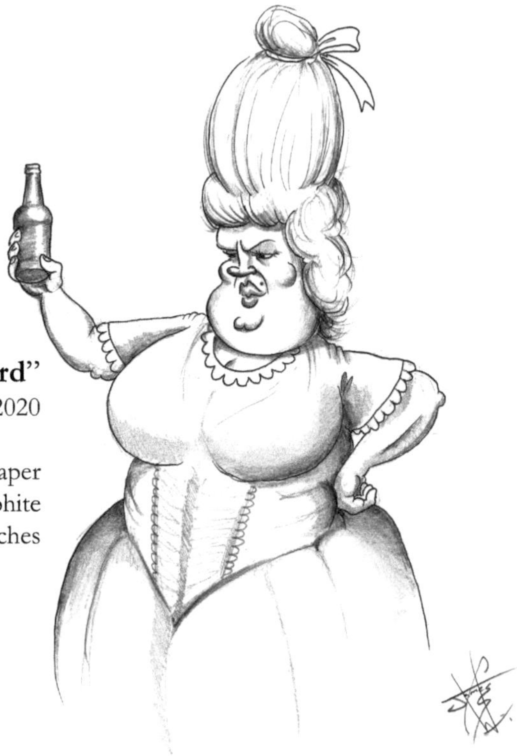

Commissioned Book Illustrations
“<u>The Bottlecap Score</u>”
Published in 2020 by Kayto & Co. Publishing
Reprinted with Permission.

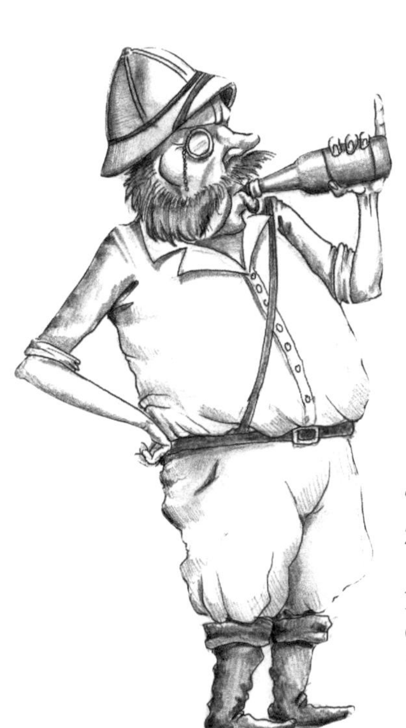

“Soda Taxonomy”
2020

Paper
Graphite
12.0 L × 9.0 W Inches

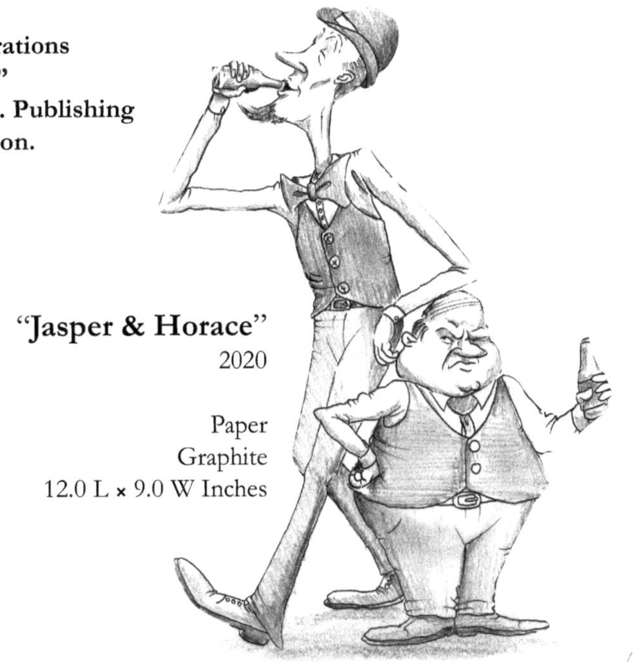

“Jasper & Horace”
2020

Paper
Graphite
12.0 L × 9.0 W Inches

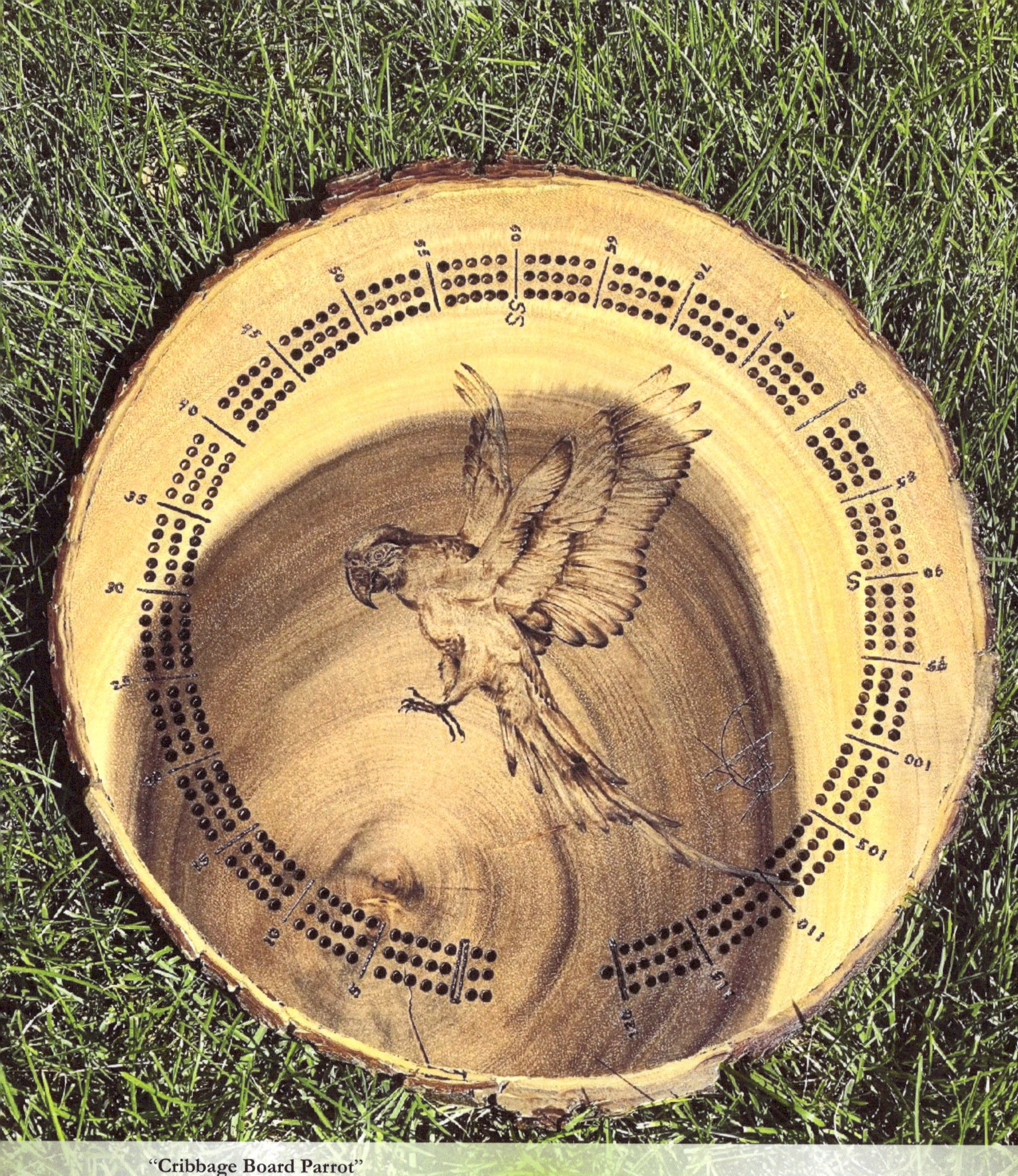

"Cribbage Board Parrot"
2019

Live Edge, Finished Acacia Wood Board
Woodburn, Laquer
13.5 L × 13.5 W Inches

Commissioned for Display
in the Private Art Collection of
Casa del Flamingo, Minnesota
Reprinted with Permission

"1814 Gator That Lost His Mind"

2019

Polymer Clay
5.0 H × 2.5 W x 4 L Inches

**In the Archives of the
James William Christenson Art Gallery
Prior Lake, Minnesota**

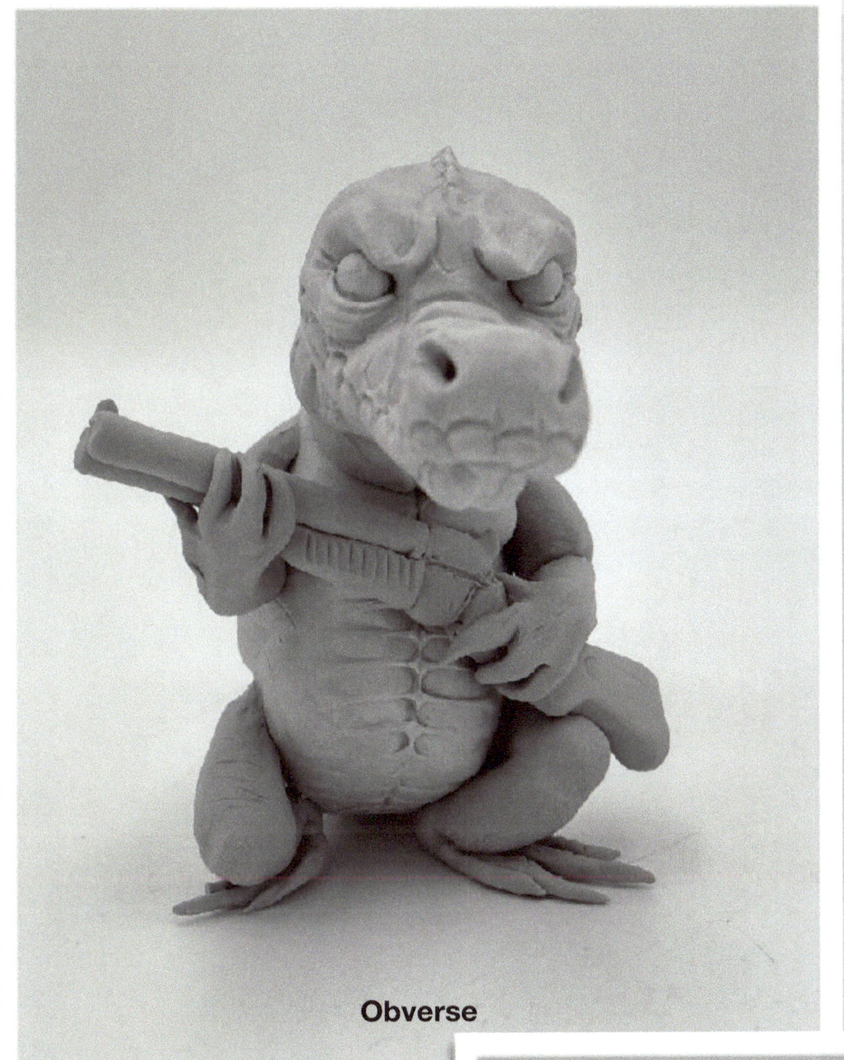

Obverse

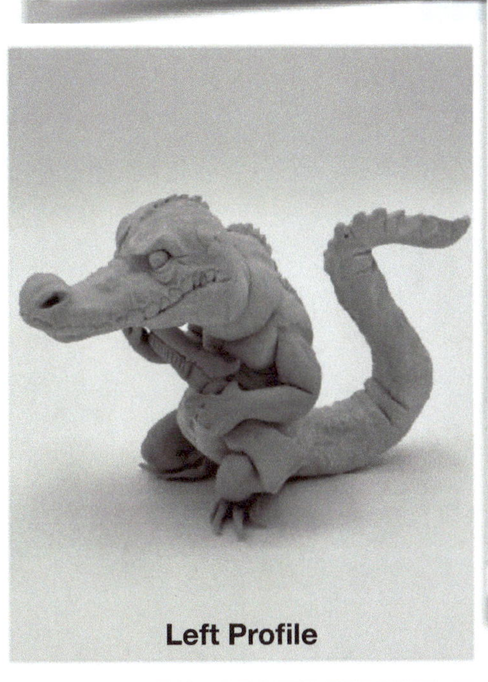

Left Profile

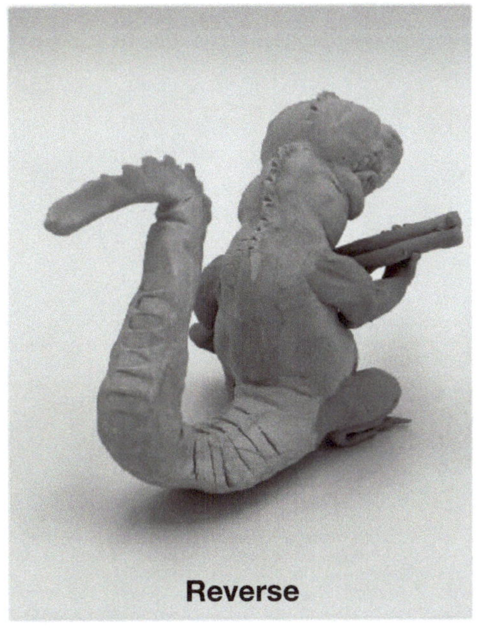

Reverse

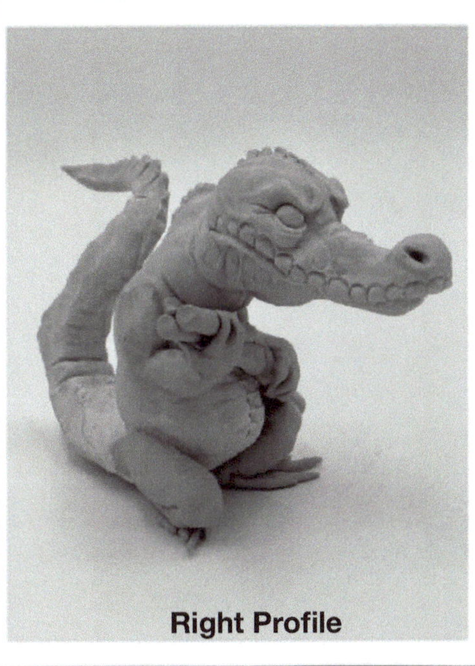

Right Profile

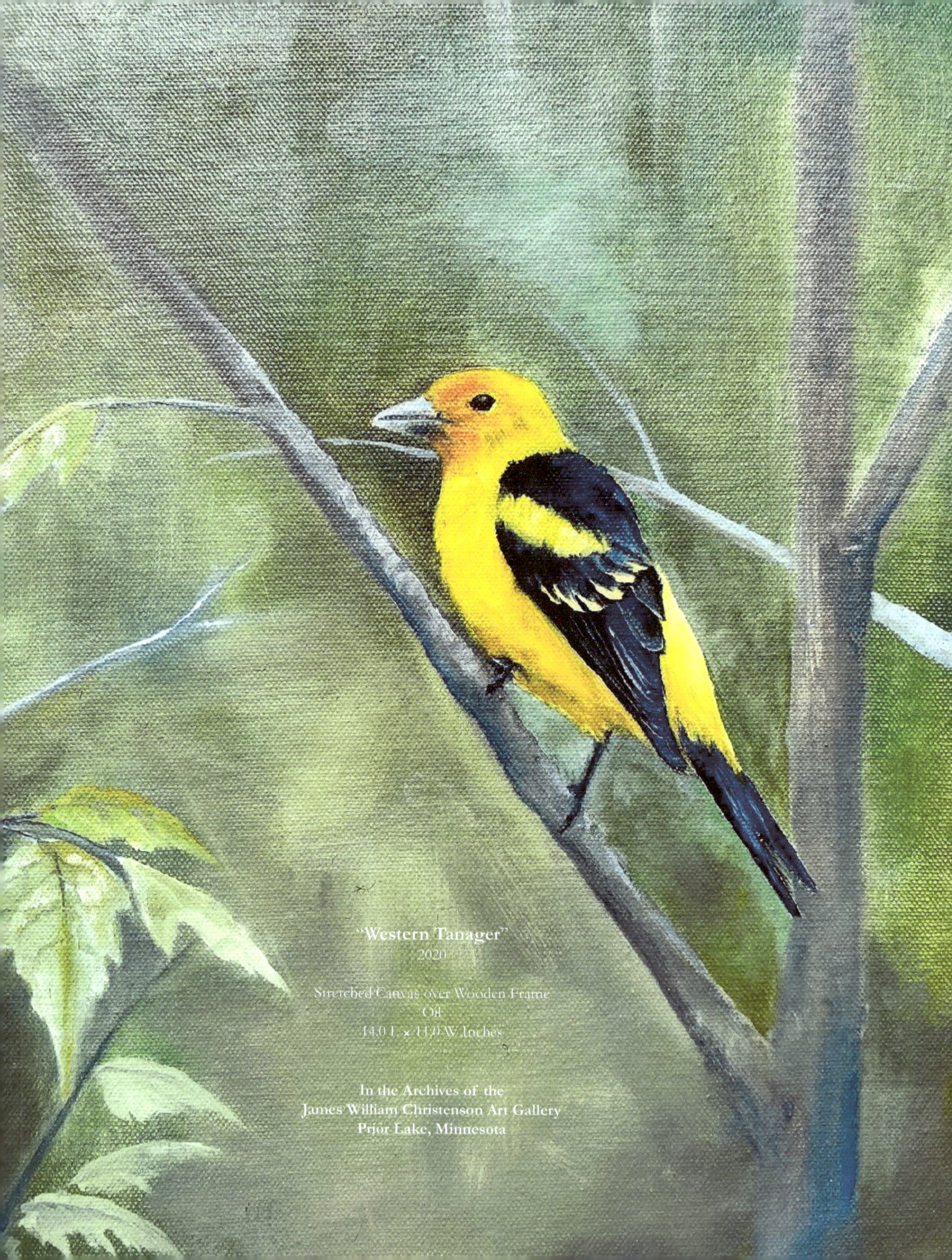

"Western Tanager"
2020

Stretched Canvas over Wooden Frame
Oil
14.0 L x 11.0 W Inches

In the Archives of the
James William Christenson Art Gallery
Prior Lake, Minnesota

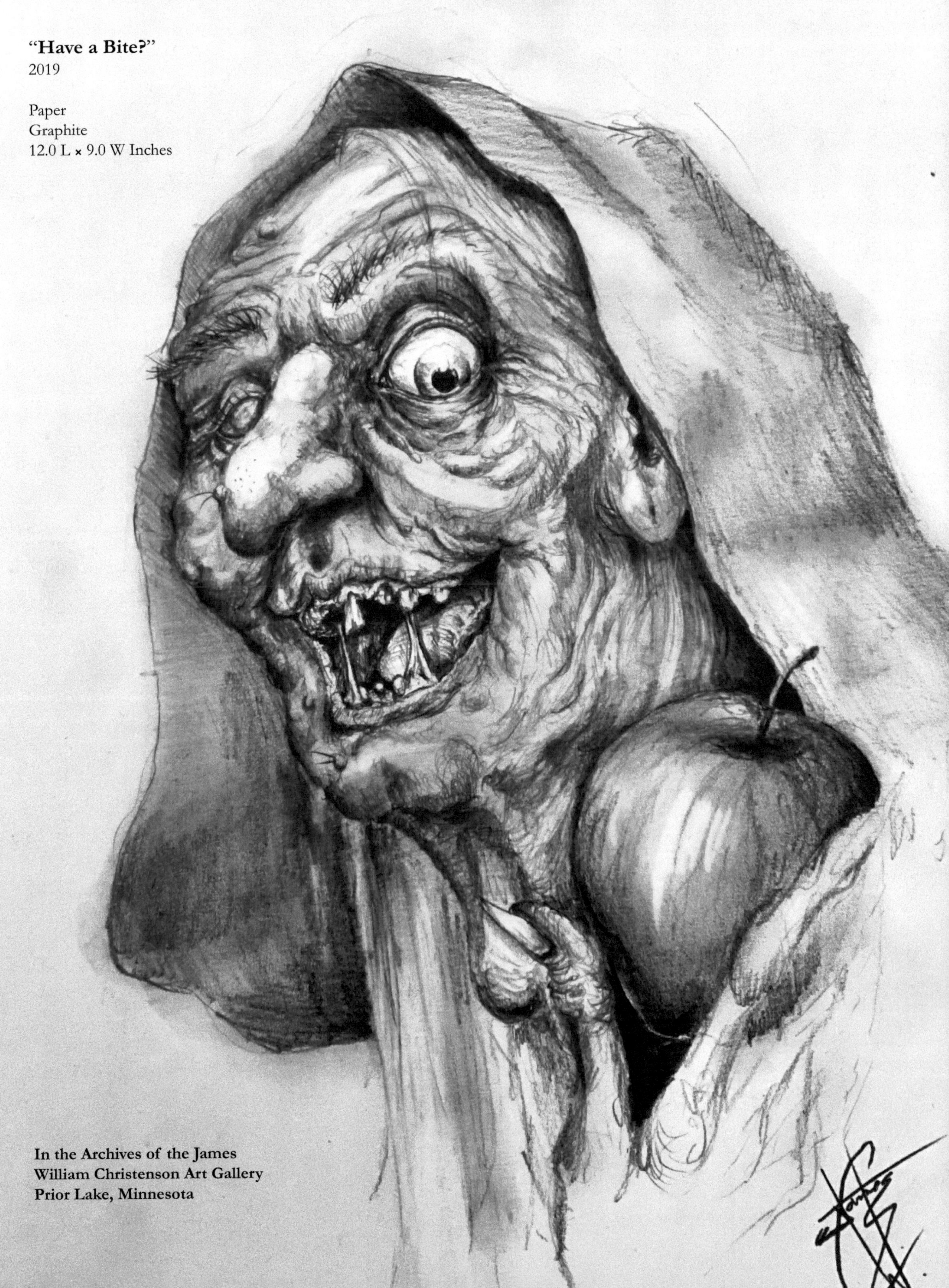

"Have a Bite?"
2019

Paper
Graphite
12.0 L × 9.0 W Inches

In the Archives of the James William Christenson Art Gallery Prior Lake, Minnesota

"Yellow Jacket"
[Vespula Vulgaris]
2020

Watercolor Paper
Oil
12.0 L × 9.0 W Inches

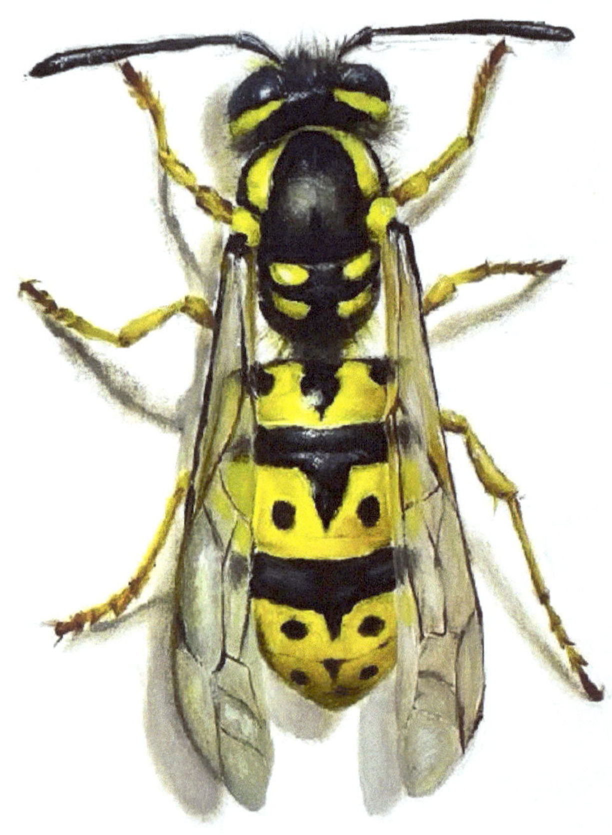

ENTOMOLOGY I.D.
NO: 61611372
DATE: JUN.1.2020
NAME: yellow Jacket

In the Archives of the
James William Christenson Art Gallery
Prior Lake, Minnesota

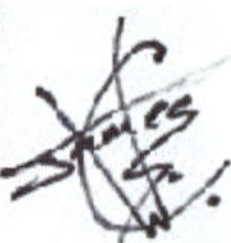

“Lucy”
[Lucilia Sericata]
2020

Watercolor Paper
Oil
12.0 L × 9.0 W Inches

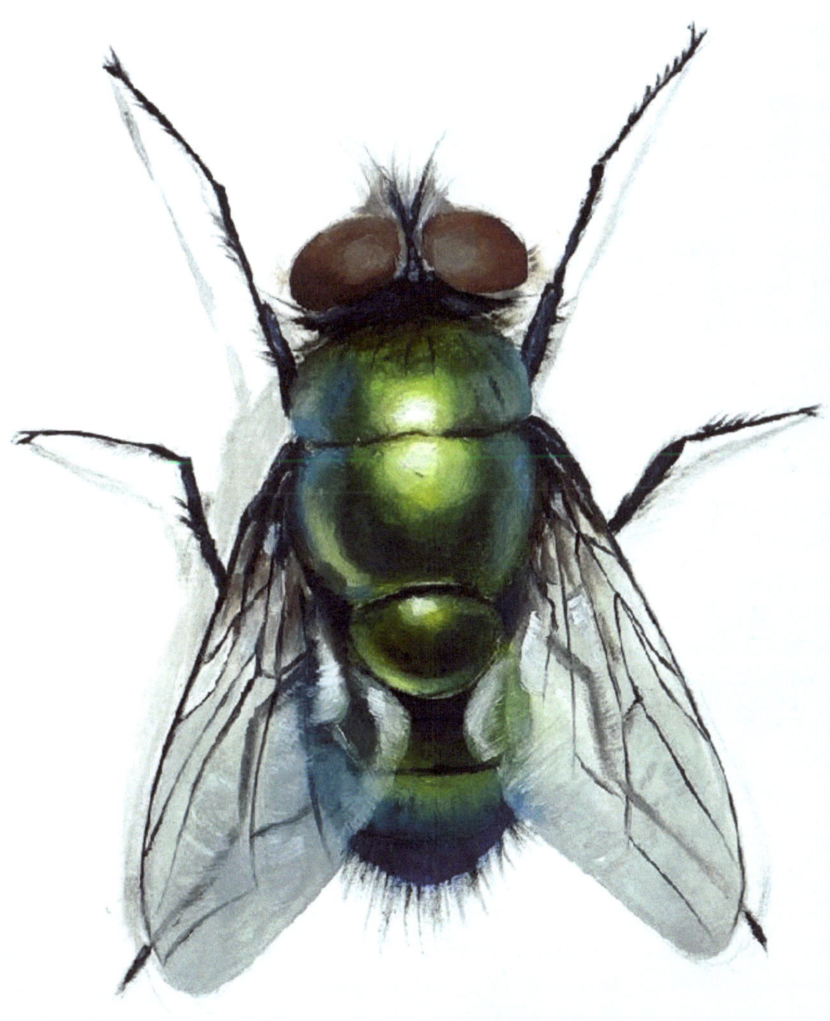

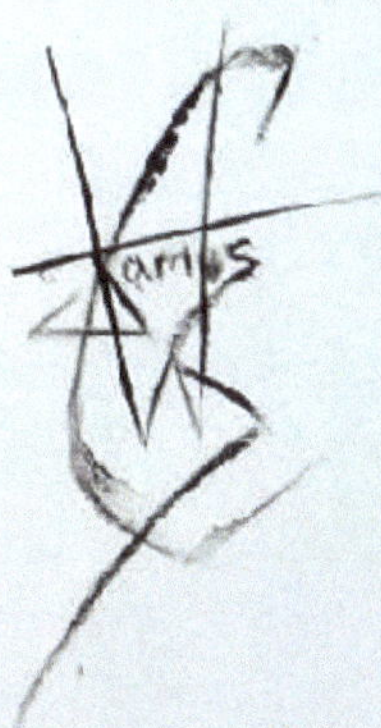

In the Archives of the
James William Christenson Art Gallery
Prior Lake, Minnesota

"Wish You Were Here"
Postcard Front
2020

Watercolor Cardstock
Pen, Brush Tip Marker
4.0 L × 6.0 W Inches

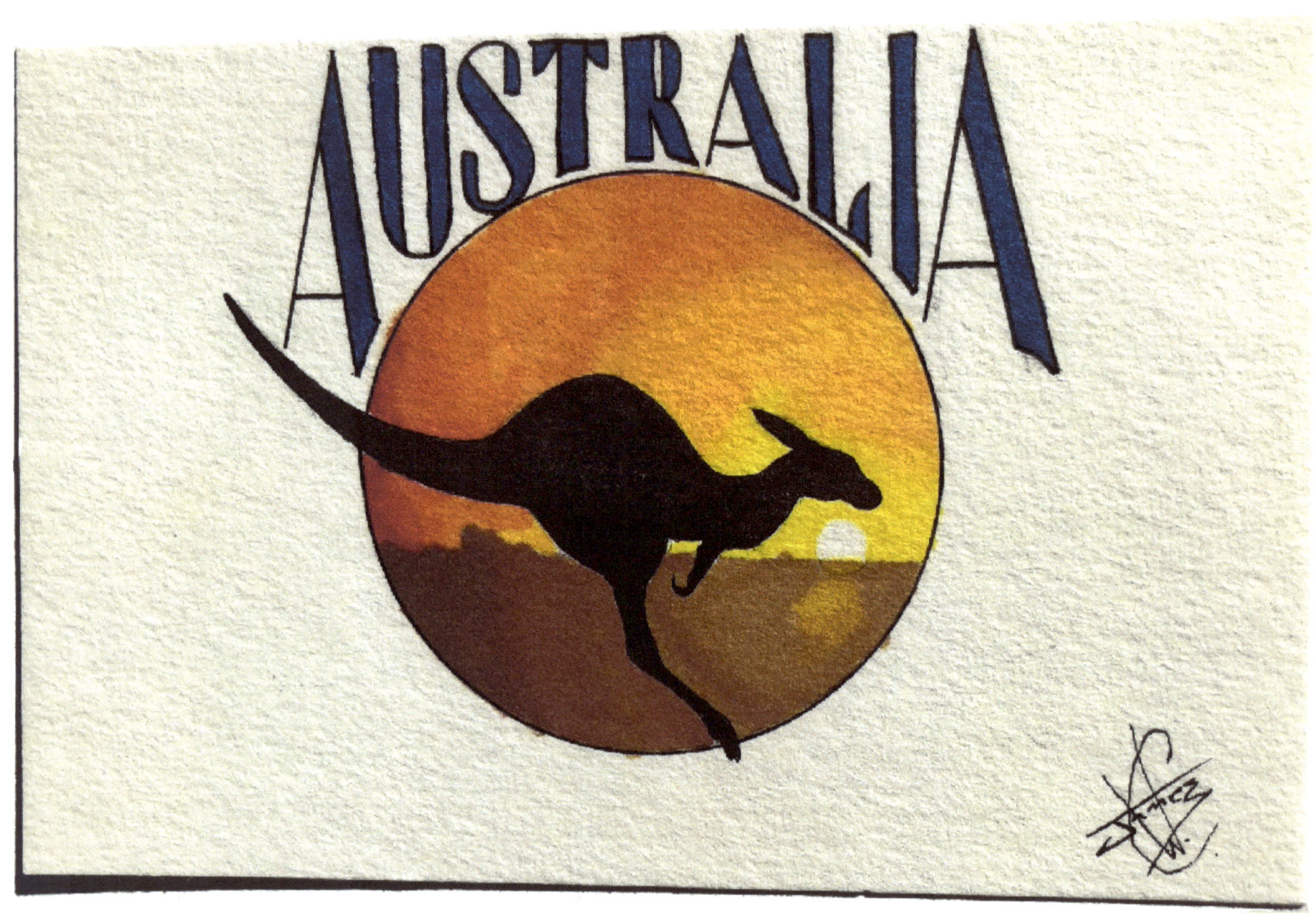

Presented as a Gift.
Private Art Collection
Cincinnati, Ohio
Reprinted with Permission.

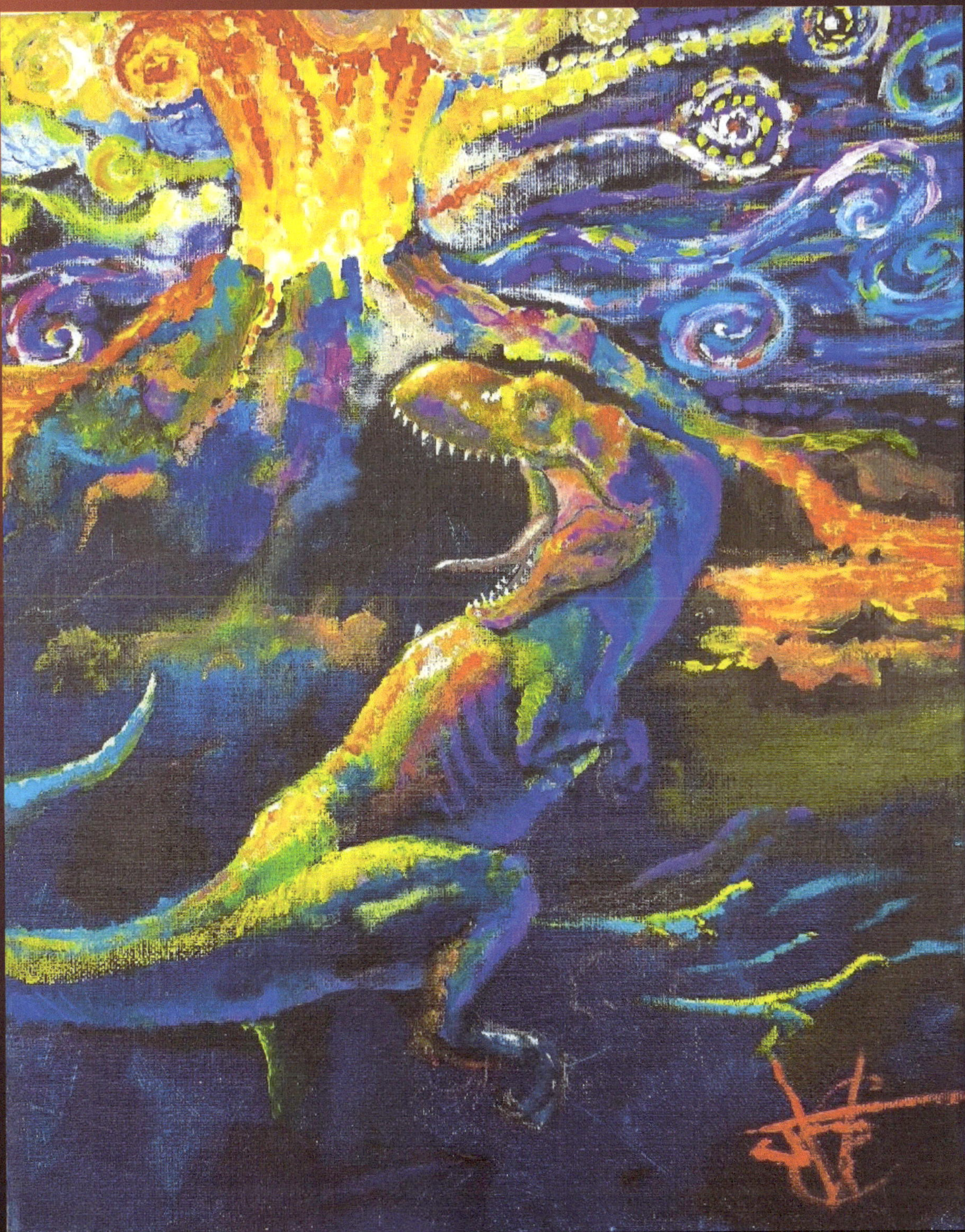

"Forgot the Brownies in the Oven"
2018

Stretched Canvass over Wooden Frame
Oil
14.0 L × 11.0 W Inches

In the Archives of the James William Christenson Art Gallery Prior Lake, Minnesota

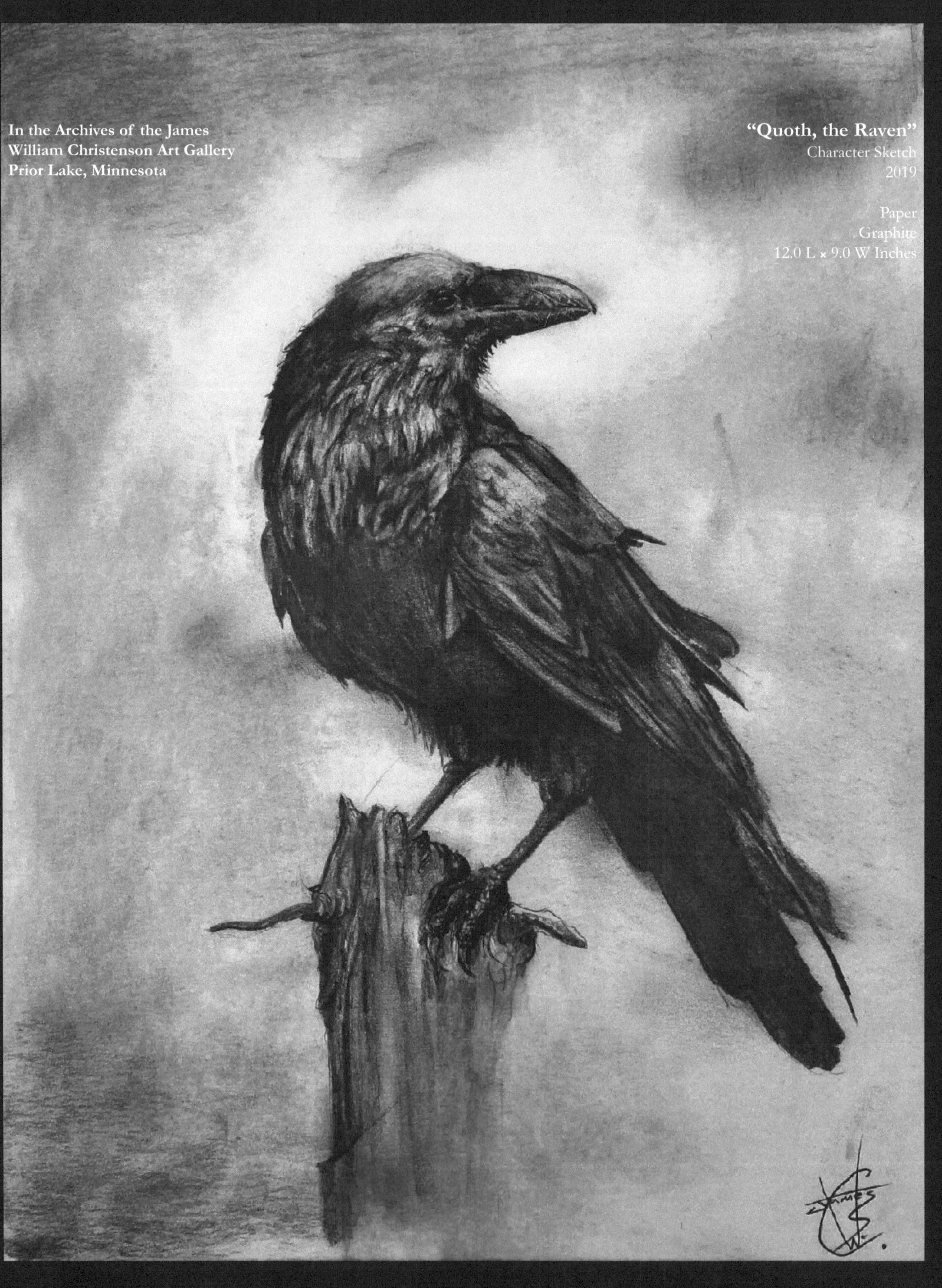
In the Archives of the James
William Christenson Art Gallery
Prior Lake, Minnesota
"Quoth, the Raven"
Character Sketch
2019
Paper
Graphite
12.0 L × 9.0 W Inches

"The Urn of Whispering Warriors"
2016

Vase
Oil Markers
11.0 H × 7.0 W Inches

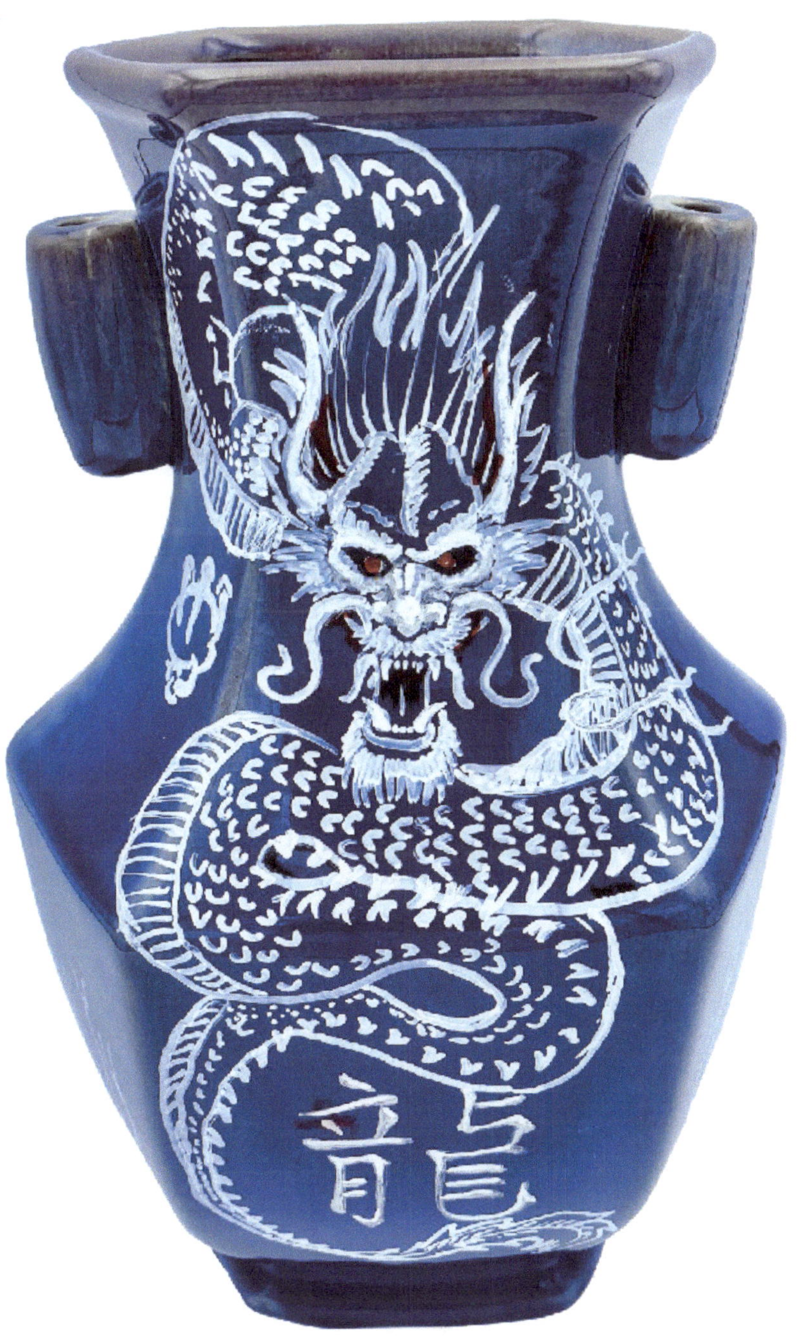

In the Archives of the James William Christenson Art Gallery Prior Lake, Minnesota

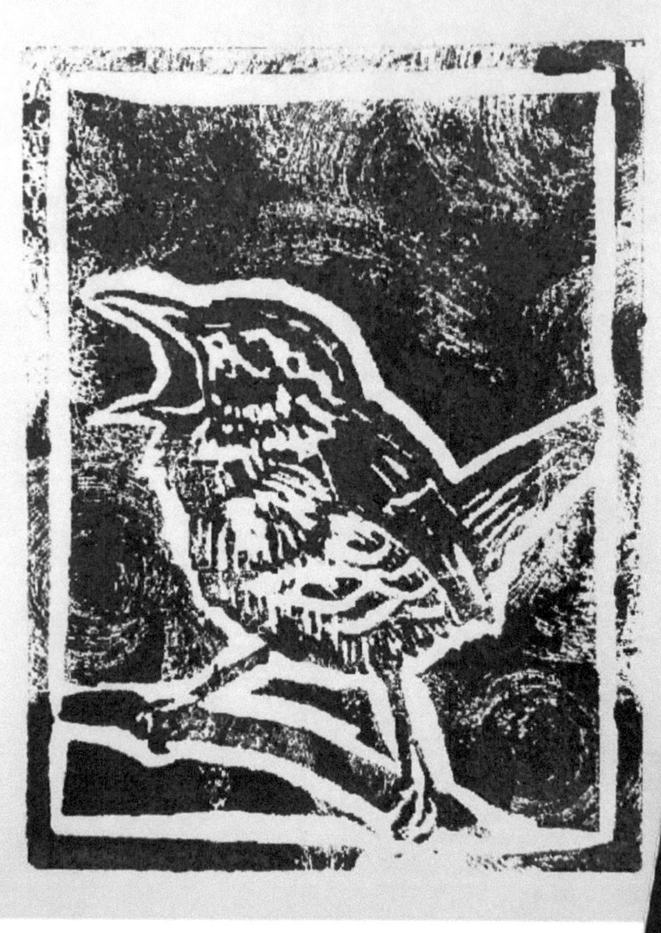

"Woodblock Troglodytidae"
2020

Carved Laminate, Paper
Ink
4.0 L × 3.0 W Inches

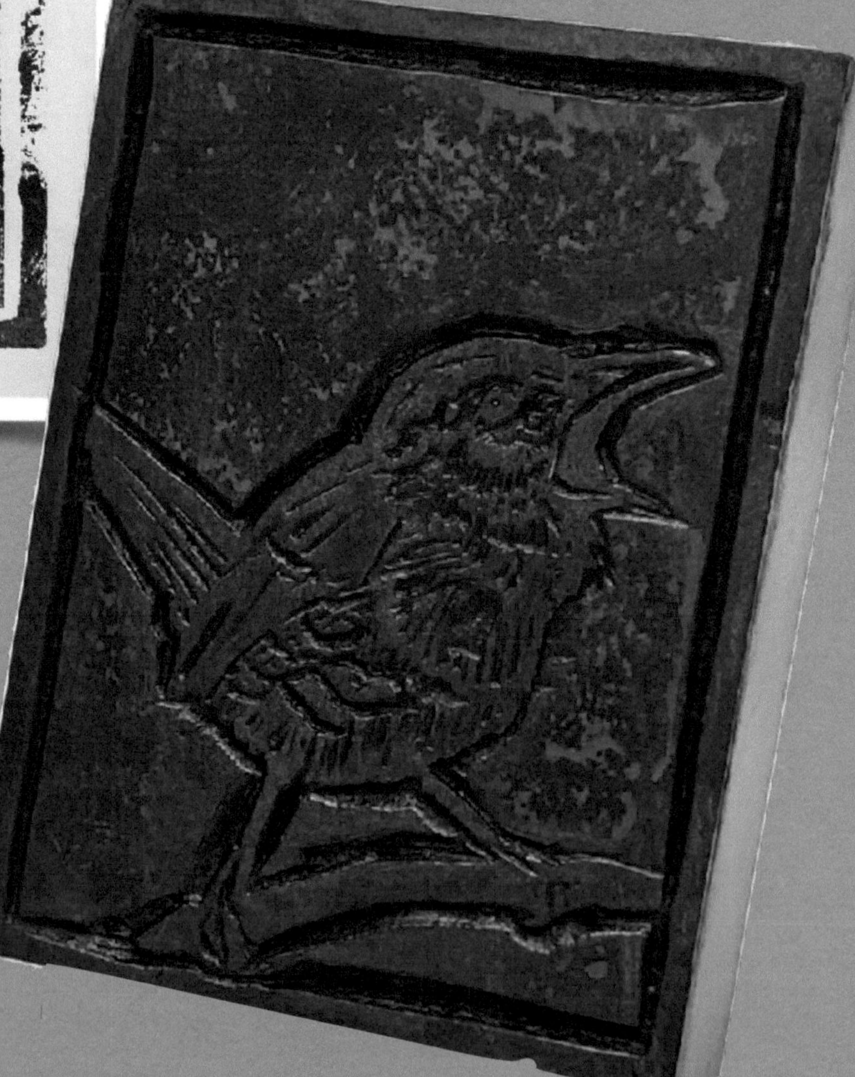

In the Archives of the
James William Christenson Art Gallery
Prior Lake, Minnesota

"Blue Jay?"
2018

Paper
Ink, Watercolor
12.0 L × 9.0 W Inches

In the Archives of the James
William Christenson Art Gallery
Prior Lake, Minnesota

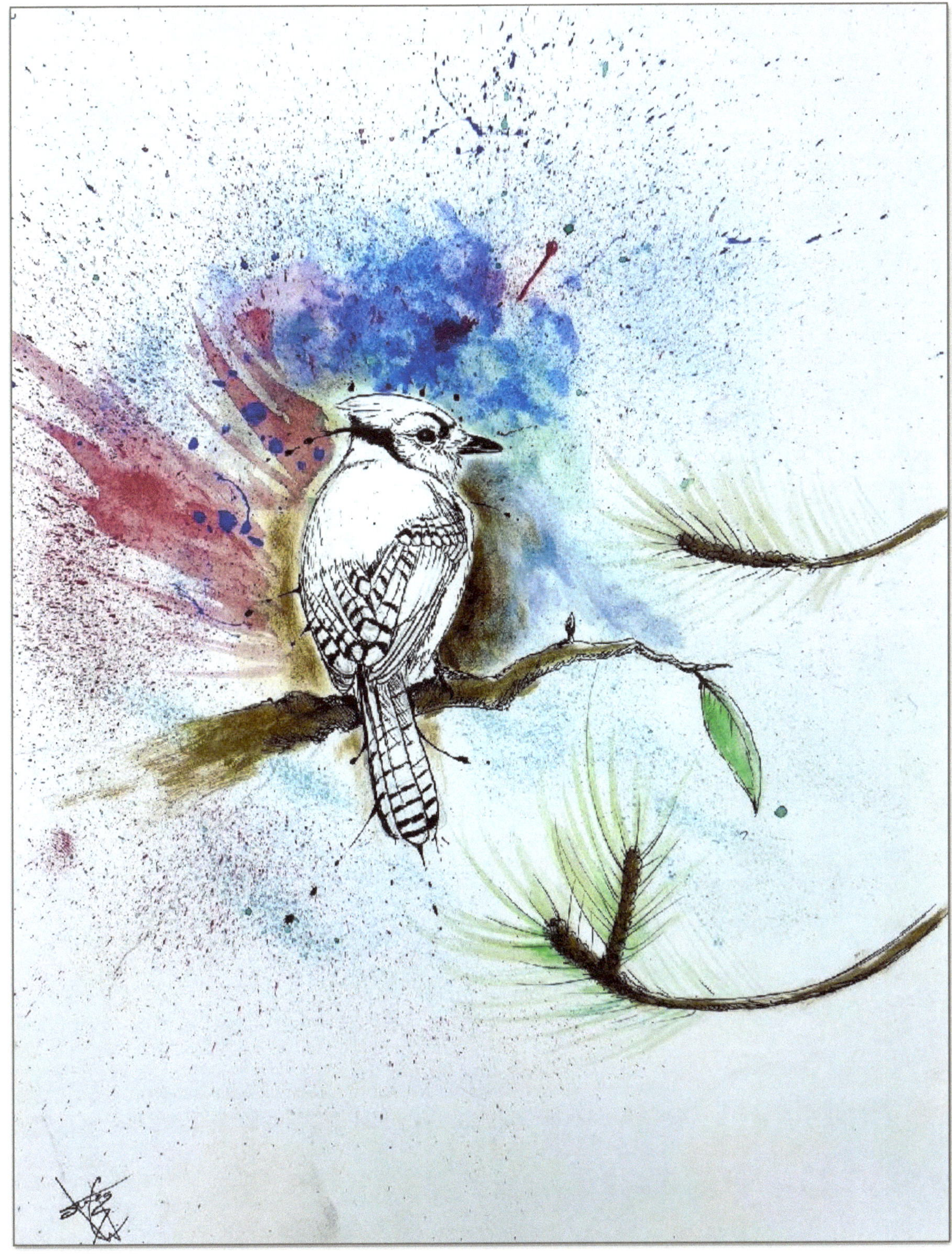

"Flip Book"
2020
Paper
Graphite, Ink
3.0 L × 1.0 W Inches

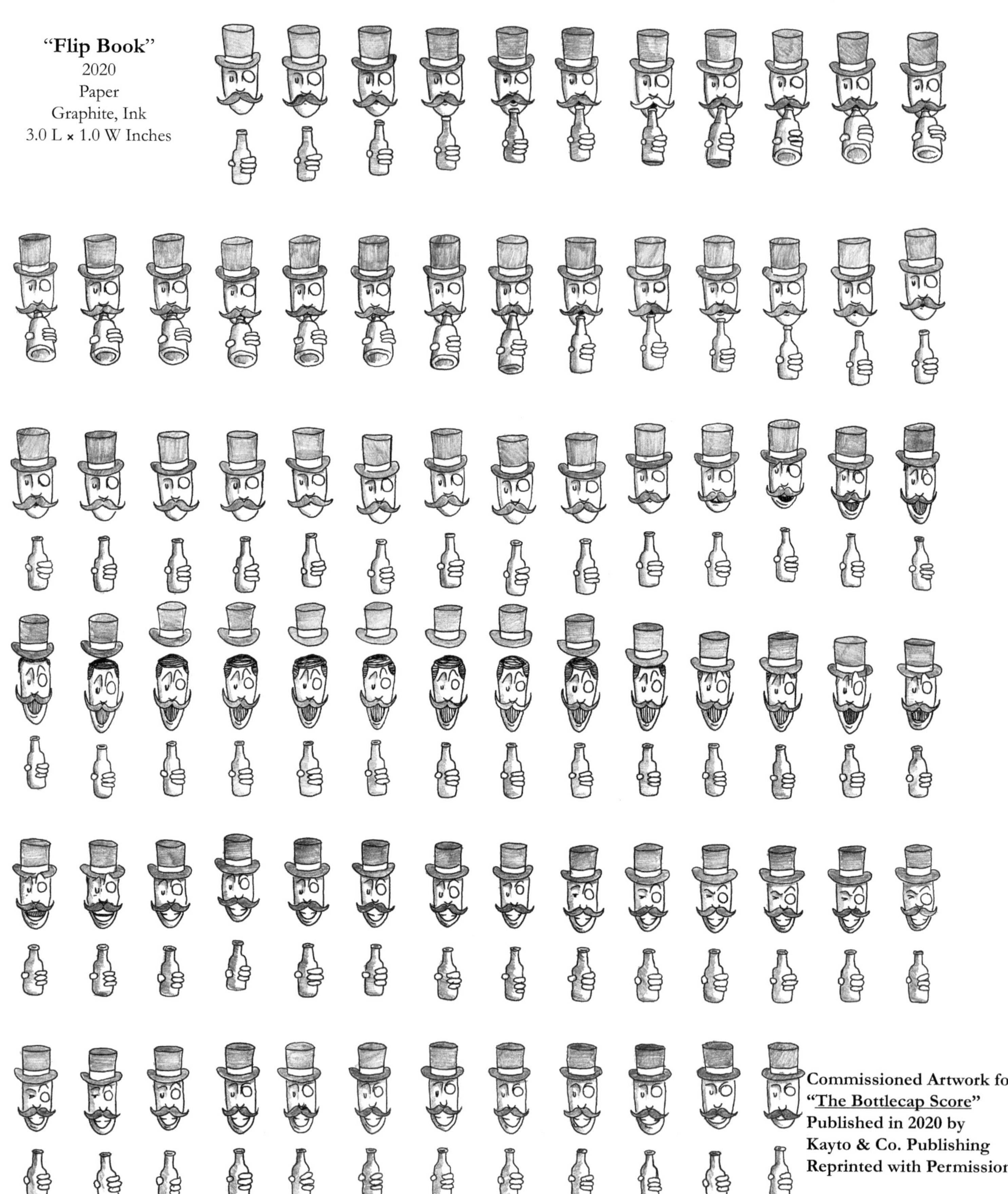

Commissioned Artwork for "The Bottlecap Score" Published in 2020 by Kayto & Co. Publishing Reprinted with Permission.

“Serenissima”
2016

Mat Board
Gouache
7.5 L × 5.0 W Inches

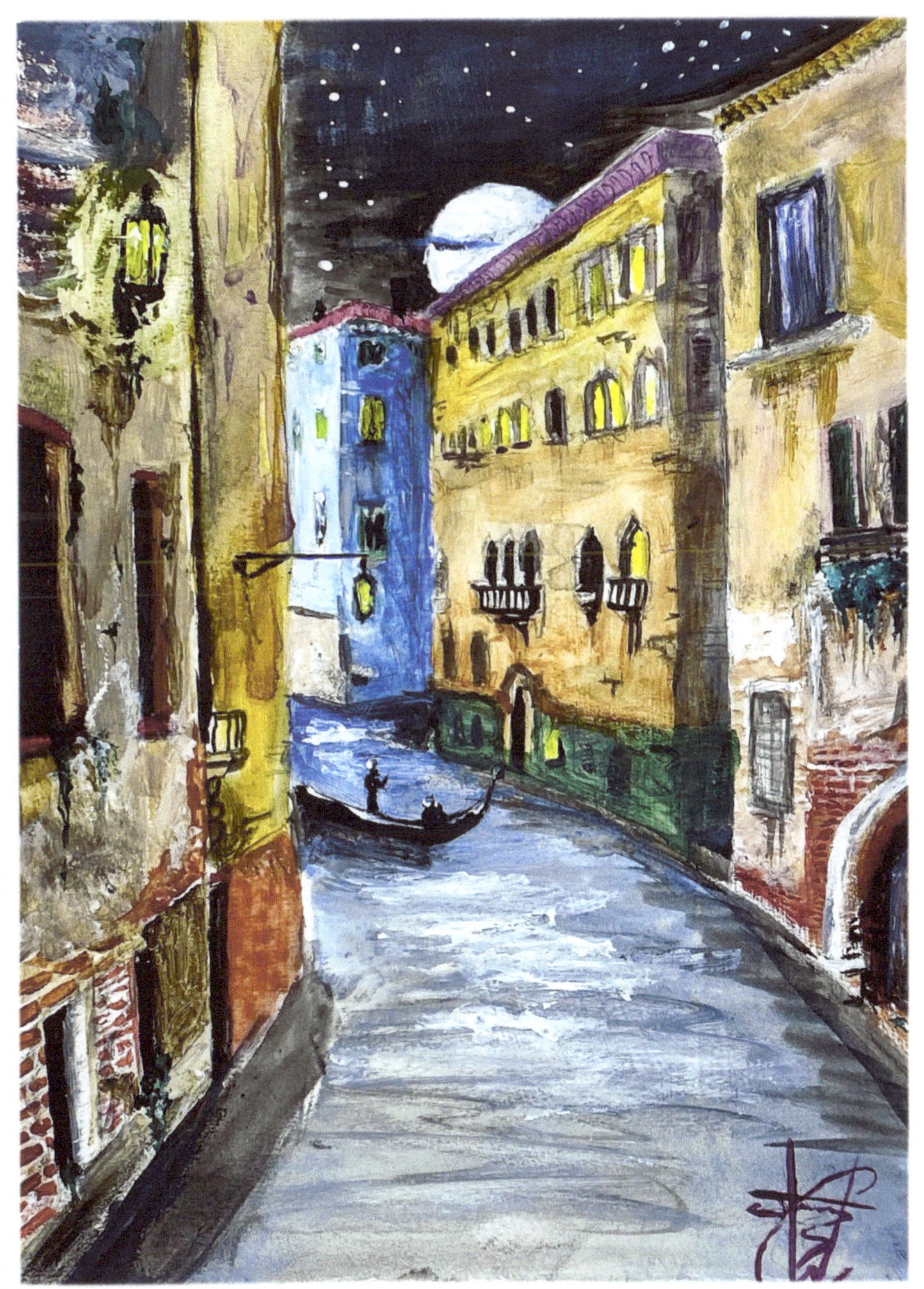

In the Archives of the
James William Christenson Art Gallery
Prior Lake, Minnesota

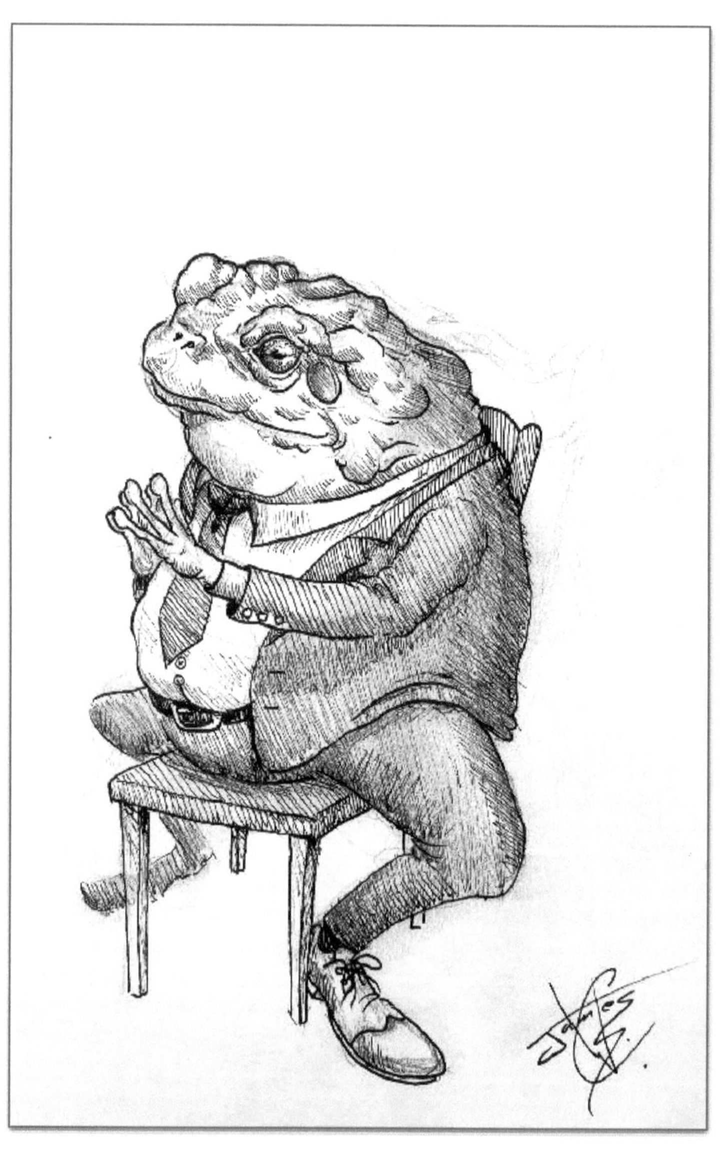

"Mr. Toad"
2020

Paper
Pen, Graphite
8.5 L × 5.5 W Inches

In the Archives of the
James William Christenson Art Gallery
Prior Lake, Minnesota

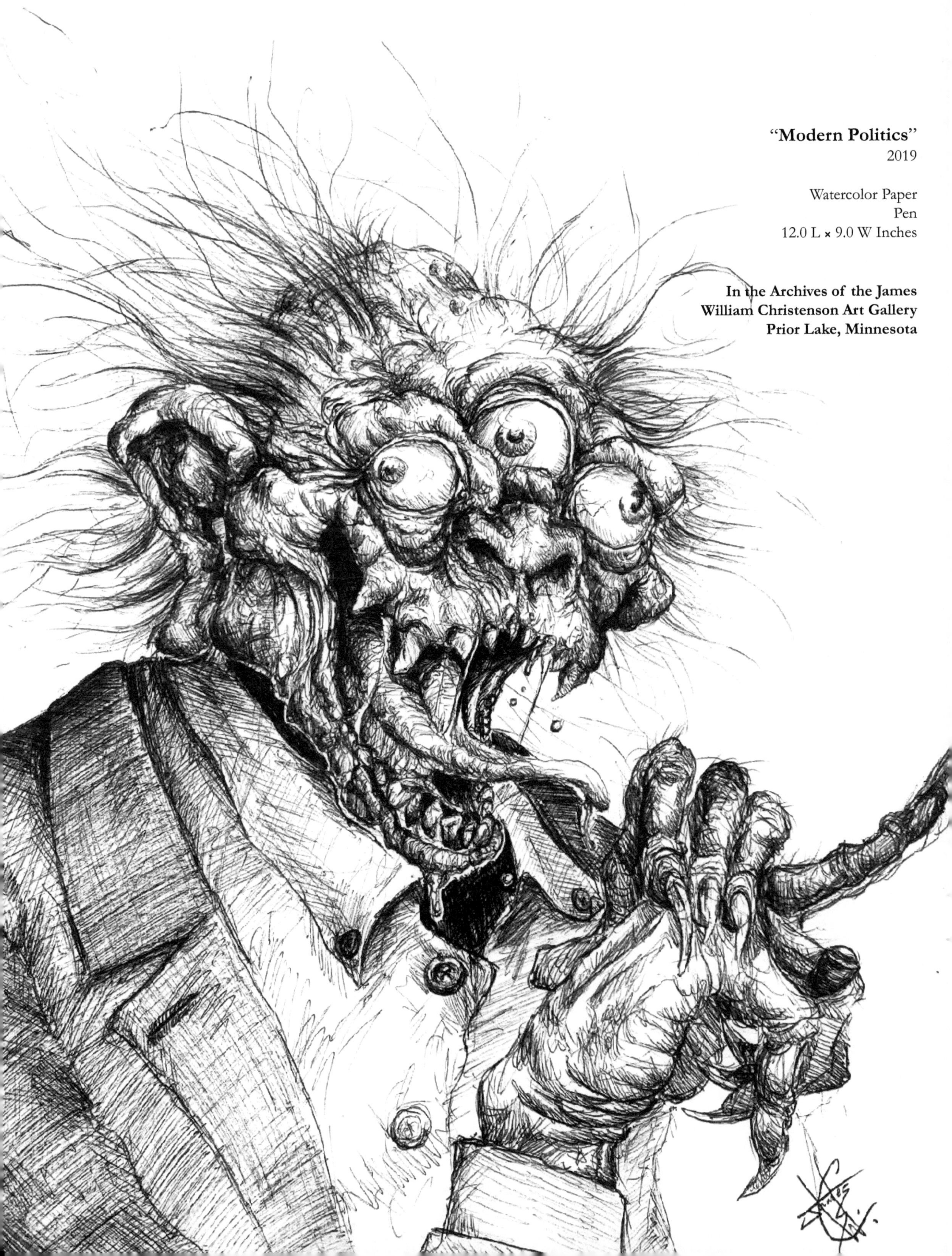

"Modern Politics"
2019

Watercolor Paper
Pen
12.0 L × 9.0 W Inches

In the Archives of the James William Christenson Art Gallery Prior Lake, Minnesota

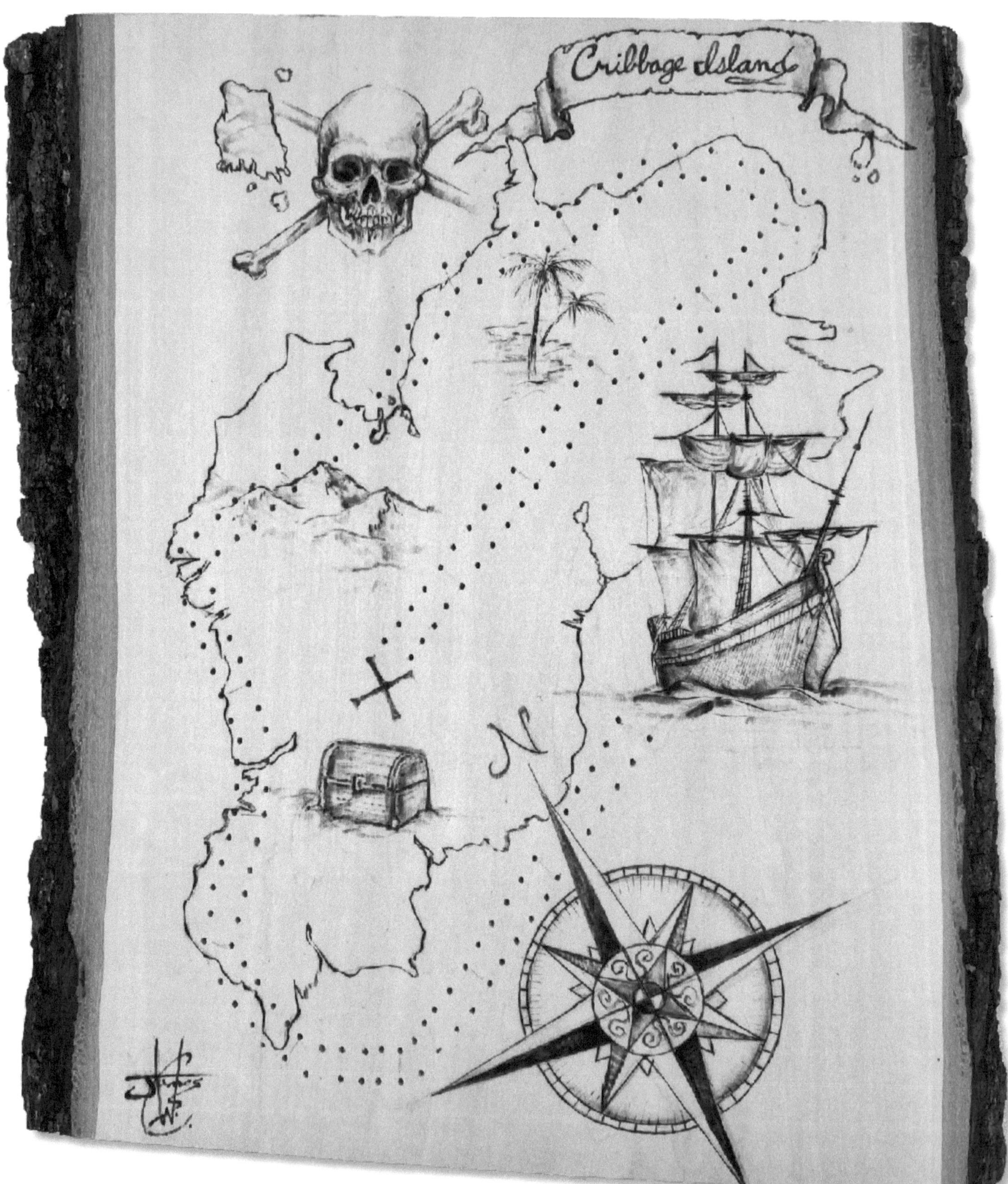
Cribbage Island
N

FACING PAGE

"Cribbage Island"
2019

Live Edge Unfinished Basswood Board
Woodburn
11.25 L × 9.5 W Inches

Presented as a Gift.
Private Art Collection
Cedarville, Ohio
Reprinted with Permission.

RIGHT

"Fancy"
Non Finito
2019

Mat Board
Graphite, Ink
20.0 L × 10.0 W Inches

In the Archives of the
James William Christenson Art Gallery
Prior Lake, Minnesota

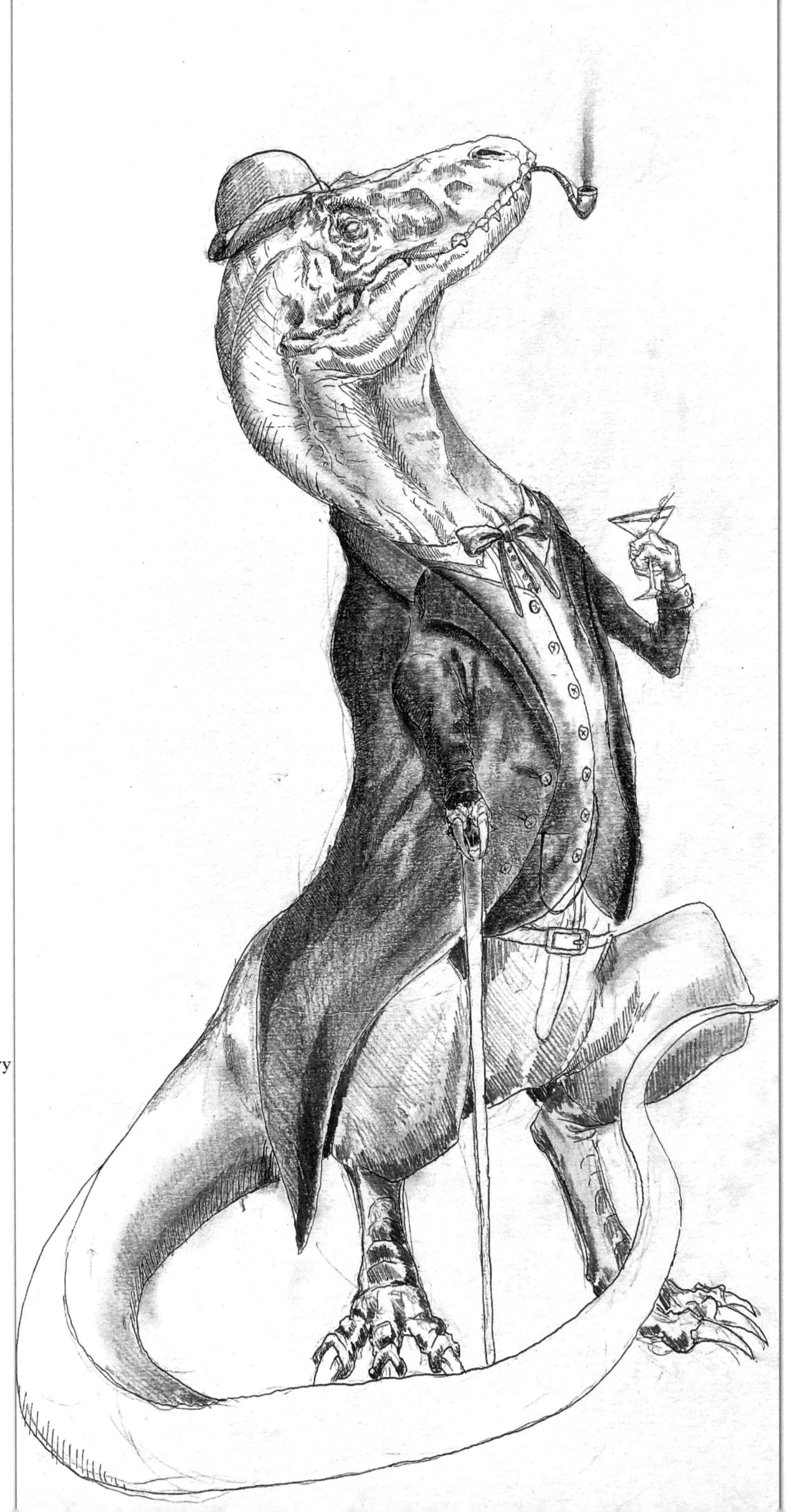

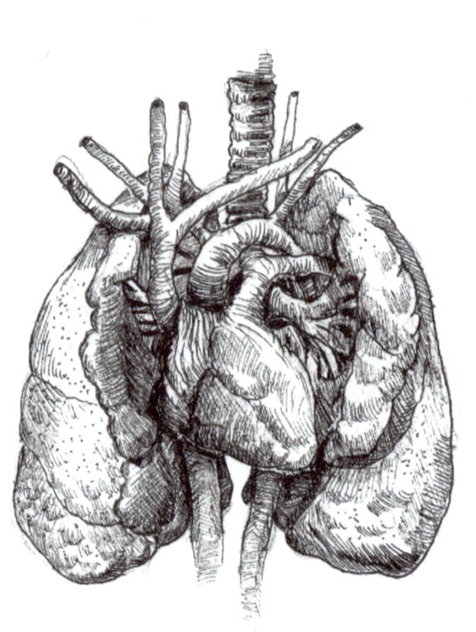

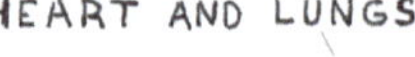

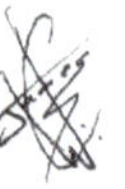

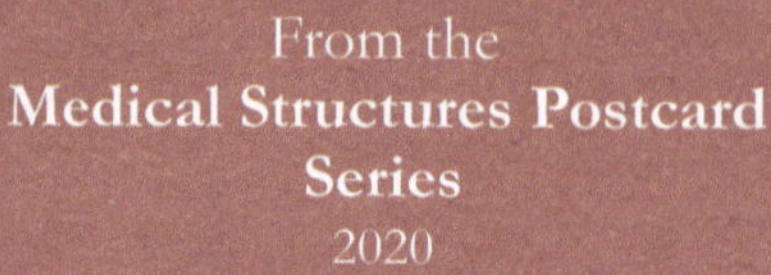

From the
Medical Structures Postcard Series
2020

Watercolor Paper
Ink
6.0 L × 4.0 W Inches

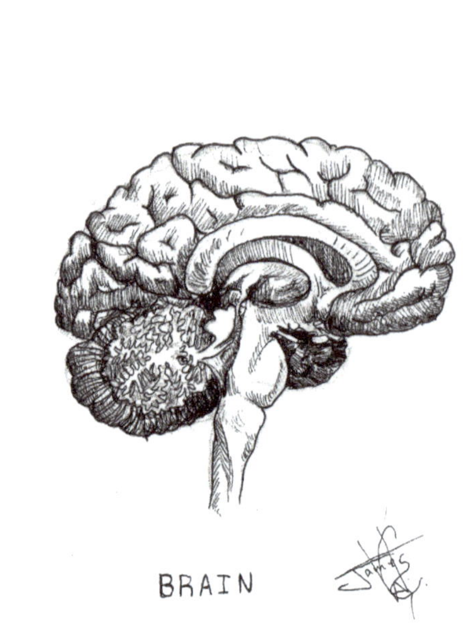

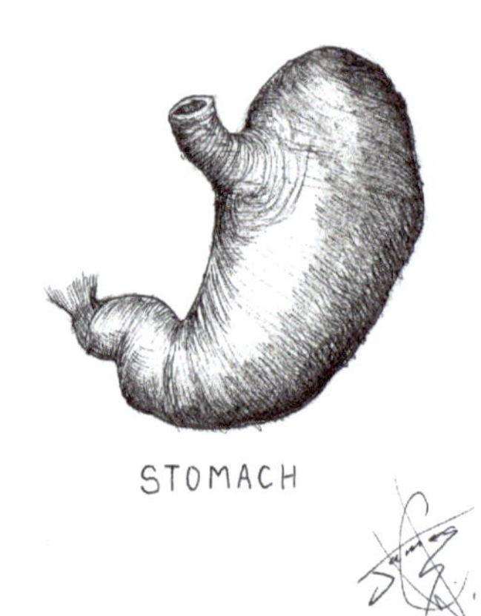

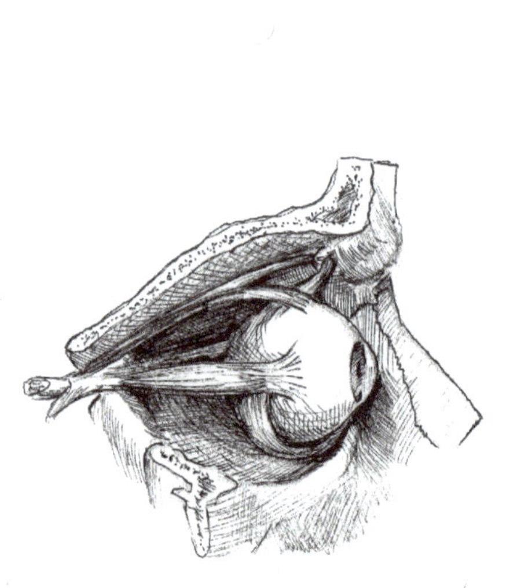

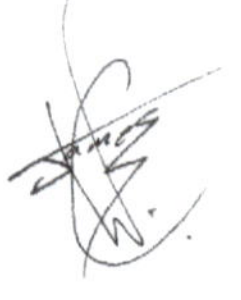

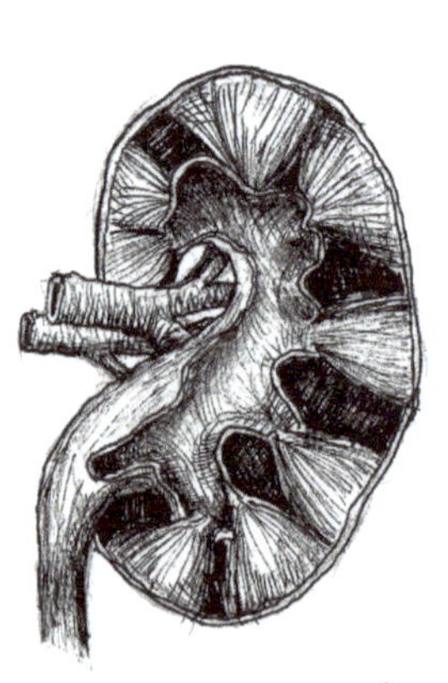

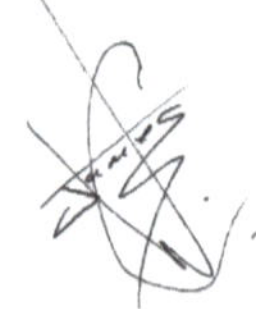

Presented as a Gift.
Private Art Collection
Cincinnati, Ohio
Reprinted with Permission.

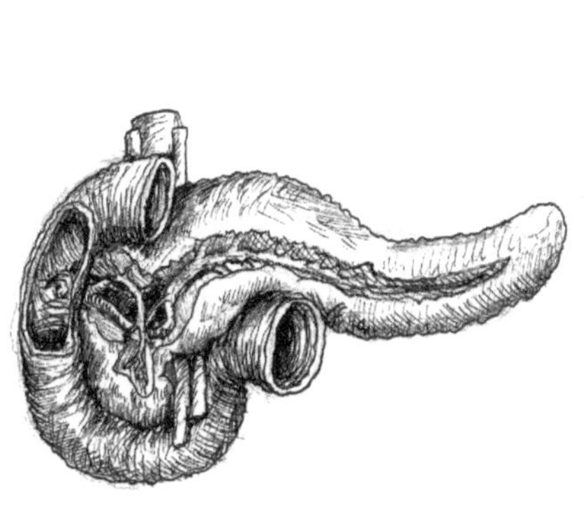

PANCREAS

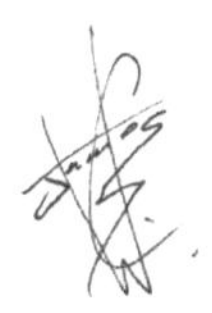

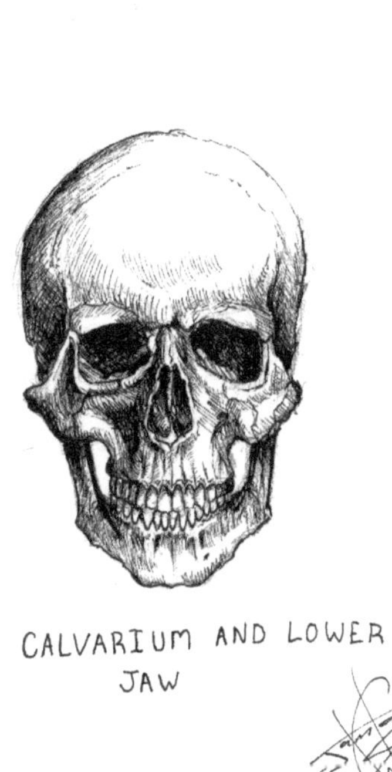

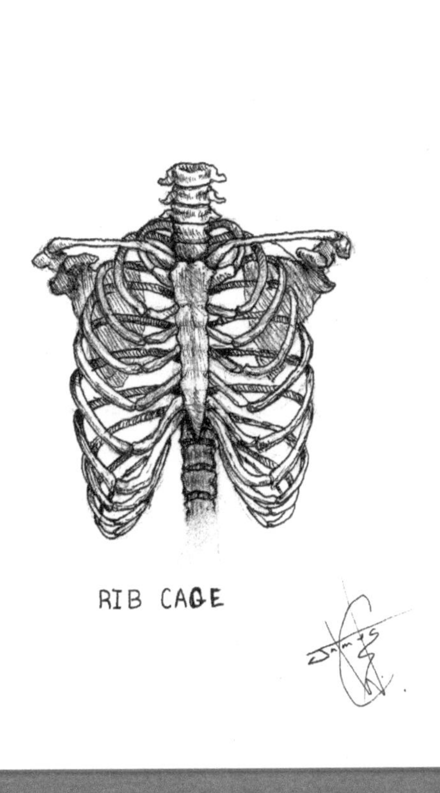

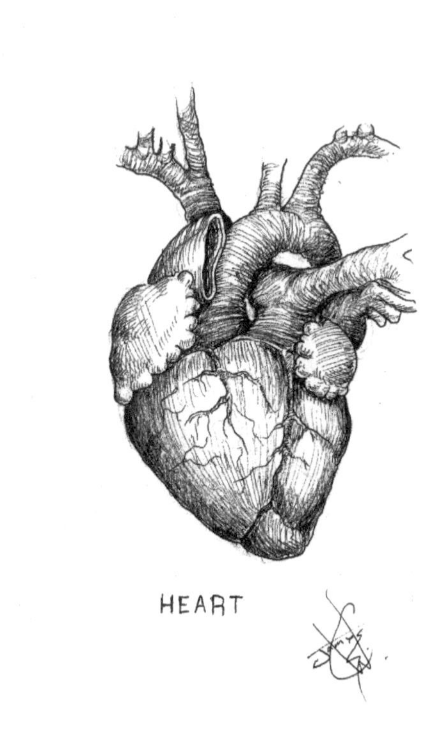

"Adventure Journal"
2019

Leather, Parchment, Ink, Gold
8.0 L × 6.0 W x 2.25 H Inches

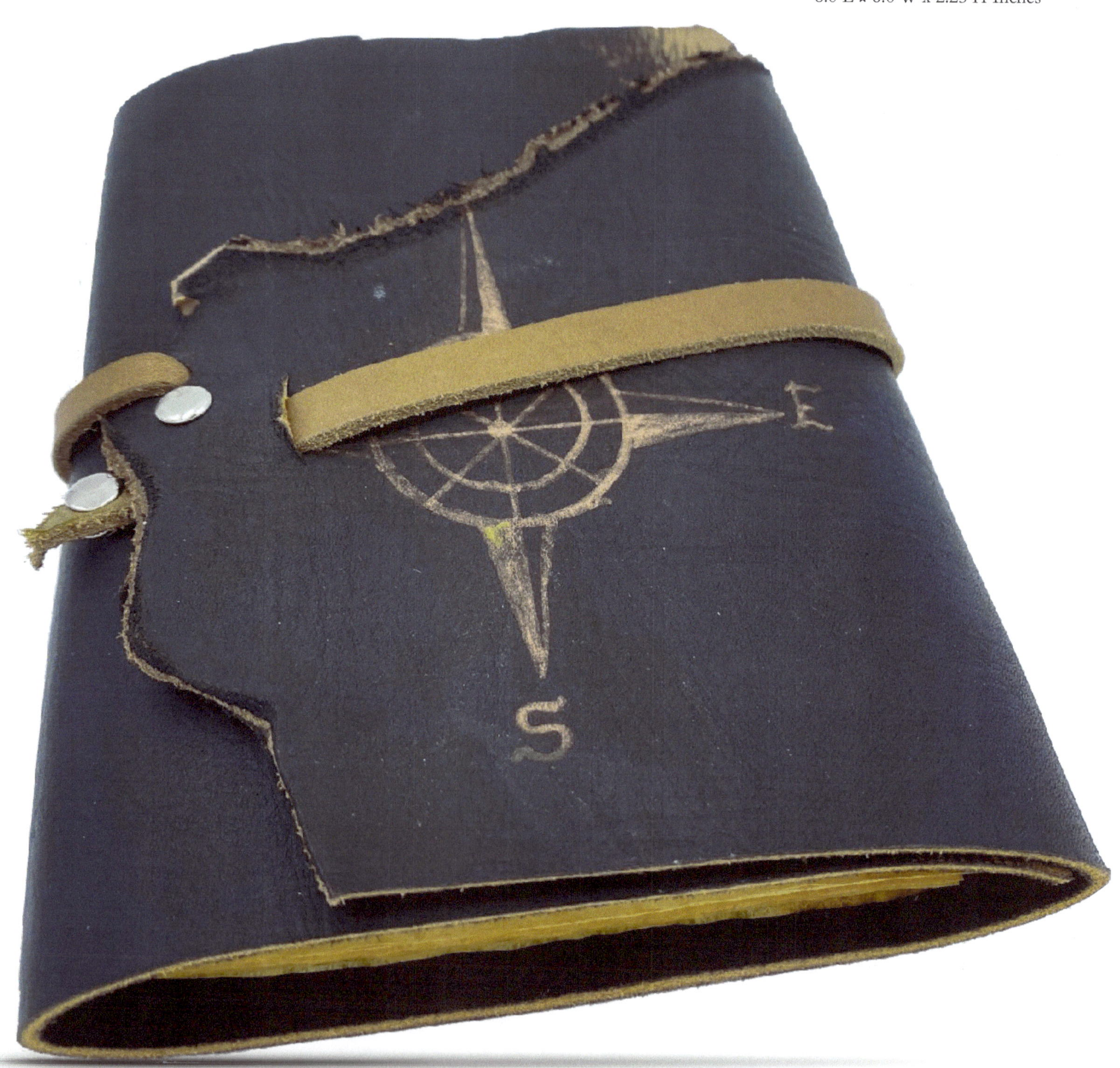

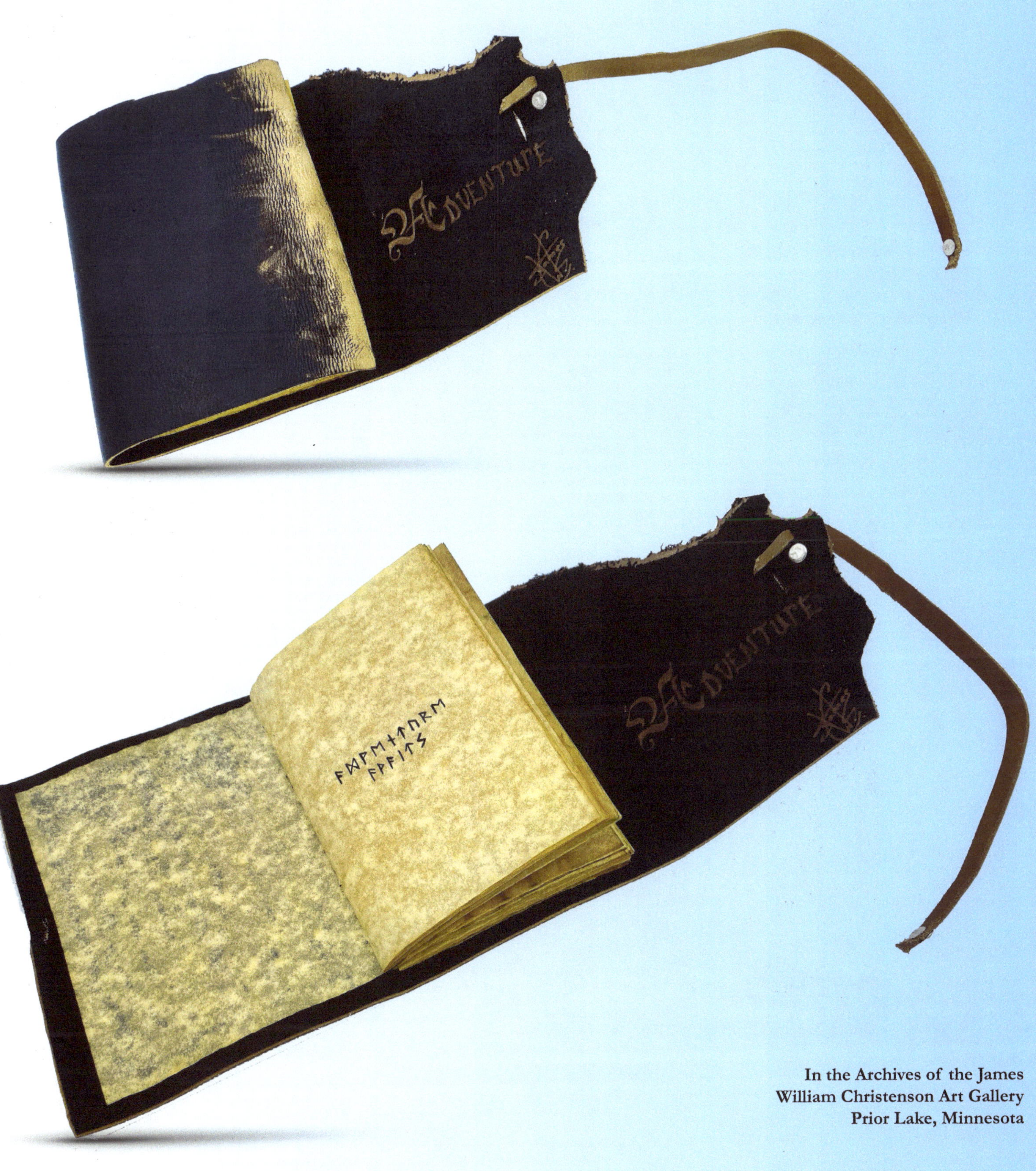

In the Archives of the James
William Christenson Art Gallery
Prior Lake, Minnesota

RIGHT

"Death of the Hashtag"
Actual Size
2017

Atlantic Seashore Rock
Acrylic
2 L × 1.5 W Inches

In the Archives of the
James William Christenson Art Gallery
Prior Lake, Minnesota

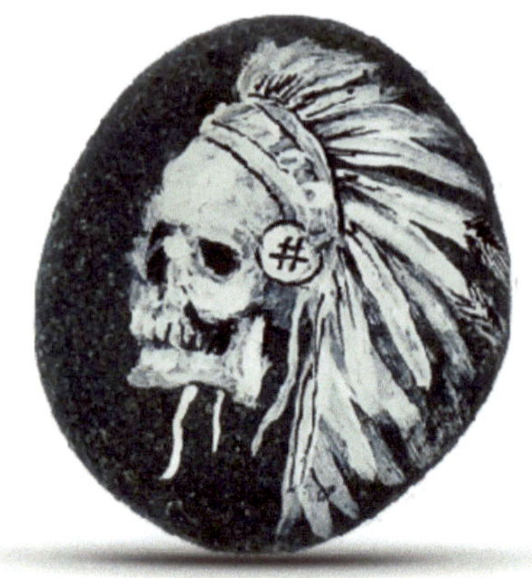

BELOW

"Rough Beast Slouches"
2020

Bristol Paper
Graphite
9.0 L × 12.0 W Inches

In the Archives of the
James William Christenson Art Gallery
Prior Lake, Minnesota

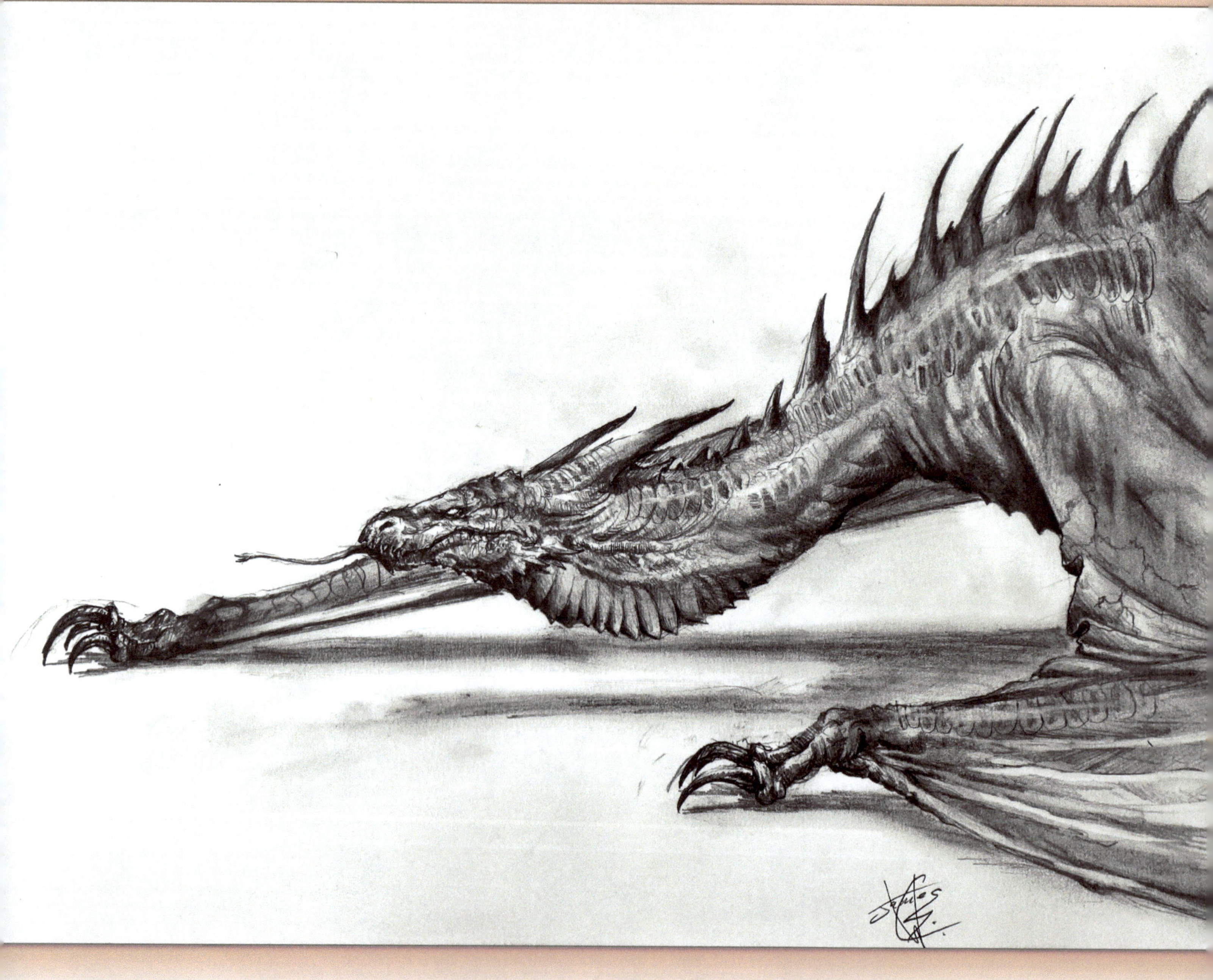

“**Dead Woman’s Jam**”
(It’s a long story…)
2018

Paper
Ink, Marker, Graphite
11.0 L × 8.5 W Inches

Commissioned by Casa del Flamingo
On Loan to the James William
Christenson Art Gallery
Plymouth, Minnesota

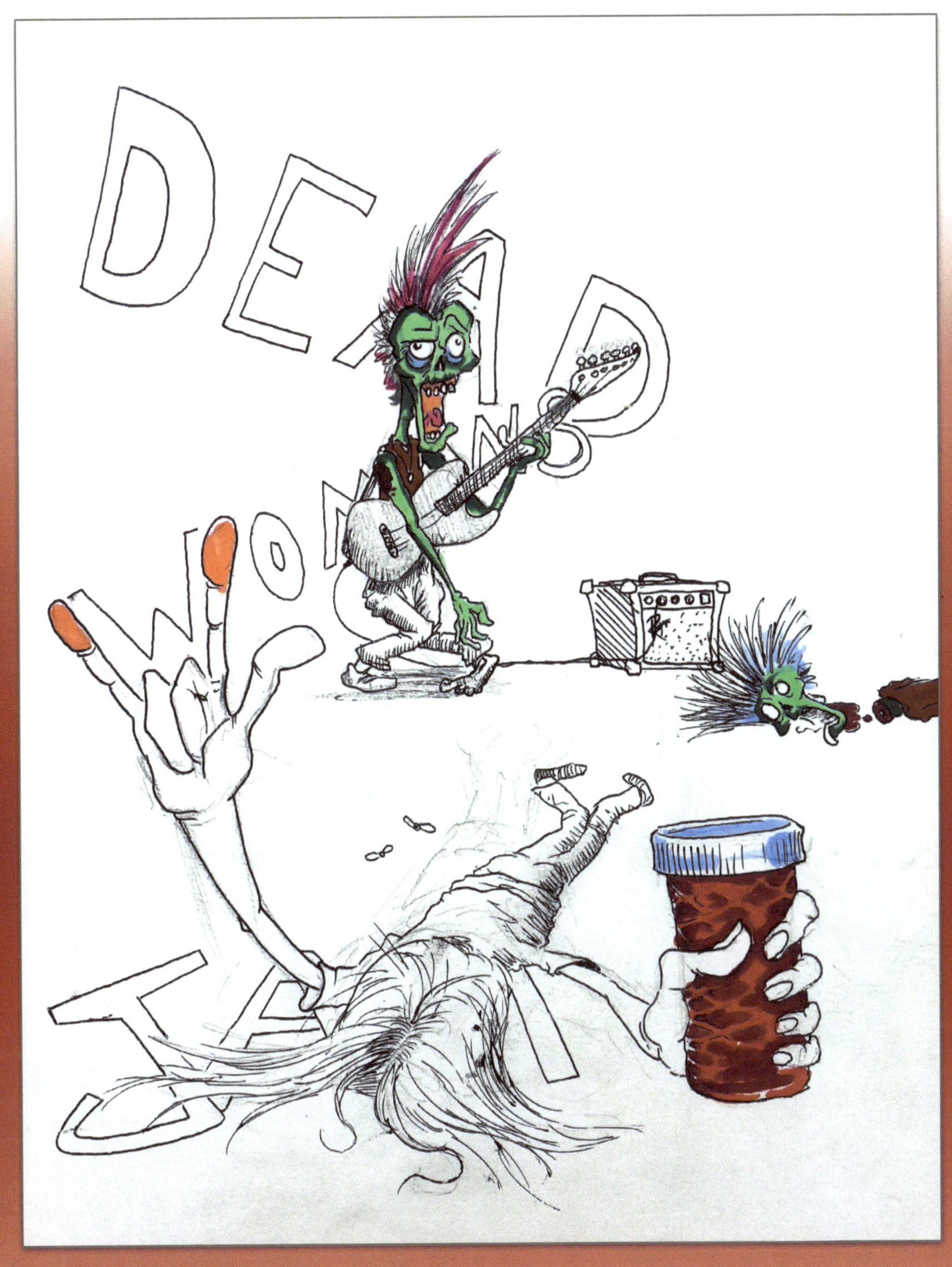

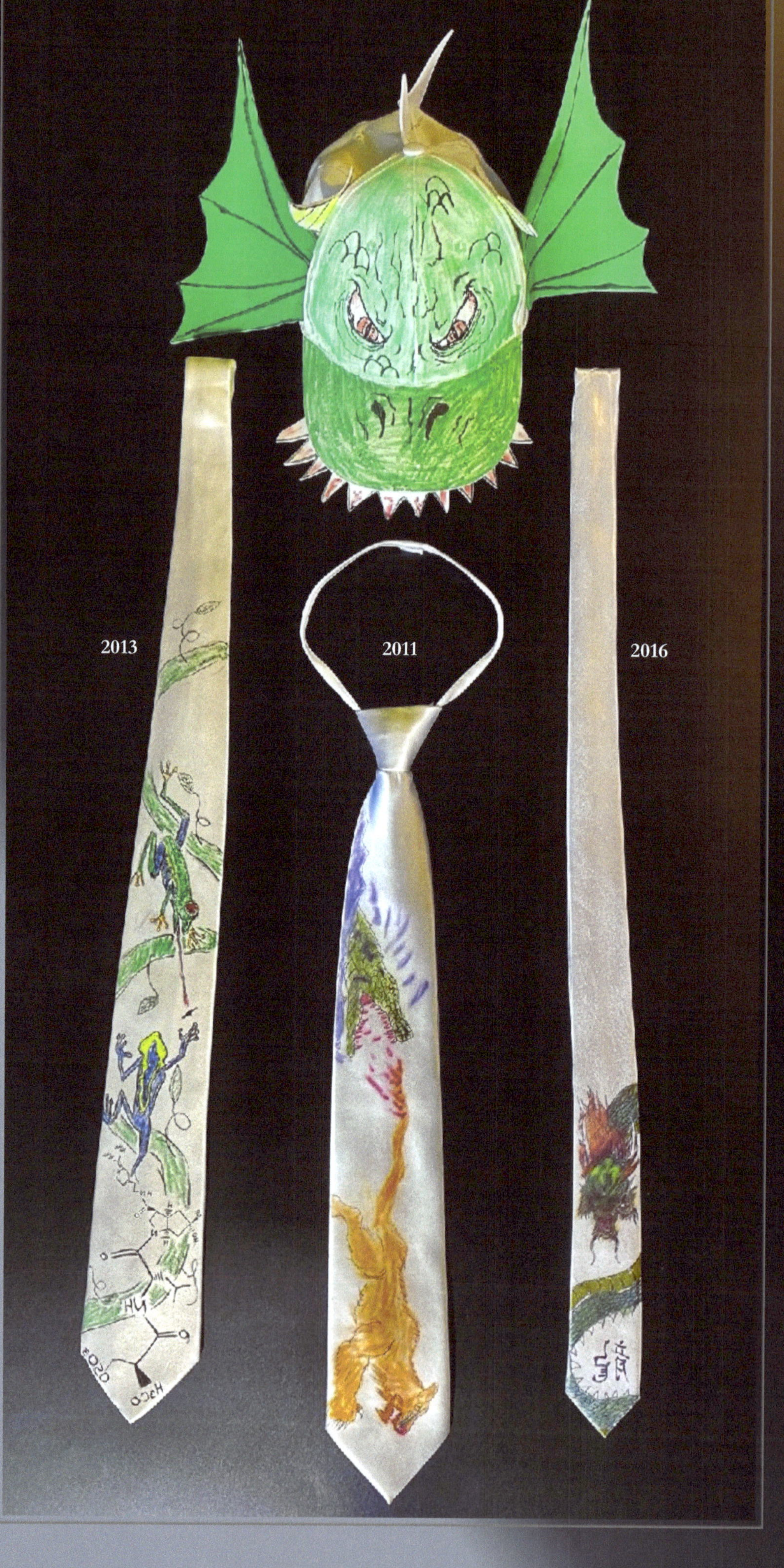

"Dragon Hat"
2013

Baseball Cap, Craft Foam
Fabric Marker

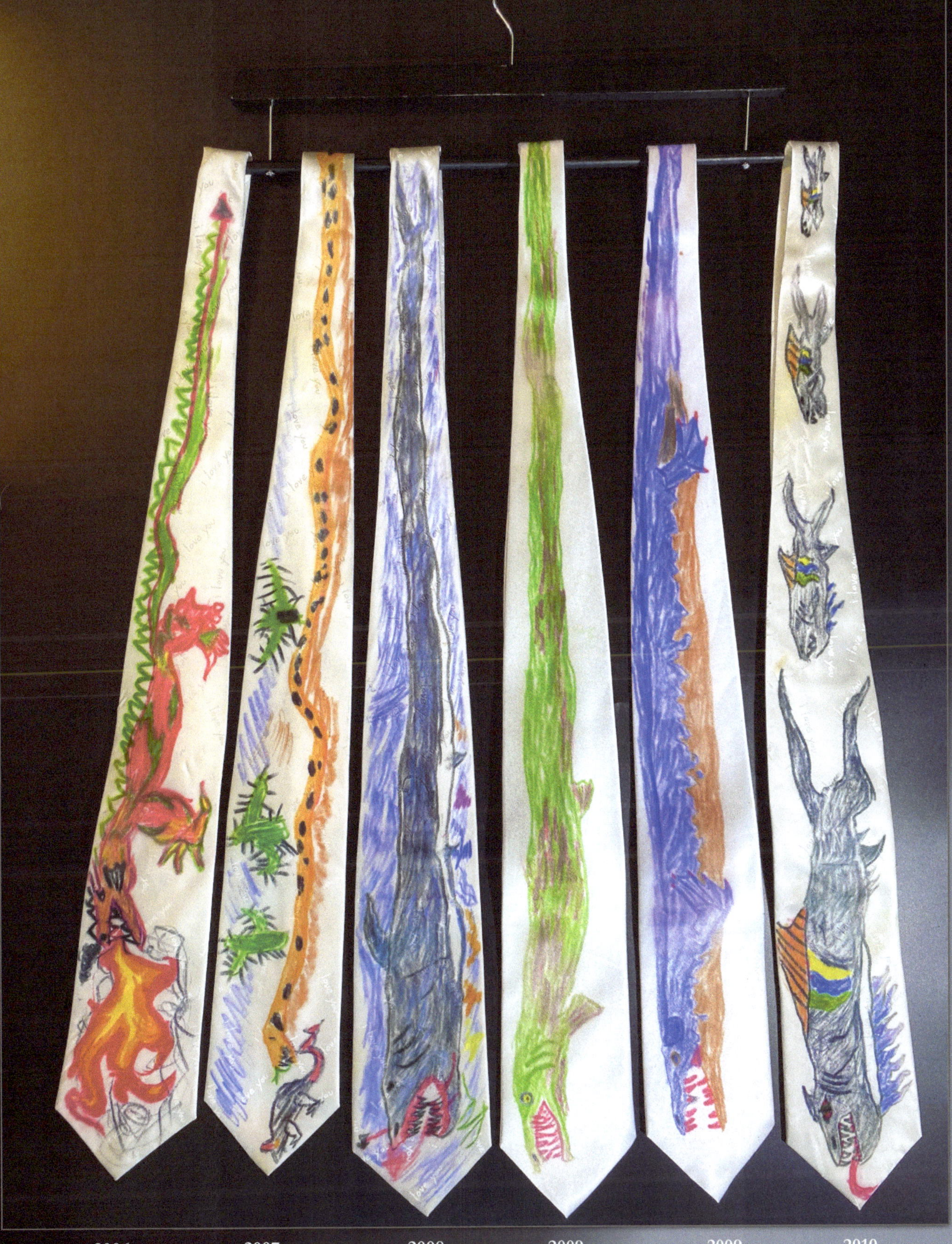

2006 2007 2008 2009 2009 2010

From the
Fearsome Tie Collection
2006 - 2016

Necktie
Ink, Fabric Marker

Presented as a Gifts.
Private Art Collection
Prior Lake, Minnesota
Reprinted with Permission.

"**Charles**"
2018

Clay, Air Dried
Acrylic, Gold Buff
6.0 L × 5.0 W x 6.0 H Inches

In the Archives of the James William Christenson Art Gallery Prior Lake, Minnesota

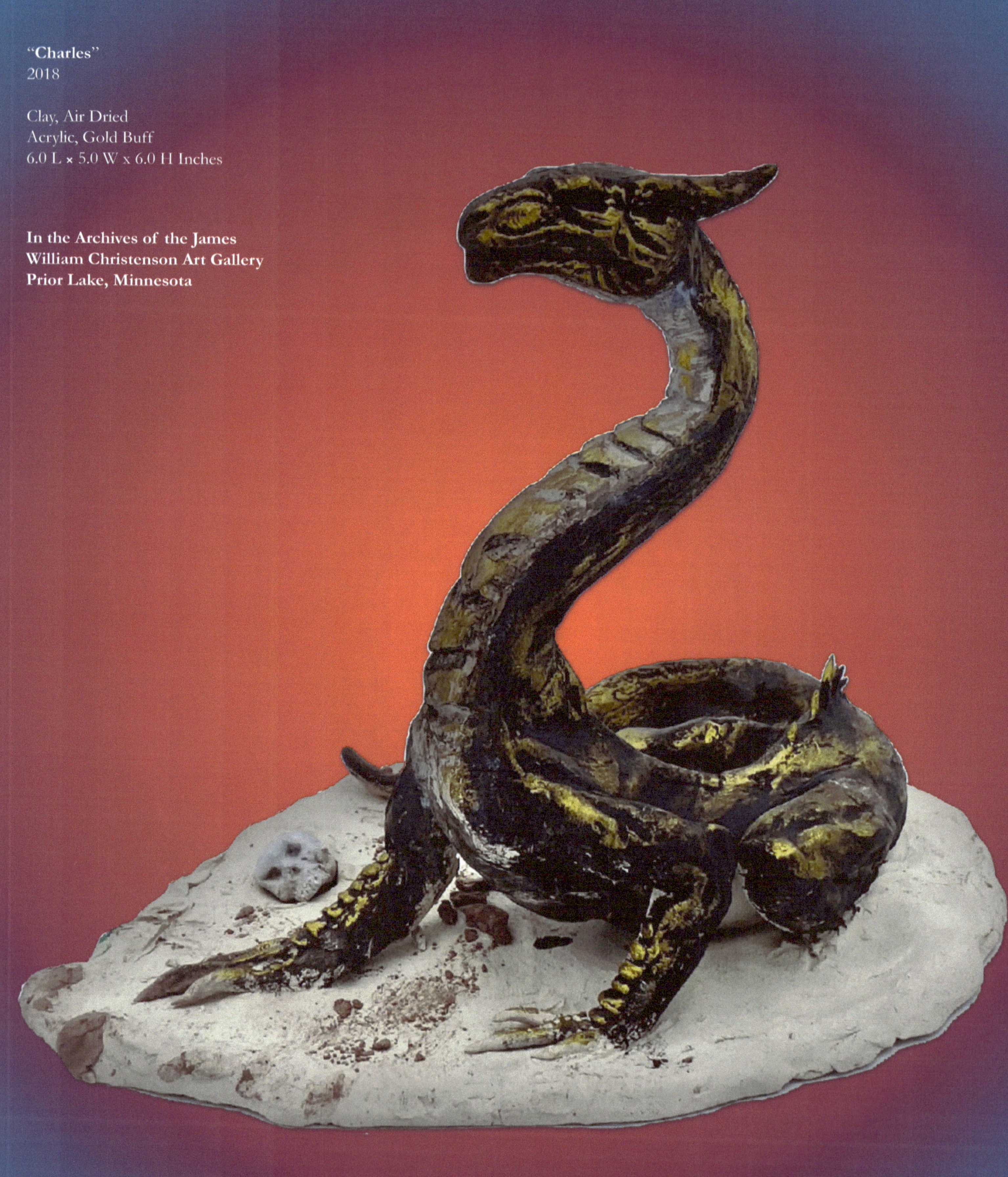

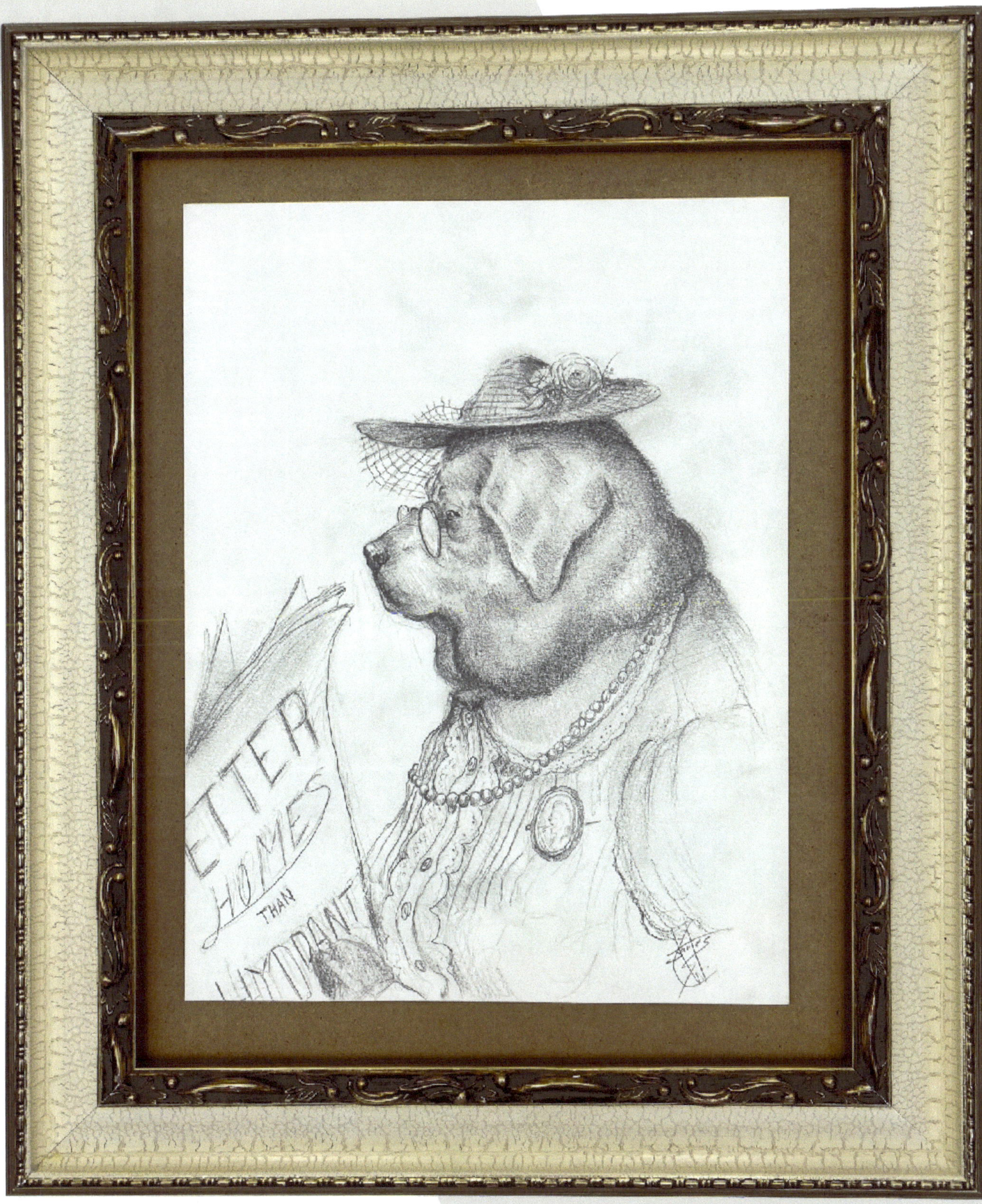

Presented as a Gift.
Private Art Collection
Savage, Minnesota
Reprinted with Permission.

"Dowdy Old Karm"
2019

Watercolor Paper
Graphite
12.0 L × 9.0 W Inches

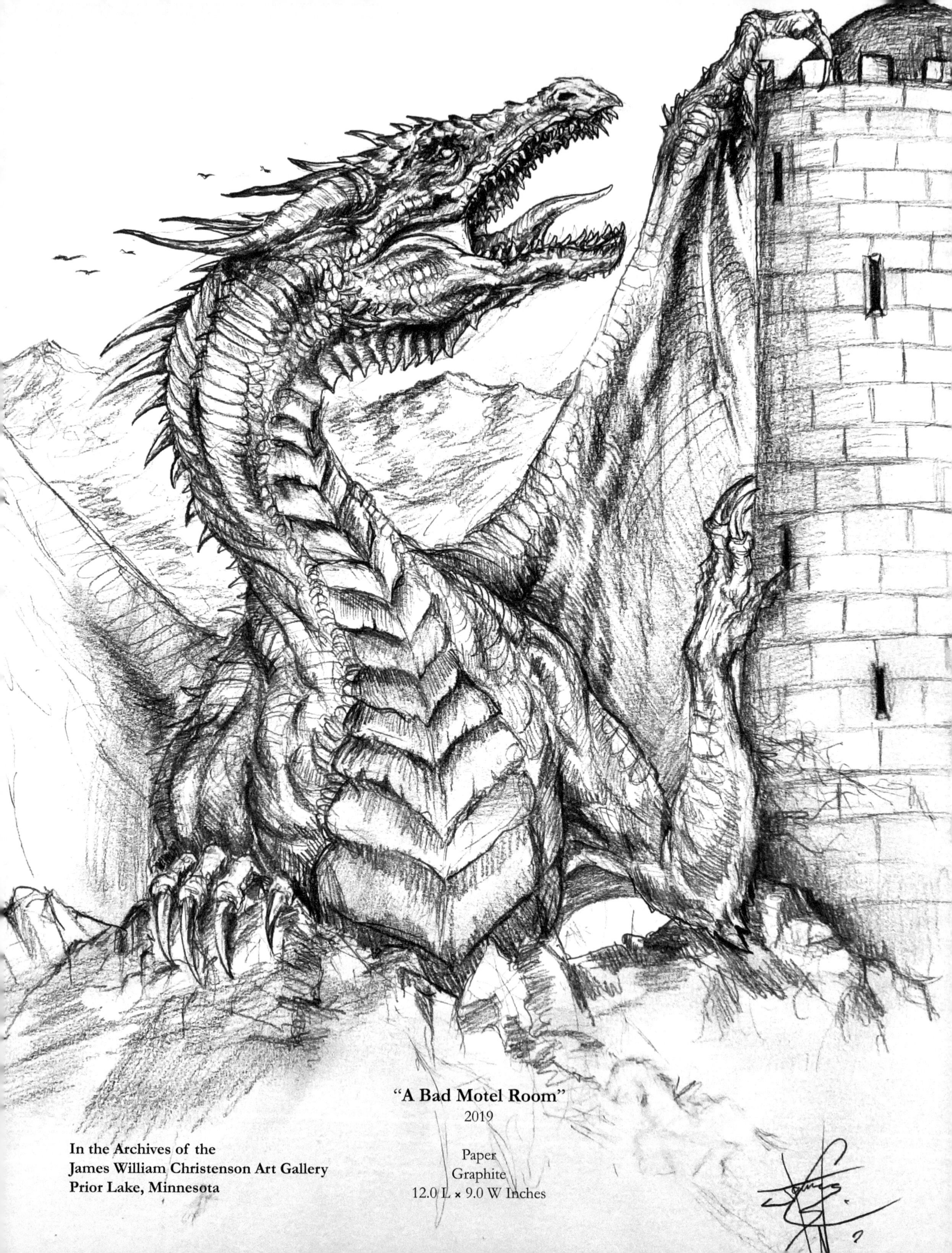

"A Bad Motel Room"
2019

In the Archives of the
James William Christenson Art Gallery
Prior Lake, Minnesota

Paper
Graphite
12.0 L × 9.0 W Inches

"**Christmas in July**"
2019

Watercolor Paper
Watercolor
9.0 L × 12.0 W Inches

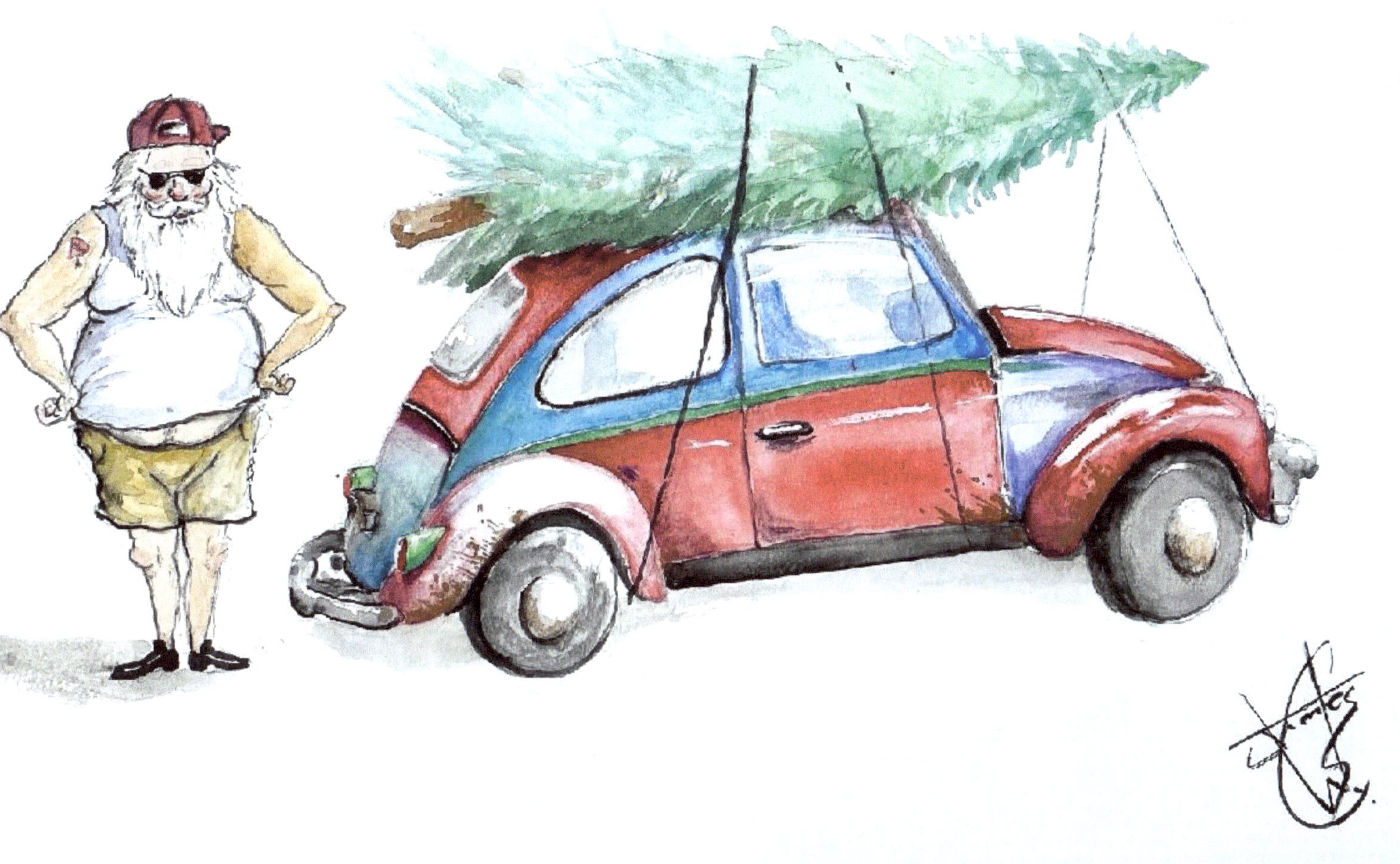

In the Archives of the
James William Christenson Art Gallery
Prior Lake, Minnesota

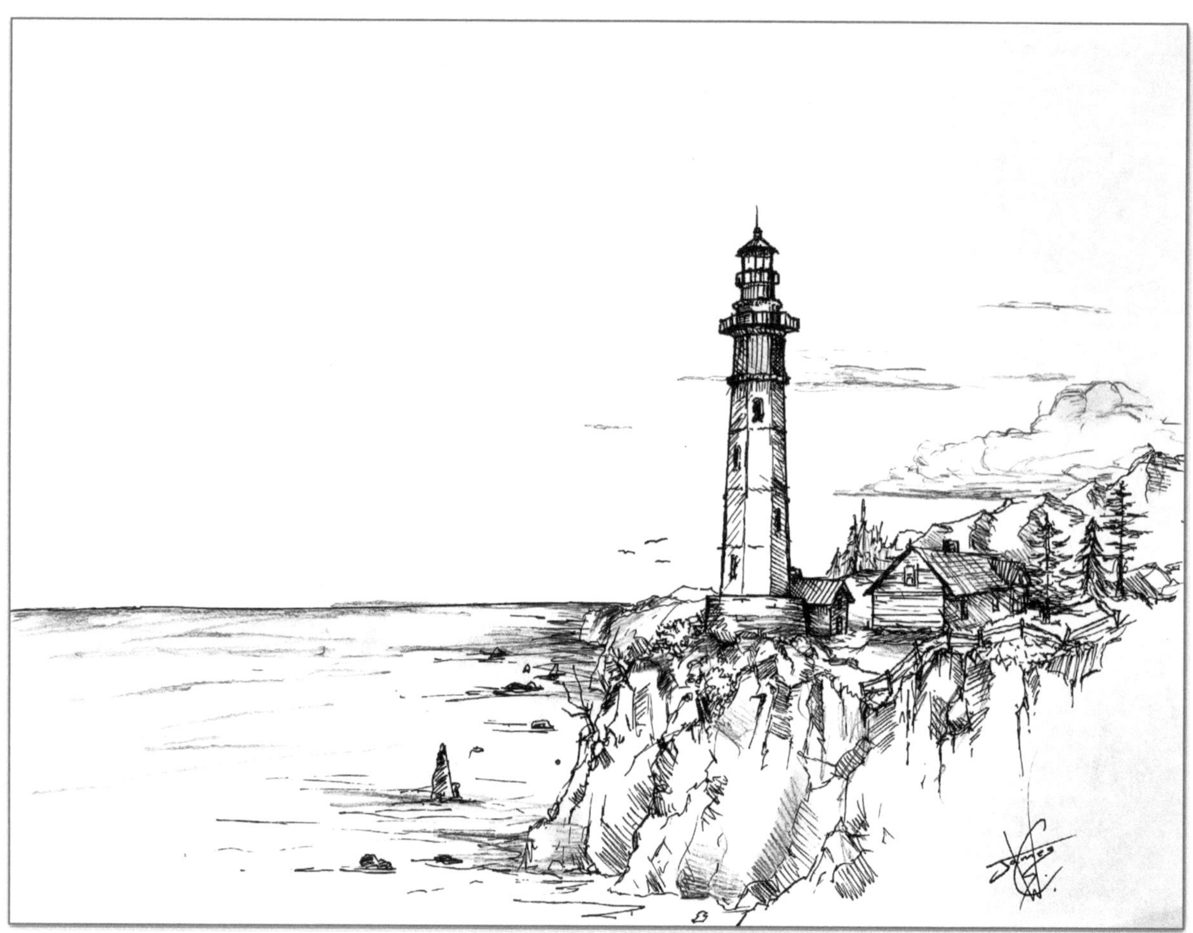

"**Maine Seashore**"
2018

Paper
Ink
9.0 L × 12.0 W Inches

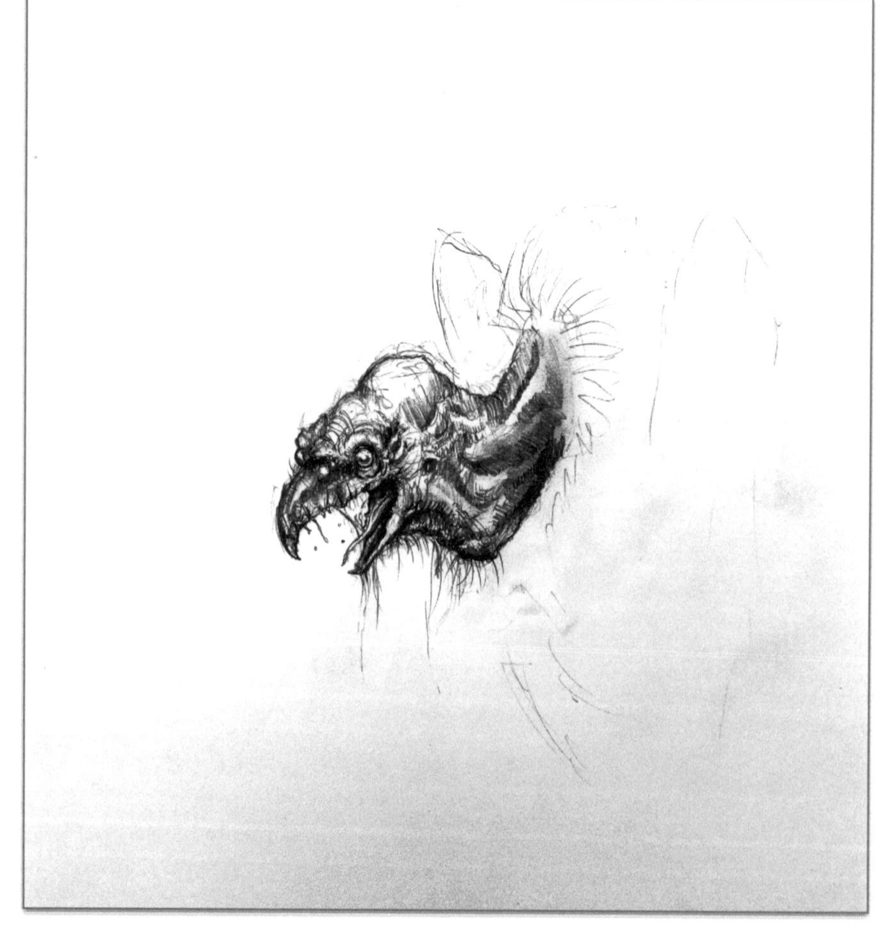

Unfinished Sketch
2018

Paper
Graphite
9.0 L × 12.0 W Inches

In the Archives of the
James William Christenson Art Gallery
Prior Lake, Minnesota

"What's in a Frame?"
2020

Canvas Over Wooden Frame
Oil
24.0 L × 12.0 W Inches

Commissioned for Private Art Collection
Cincinnati, Ohio

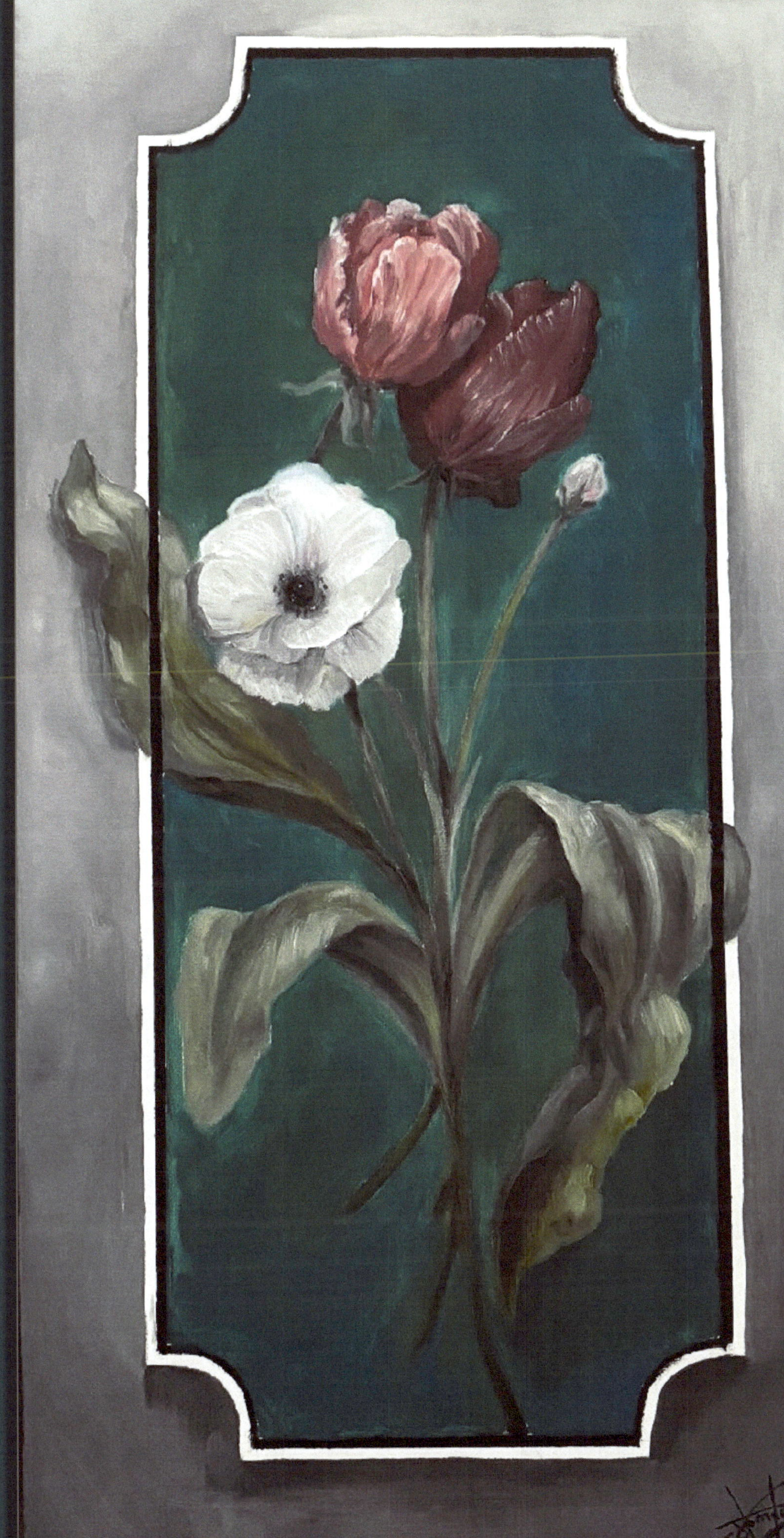

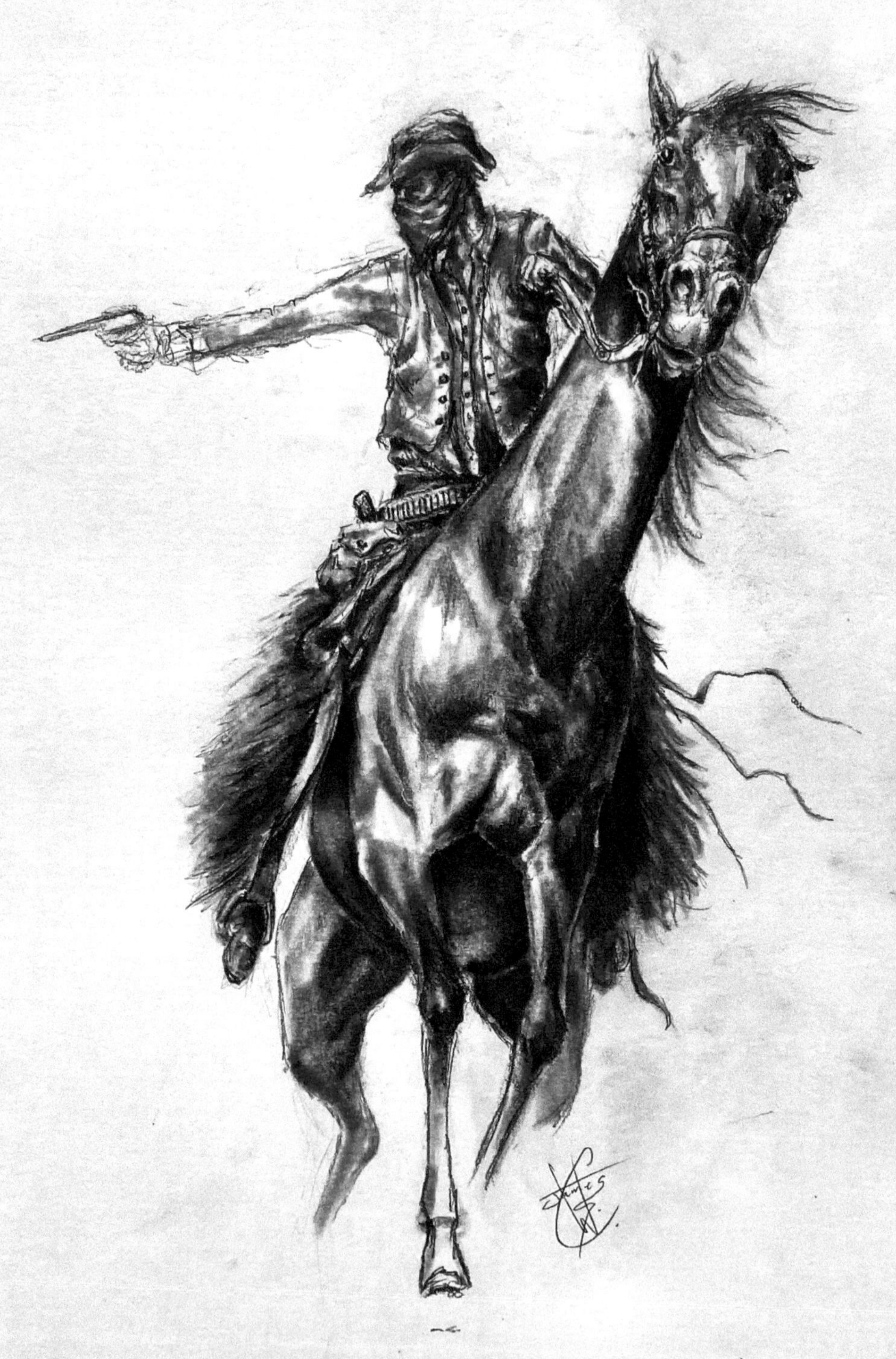

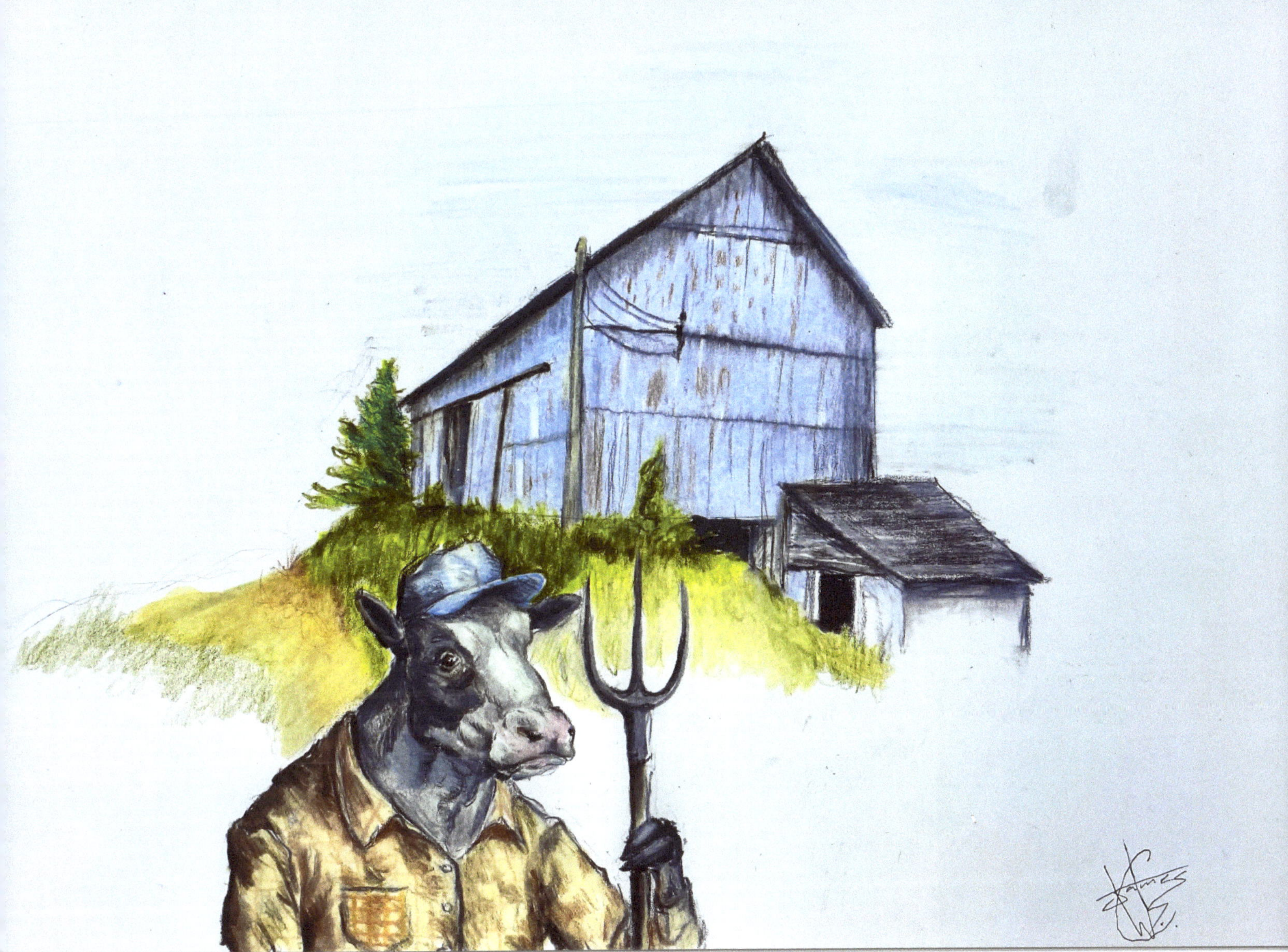

FACING PAGE

"Outlaw"
2020

Paper
Graphite
24.0 L × 19.0 W Inches

In the Archives of the
James William Christenson Art Gallery
Prior Lake, Minnesota

ABOVE

"Animal Farm"
2019

Paper
Colored Pencil
9.0 L × 12.0 W Inches

Presented as a Gift.
Private Art Collection
Savage, Minnesota
Reprinted with Permission.

"Tryouts"
2018

Paper
Pencil Sketch
11.0 L × 8.5 W Inches

In the Archives of the
James William Christenson Art Gallery
Prior Lake, Minnesota

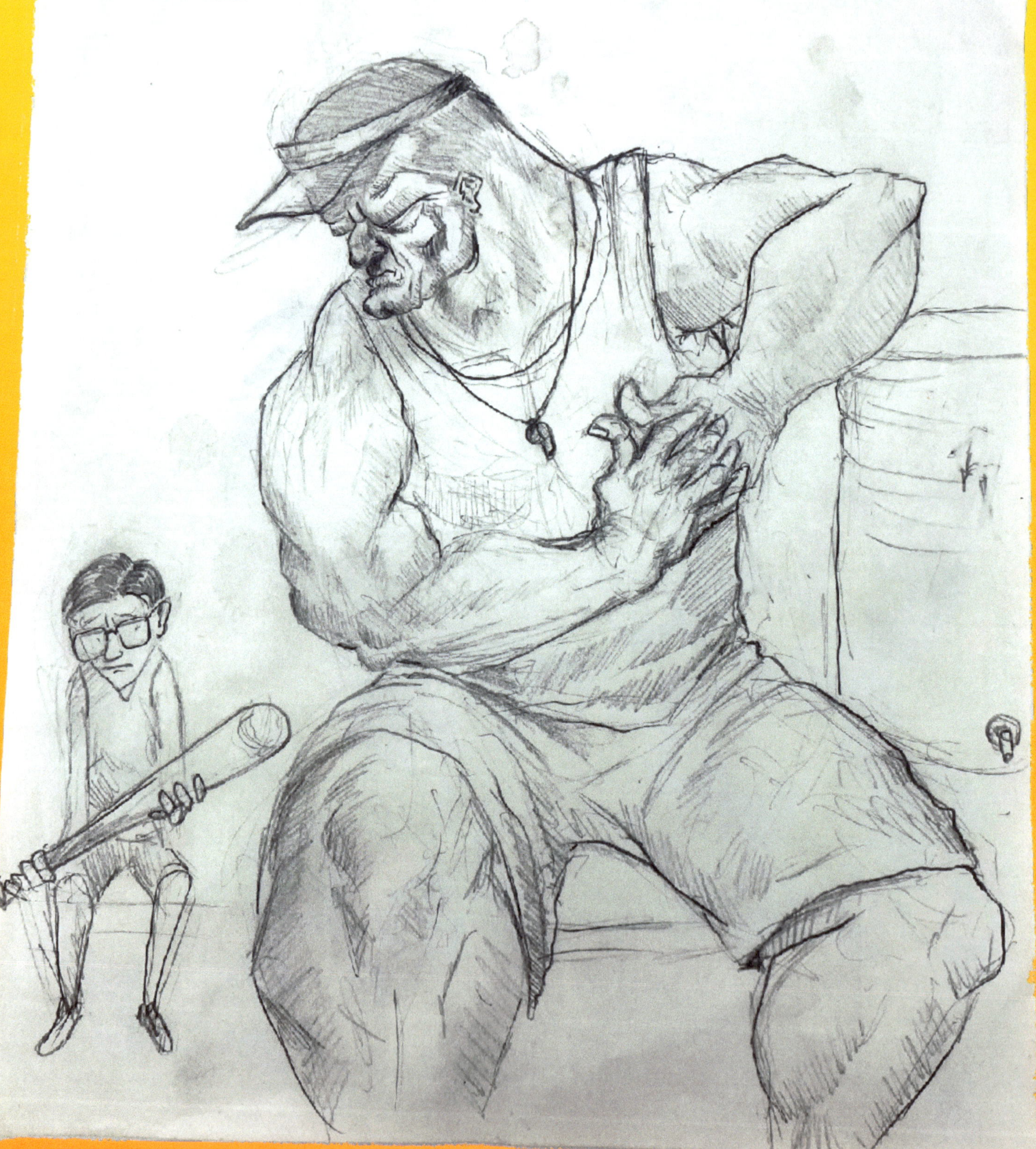

"OutStanding in Her Field"
2020

Stretched Canvas Over Wooden Frame
Oil
16.0 L × 20.0 W Inches

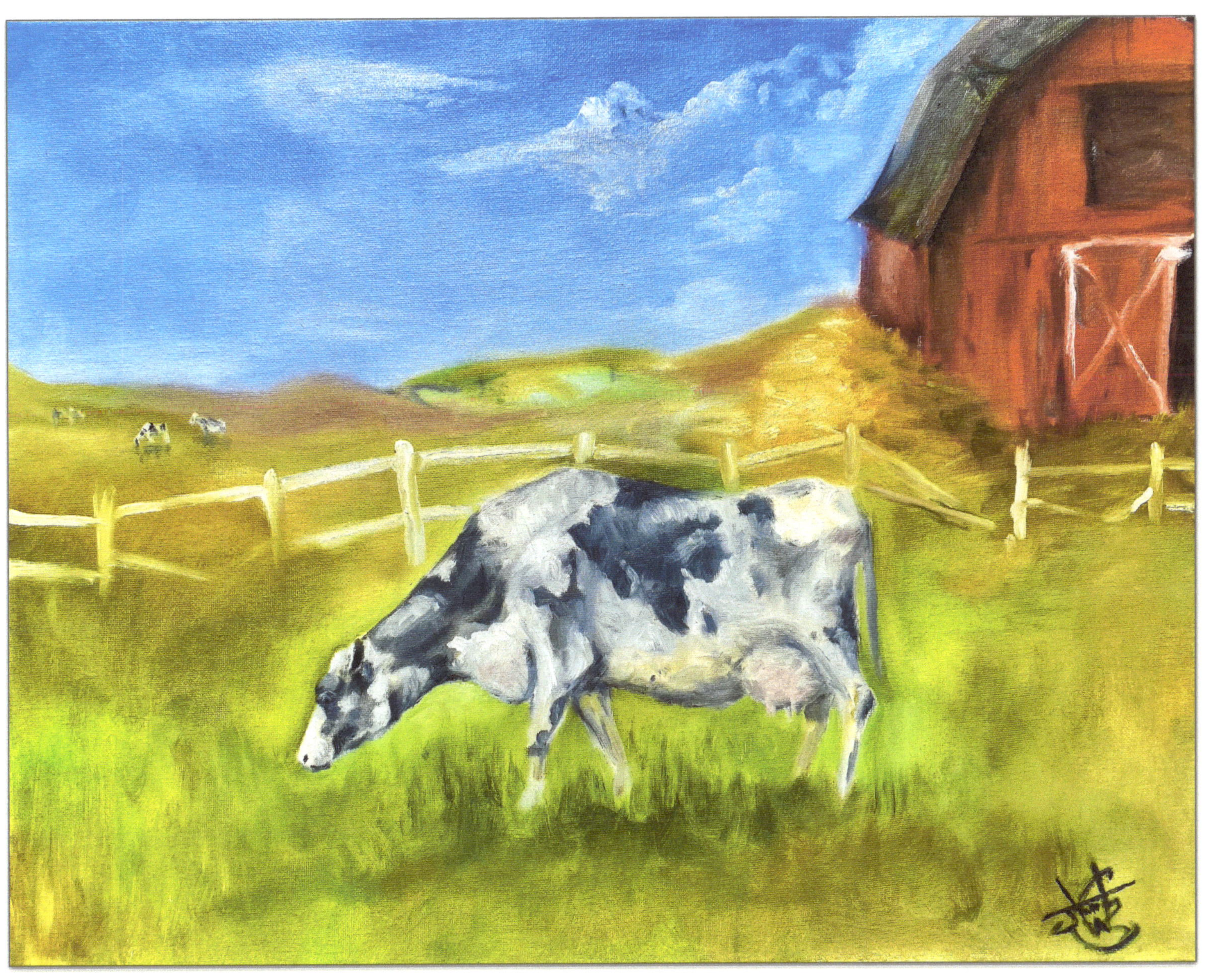

Presented as a Gift.
Private Art Collection
Savage, Minnesota
Reprinted with Permission.

UNTITLED
Sketch
2019

Paper
Graphite
9.0 L × 12.0 W Inches

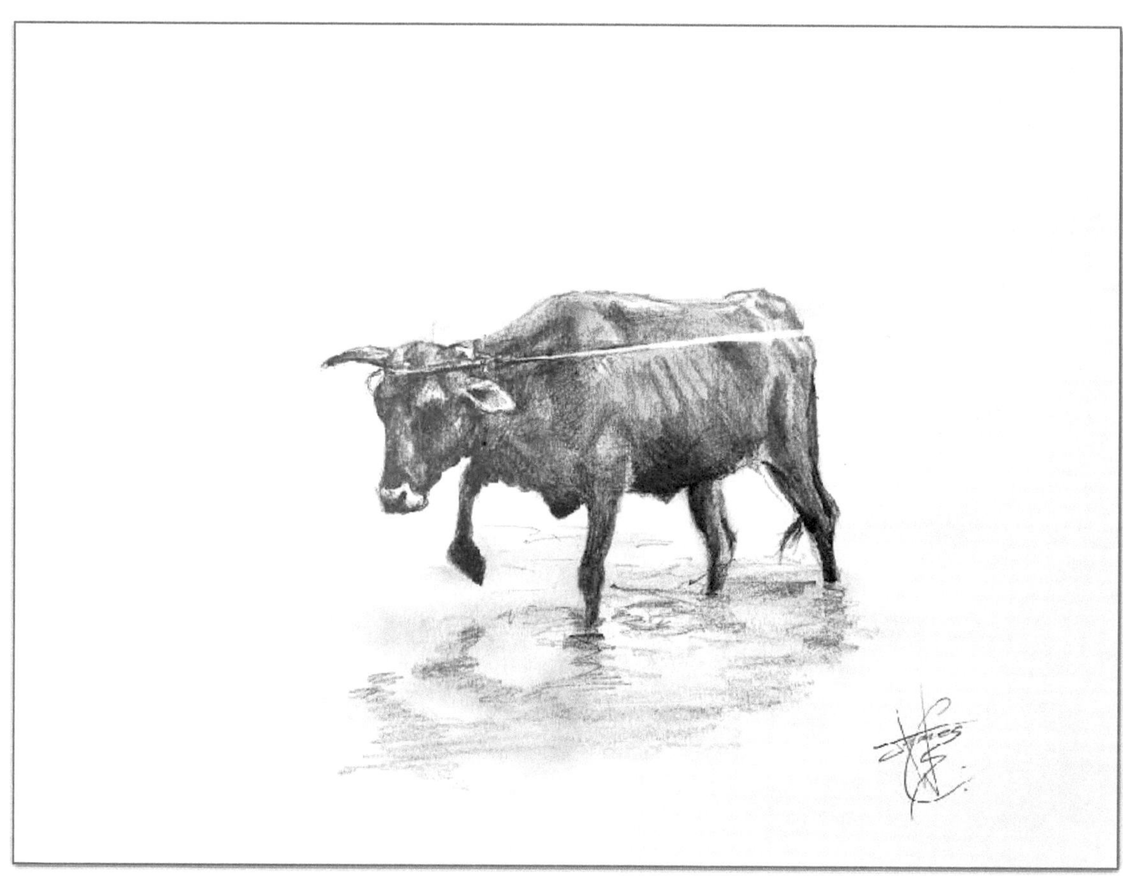

In the Archives of the
James William Christenson Art Gallery
Prior Lake, Minnesota

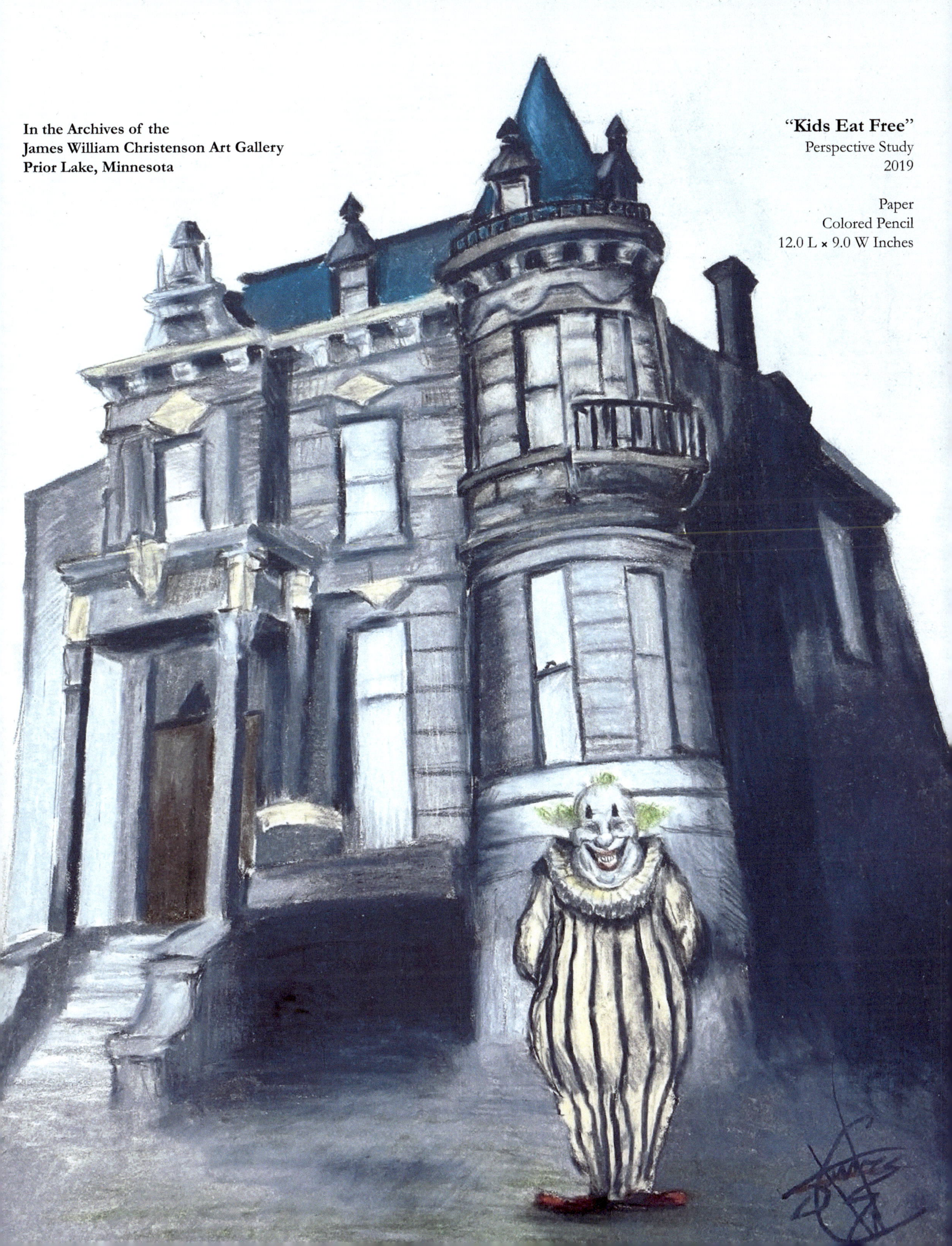
In the Archives of the
James William Christenson Art Gallery
Prior Lake, Minnesota
"Kids Eat Free"
Perspective Study
2019
Paper
Colored Pencil
12.0 L × 9.0 W Inches

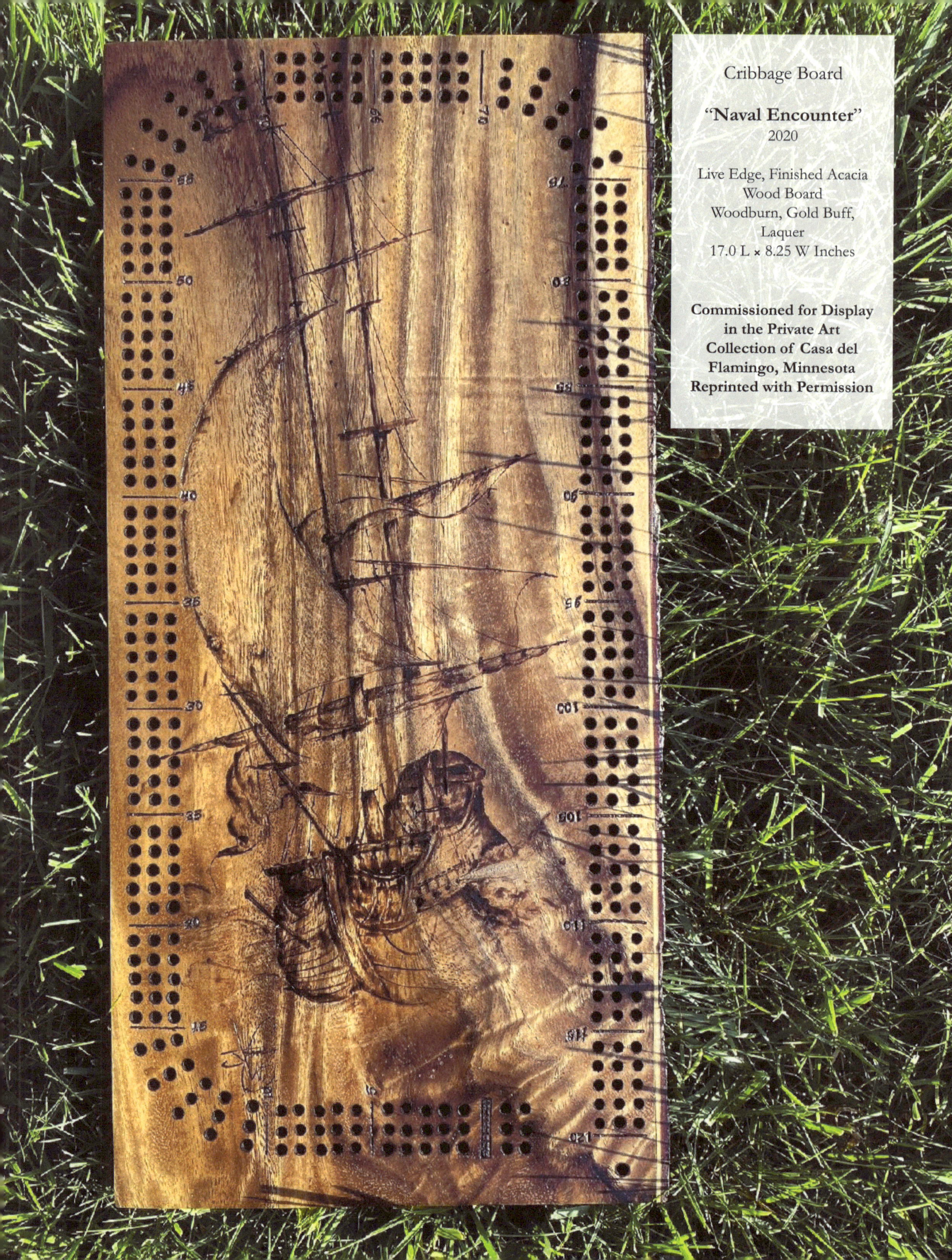

Cribbage Board

"Naval Encounter"
2020

Live Edge, Finished Acacia Wood Board
Woodburn, Gold Buff, Laquer
17.0 L × 8.25 W Inches

Commissioned for Display in the Private Art Collection of Casa del Flamingo, Minnesota
Reprinted with Permission

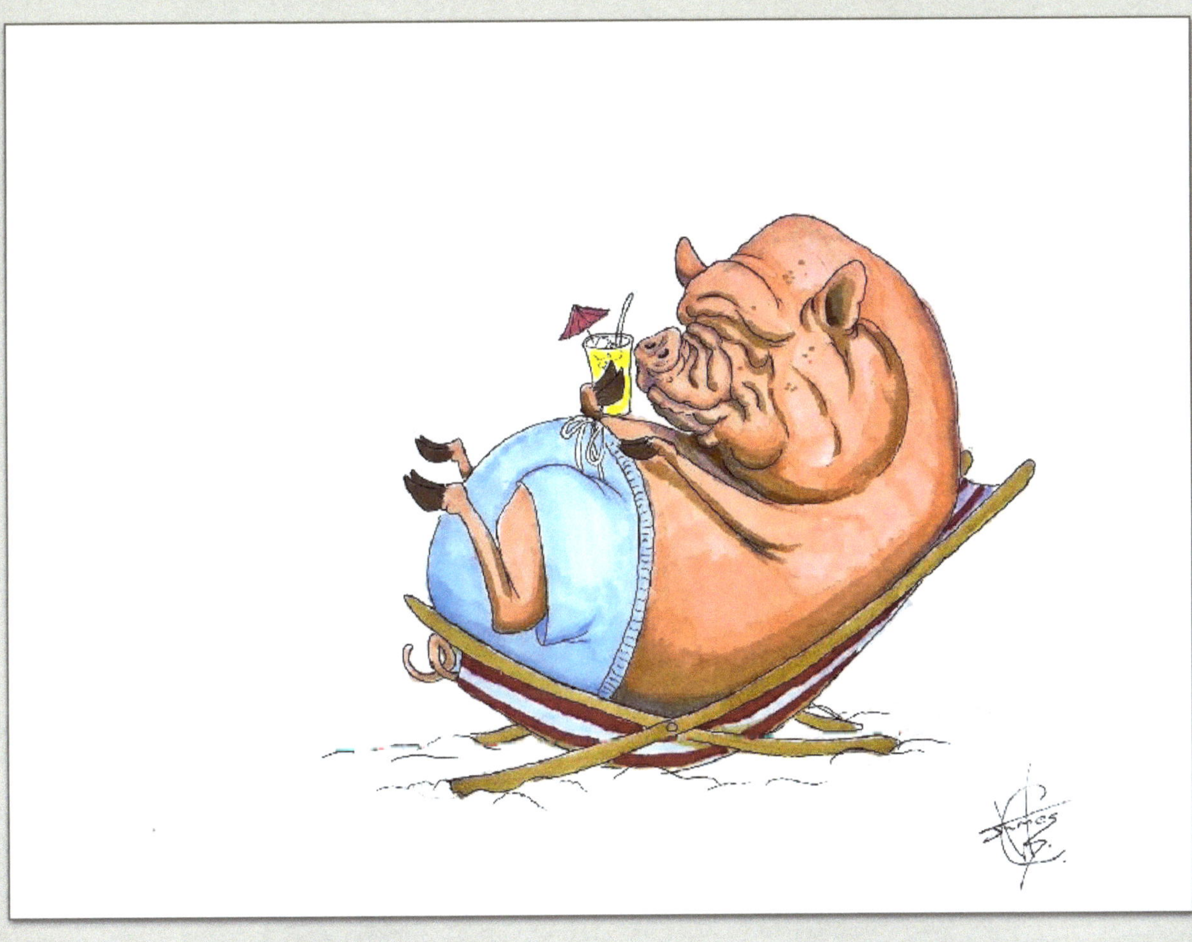

"Curing Bacon"
2019

Paper
Marker
9.0 L × 12.0 W Inches

In the Archives of the
James William Christenson
Art Gallery
Prior Lake, Minnesota

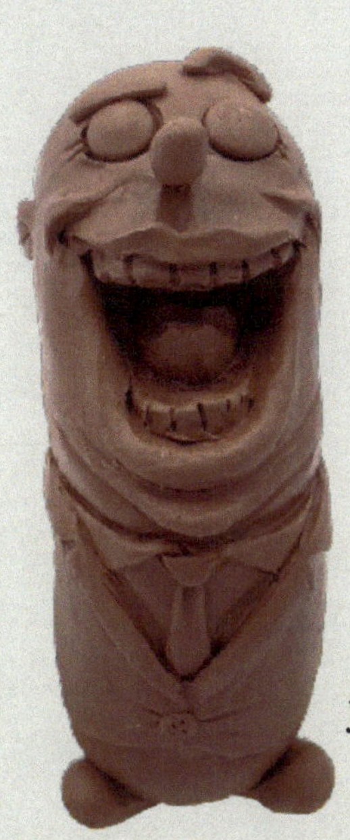

"Happy Little Moron"
Actual Size
Obverse, Left Profile
2018

Clay
3.0 L × 1.25 W Inches

In the Archives of the
James William Christenson Art Gallery
Prior Lake, Minnesota

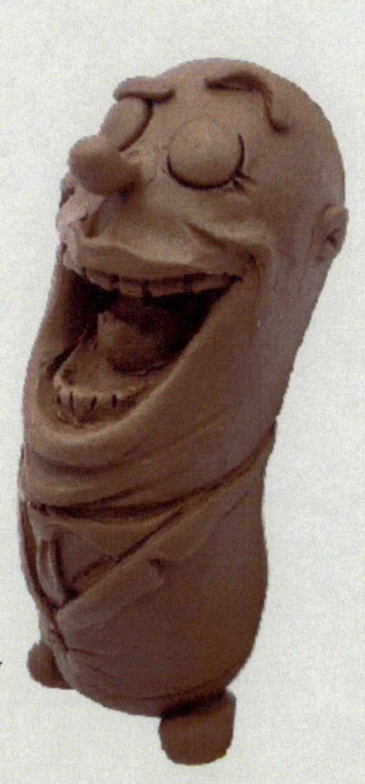

"Stanisław Paweł Stefan Jan Sebastian Skrowaczewski"
Character Sketch
2019

Paper
Ink
9.0 L × 12.0 W Inches

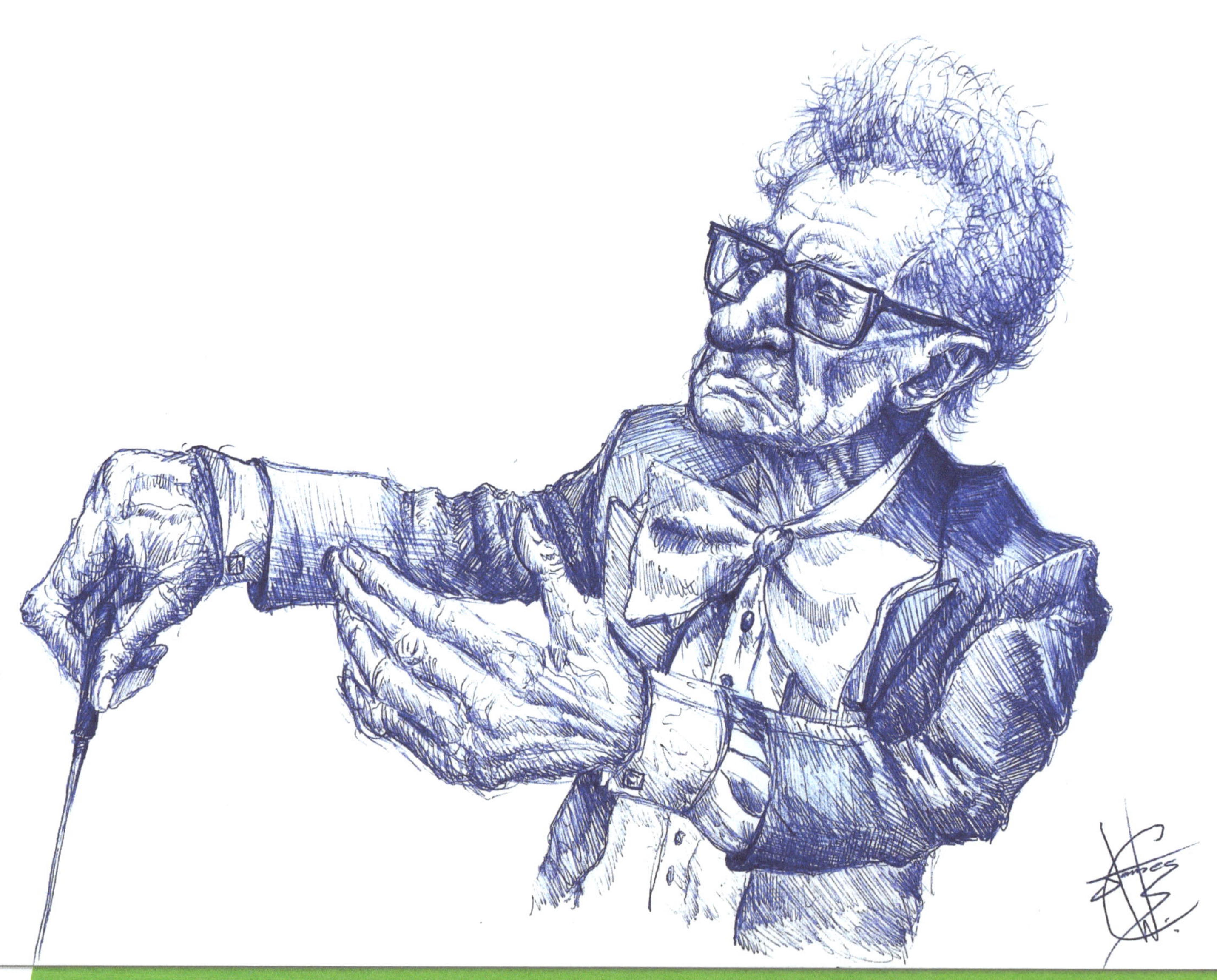

In the Archives of the
James William Christenson Art Gallery
Prior Lake, Minnesota

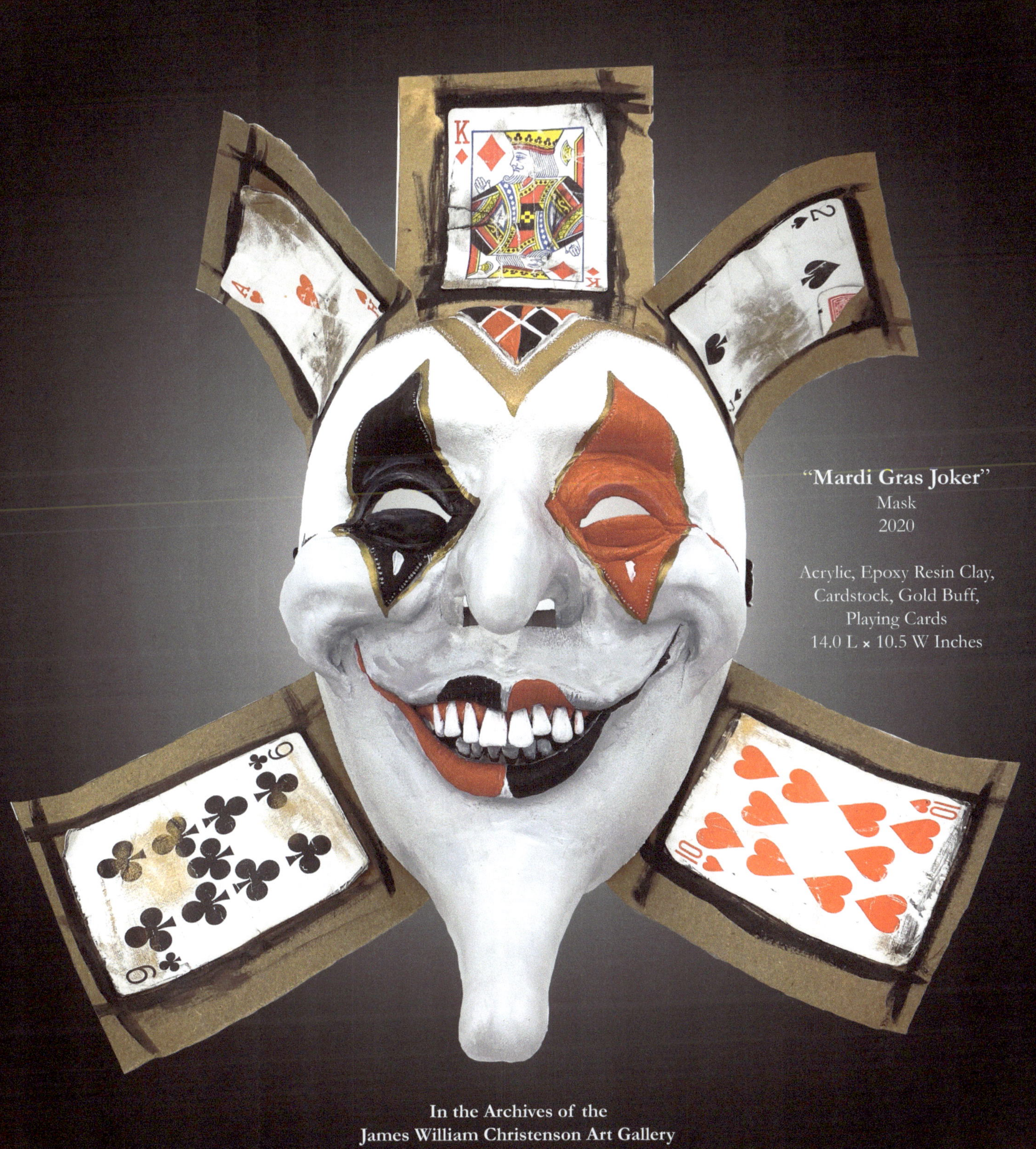

"Mardi Gras Joker"
Mask
2020

Acrylic, Epoxy Resin Clay,
Cardstock, Gold Buff,
Playing Cards
14.0 L × 10.5 W Inches

In the Archives of the
James William Christenson Art Gallery
Prior Lake, Minnesota

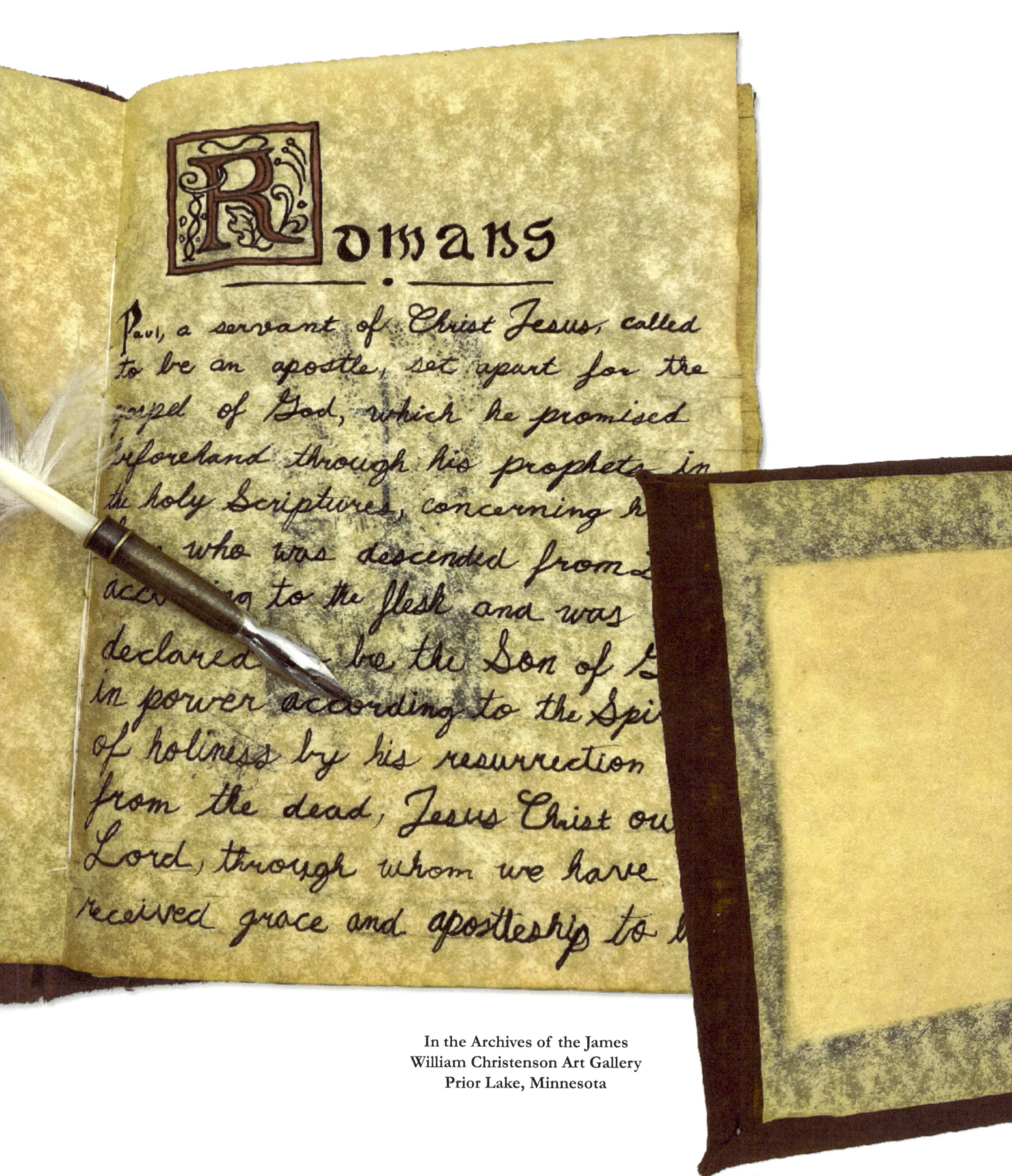

In the Archives of the James
William Christenson Art Gallery
Prior Lake, Minnesota

"Journal"
2020

Suede Leather, Belt, Parchment Paper, Marker, Ink
7.5 L × 5.5 W x 2.5 H Inches

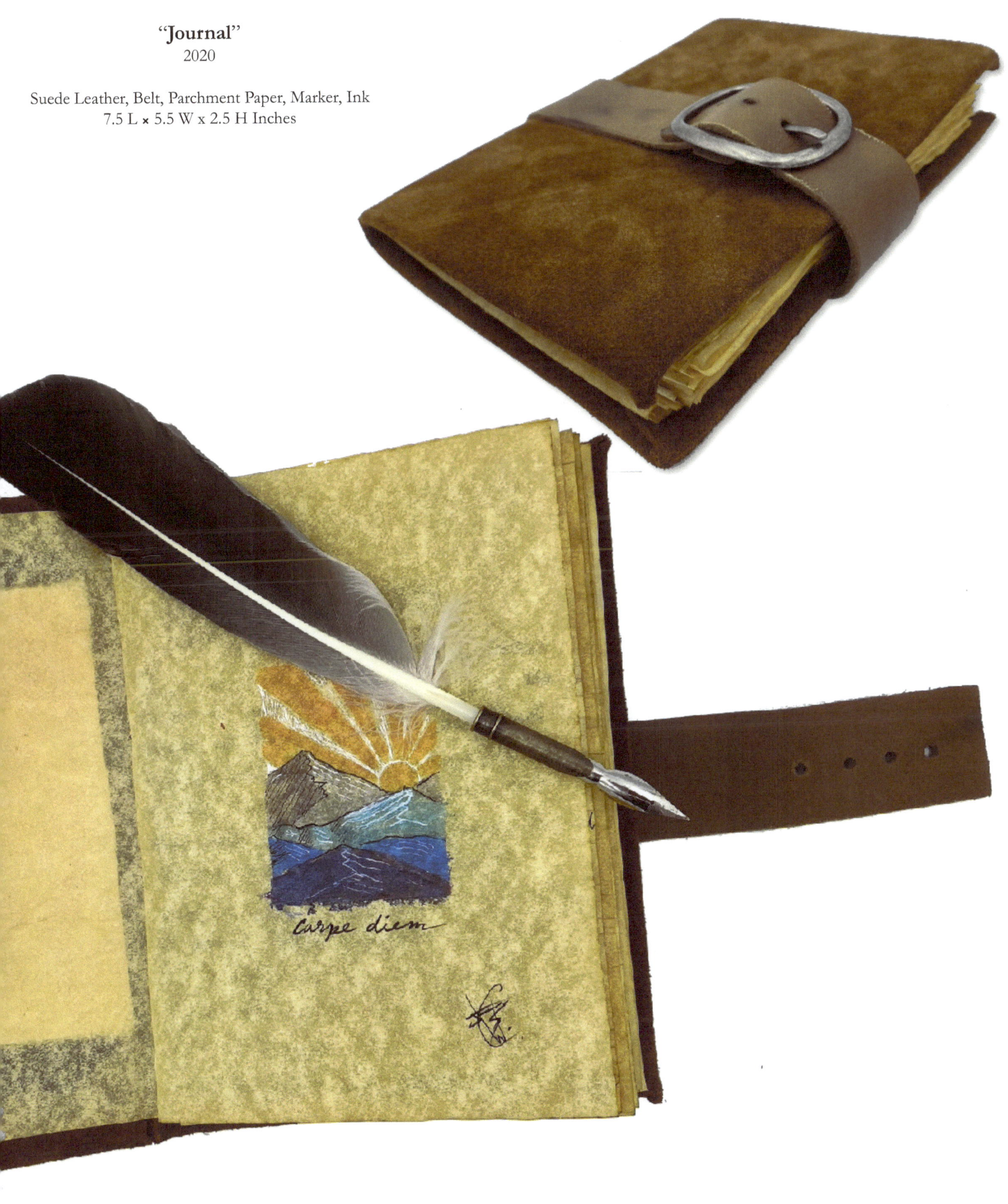

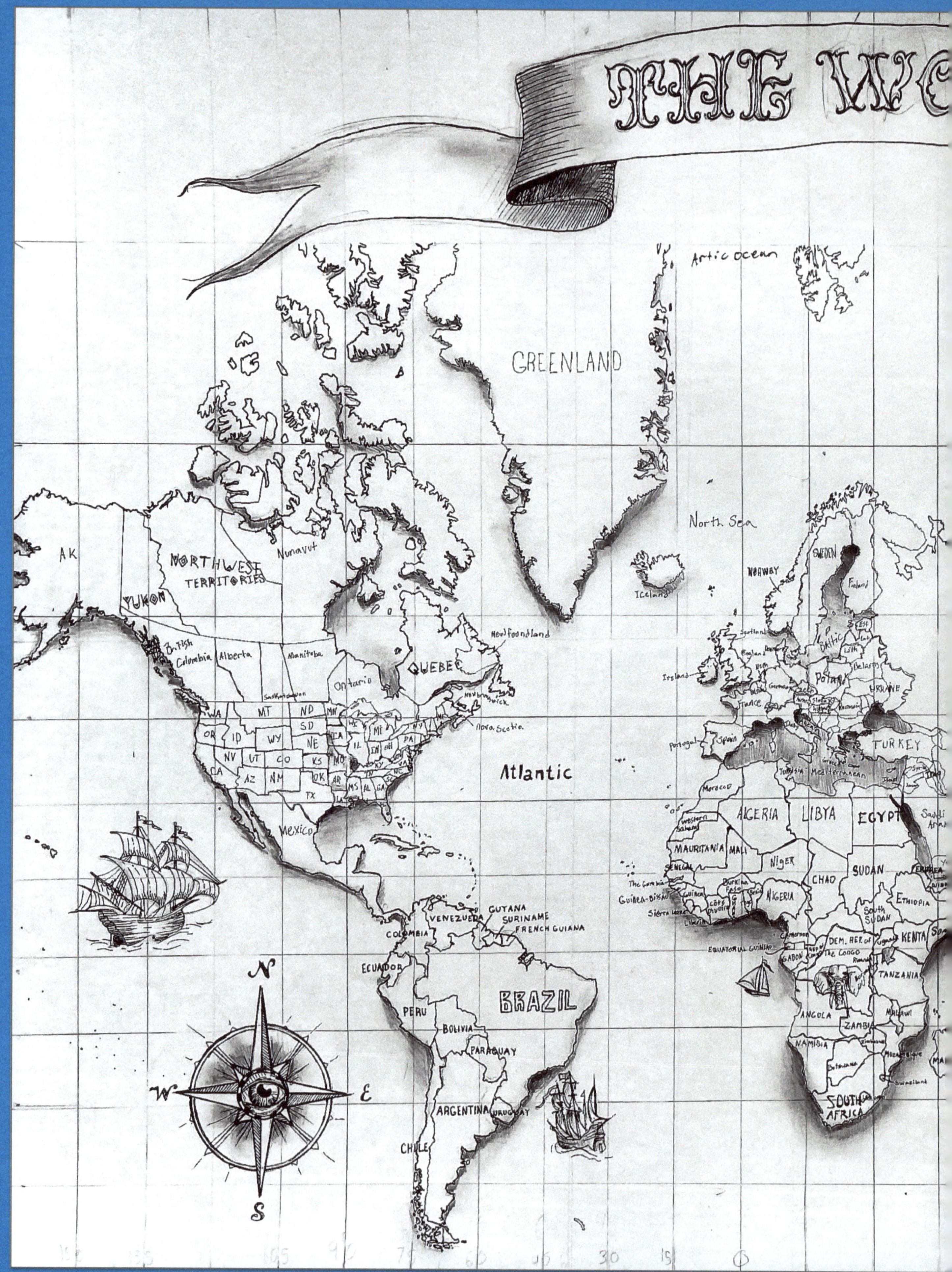
Artic ocean
GREENLAND
North Sea
Iceland
NORWAY
SWEDEN
Finland
AK
NORTHWEST TERRITORIES
YUKON
Nunavut
Alberta
Manitoba
Ontario
QUEBEC
New Foundland
Nova Scotia
WA
MT
ND
OR
ID
WY
SD
NE
NV
UT
CO
KS
CA
AZ
NM
OK
TX
Mexico
Atlantic
Scotland
England
Ireland
Portugal
Spain
France
Poland
TURKEY
Mediterranean
Morocco
ALGERIA
LIBYA
EGYPT
MAURITANIA
MALI
Niger
CHAD
SUDAN
South SUDAN
ETHIOPIA
NIGERIA
The Gambia
Guinea-Bissau
Sierra Leone
Liberia
EQUATORIAL GUINEA
GABON
DEM. REP. of The Congo
KENYA
TANZANIA
ANGOLA
ZAMBIA
MALAWI
NAMIBIA
SOUTH AFRICA
GUYANA
VENEZUELA
SURINAME
FRENCH GUIANA
COLOMBIA
ECUADOR
PERU
BRAZIL
BOLIVIA
PARAGUAY
ARGENTINA
URUGUAY
CHILE
N
W
E
S

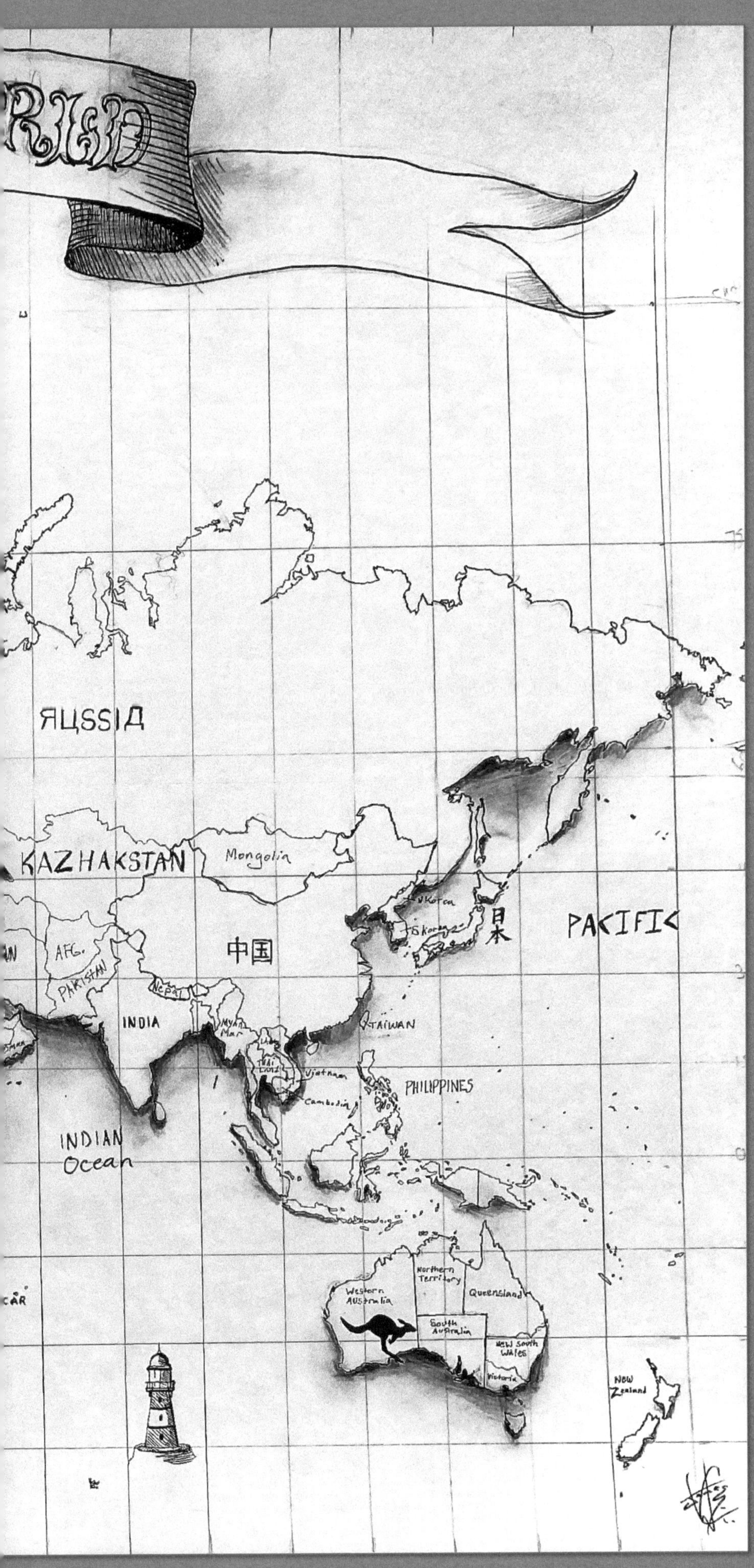

"The World Map"
2020

Mat Board
Ink, Graphite
24.0 L × 36.0 W Inches

In the Archives of the
James William Christenson Art Gallery
Prior Lake, Minnesota

FACING PAGE

"Serpent of the <u>Carta Marina</u>"
2019

Stretched Canvas Over Wooden Frame
Oil
60.0 L × 54.0 W Inches

In the Archives of the
James William Christenson Art Gallery
Prior Lake, Minnesota

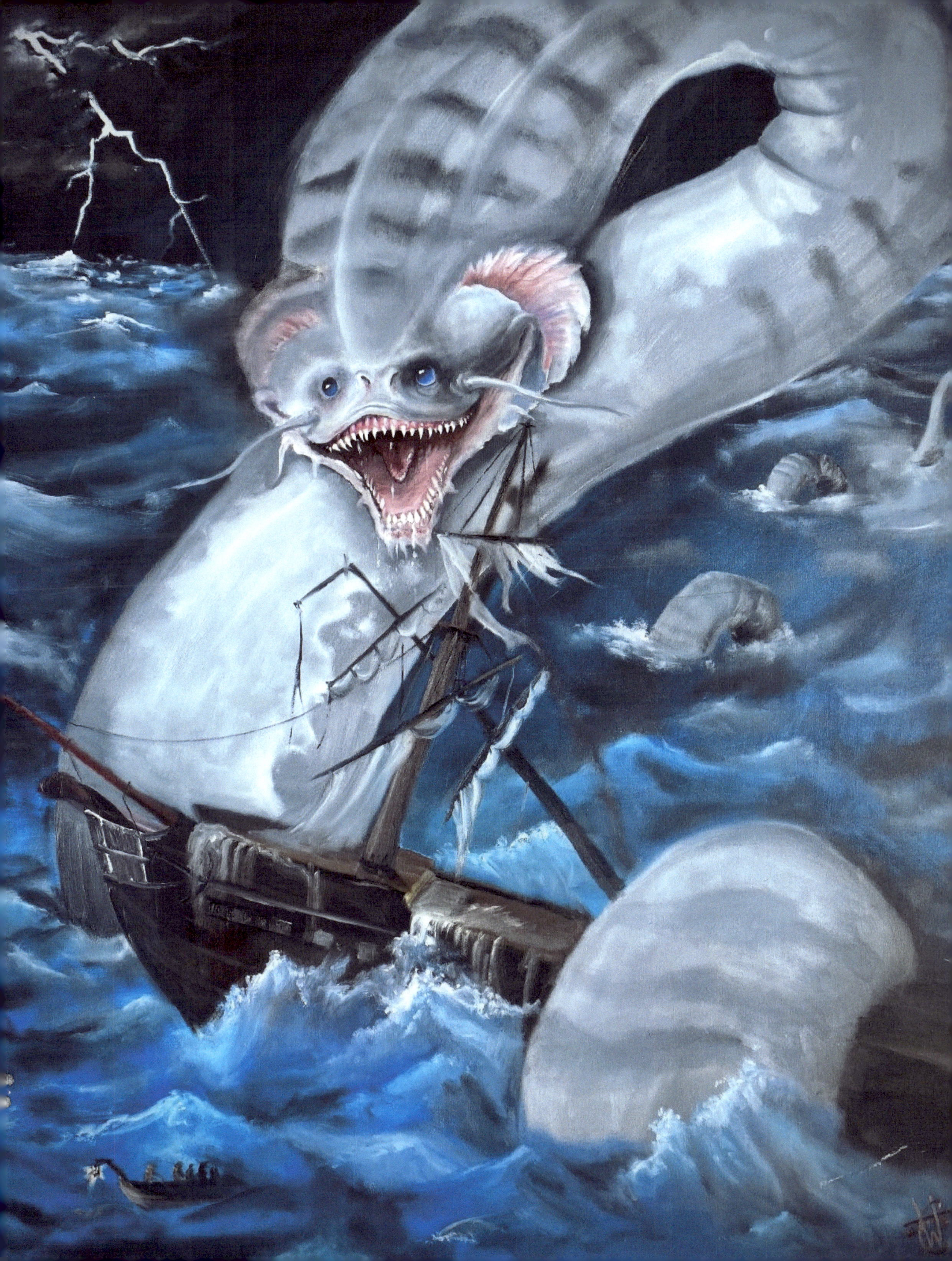

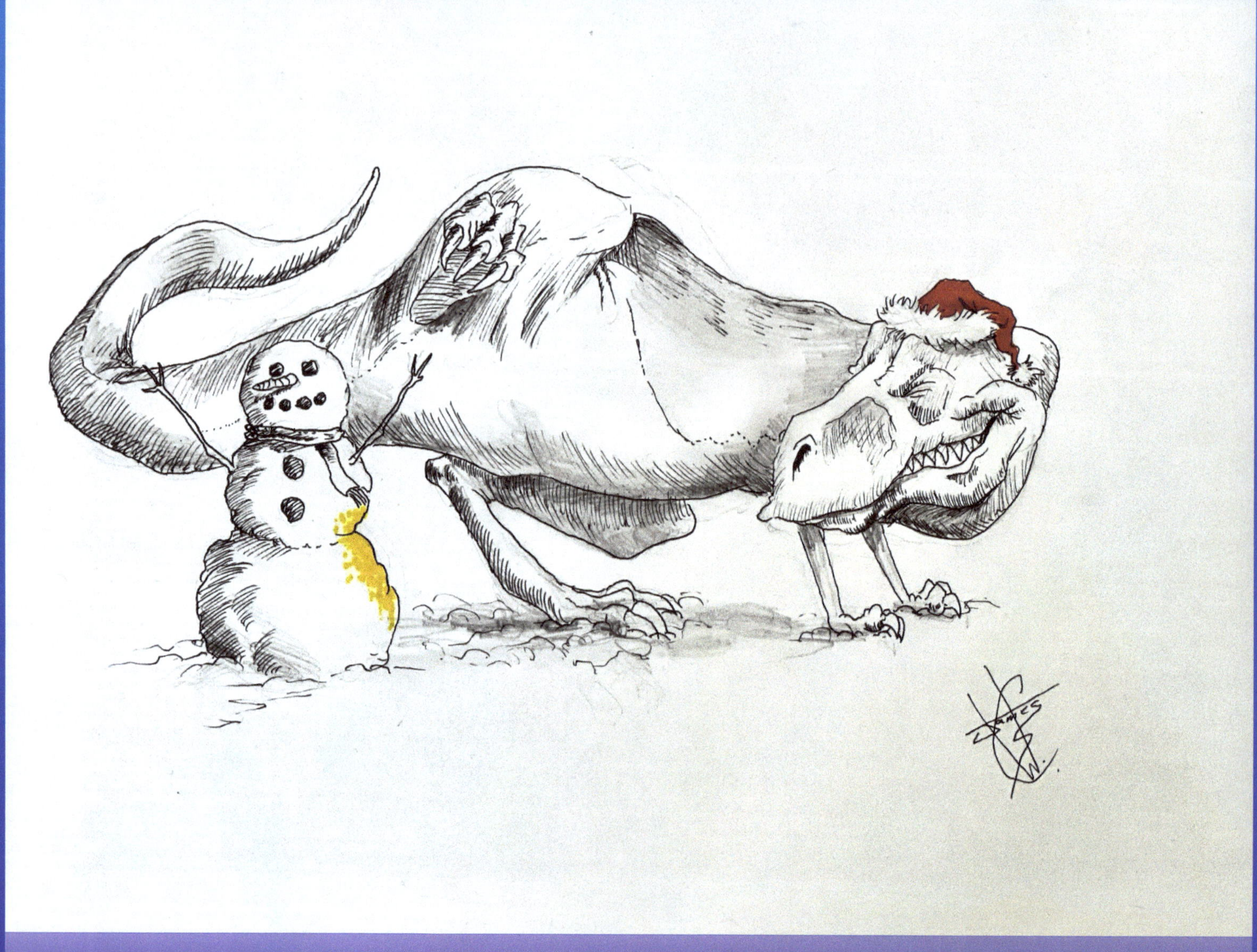

"Yellow Snow"
2019

Paper
Pencil, Ink, Marker
9.0 L × 12.0 W Inches

In the Archives of the
James William Christenson Art Gallery
Prior Lake, Minnesota

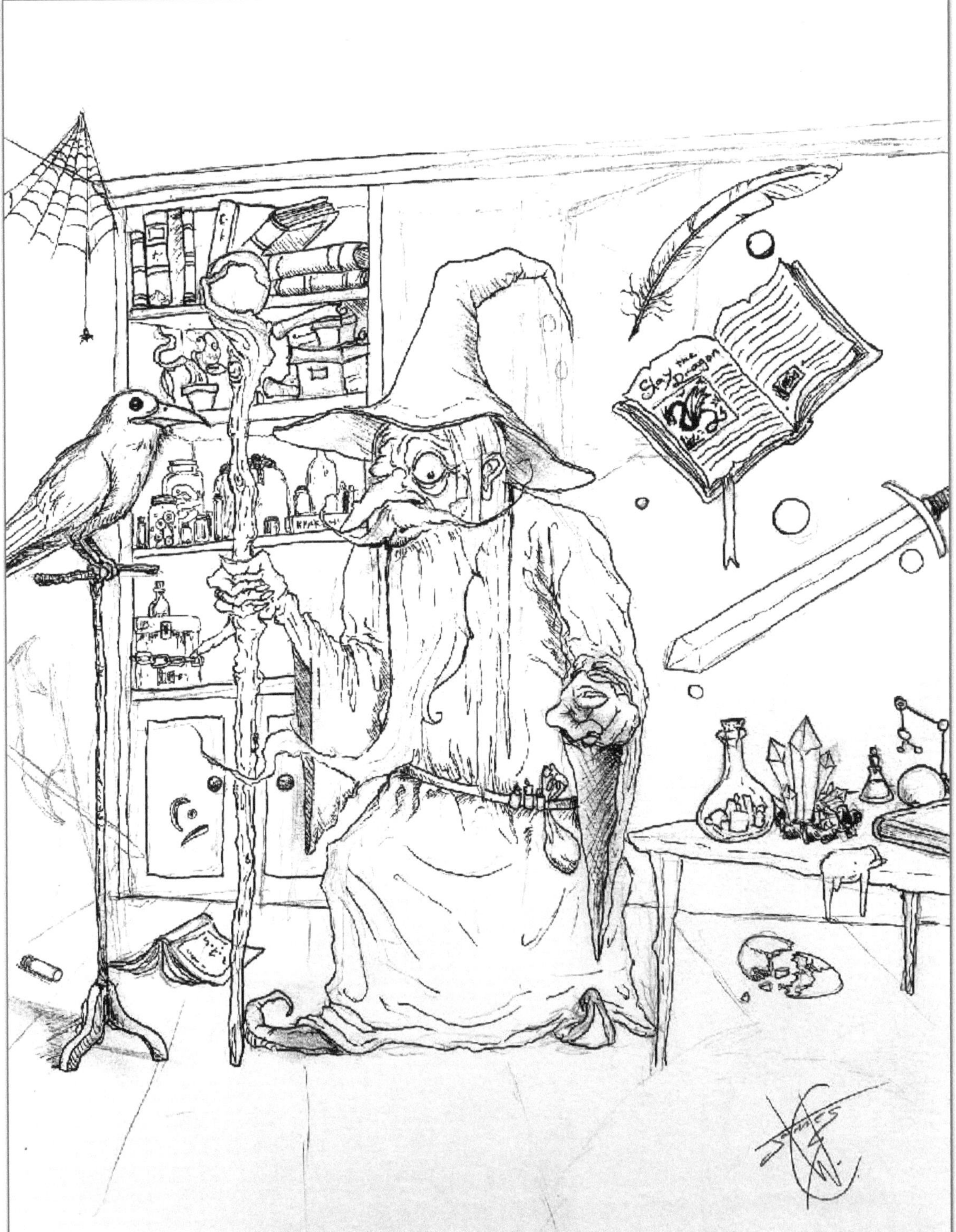

"Merlin Wants You"
2018

Watercolor Paper
Ink, Graphite
12.0 L × 9.0 W Inches

In the Archives of the
James William Christenson Art Gallery
Prior Lake, Minnesota

RIGHT
"Dr. Pluvianus, DDS"
Postcard
2010

Paper
Colored Pencil
4.0 L × 6.0 W Inches

In the Archives of the
James William Christenson Art Gallery
Prior Lake, Minnesota

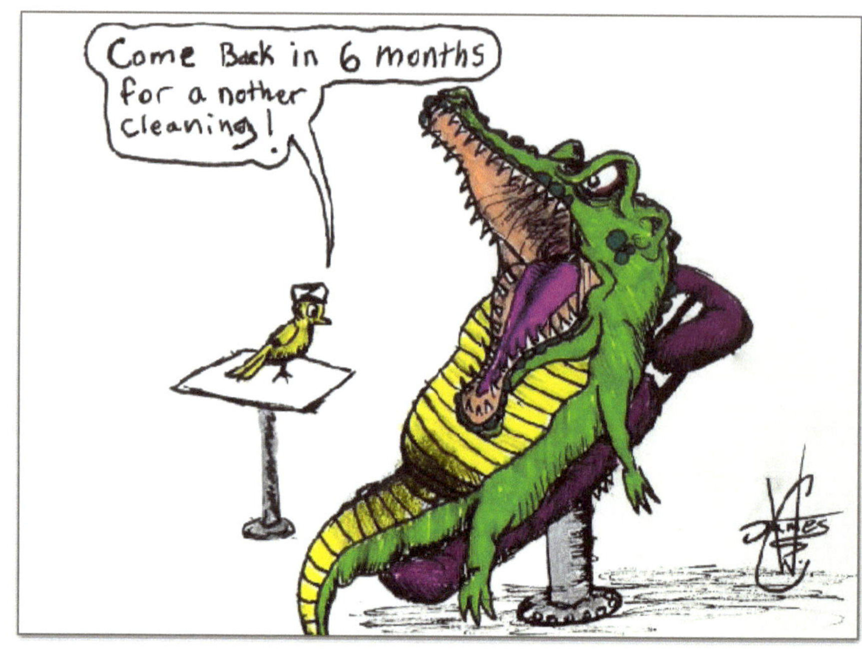

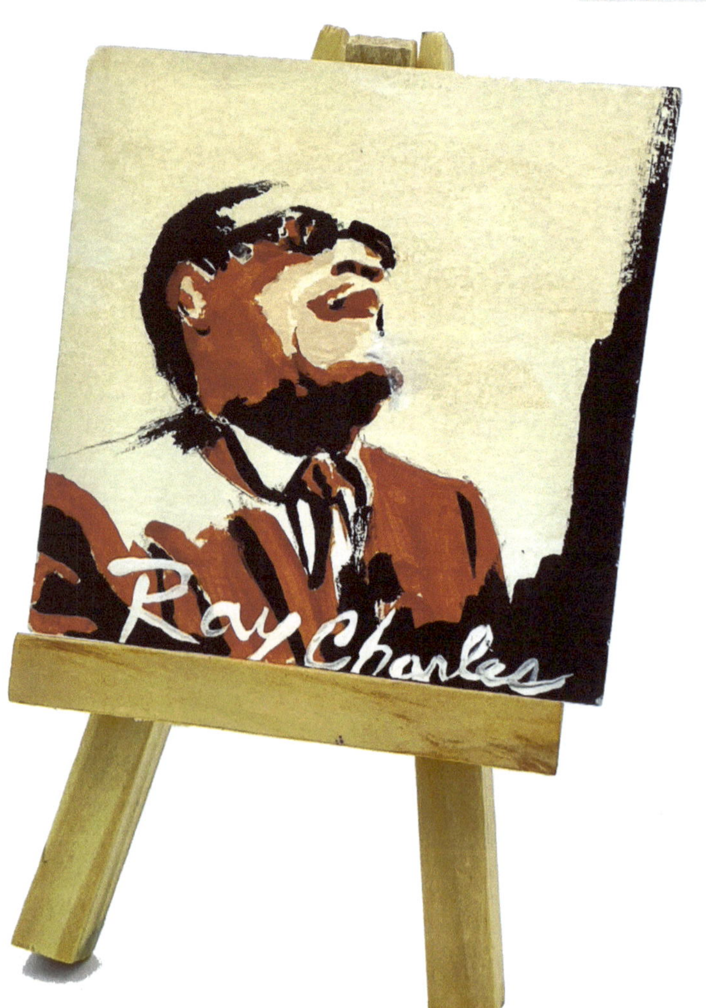

"Ray Charles"
Actual Size, Displayed on Stand
2018

Watercolor Paper
Acrylic
3.0 L × 3.0 W Inches

In the Archives of the
James William Christenson Art Gallery
Prior Lake, Minnesota

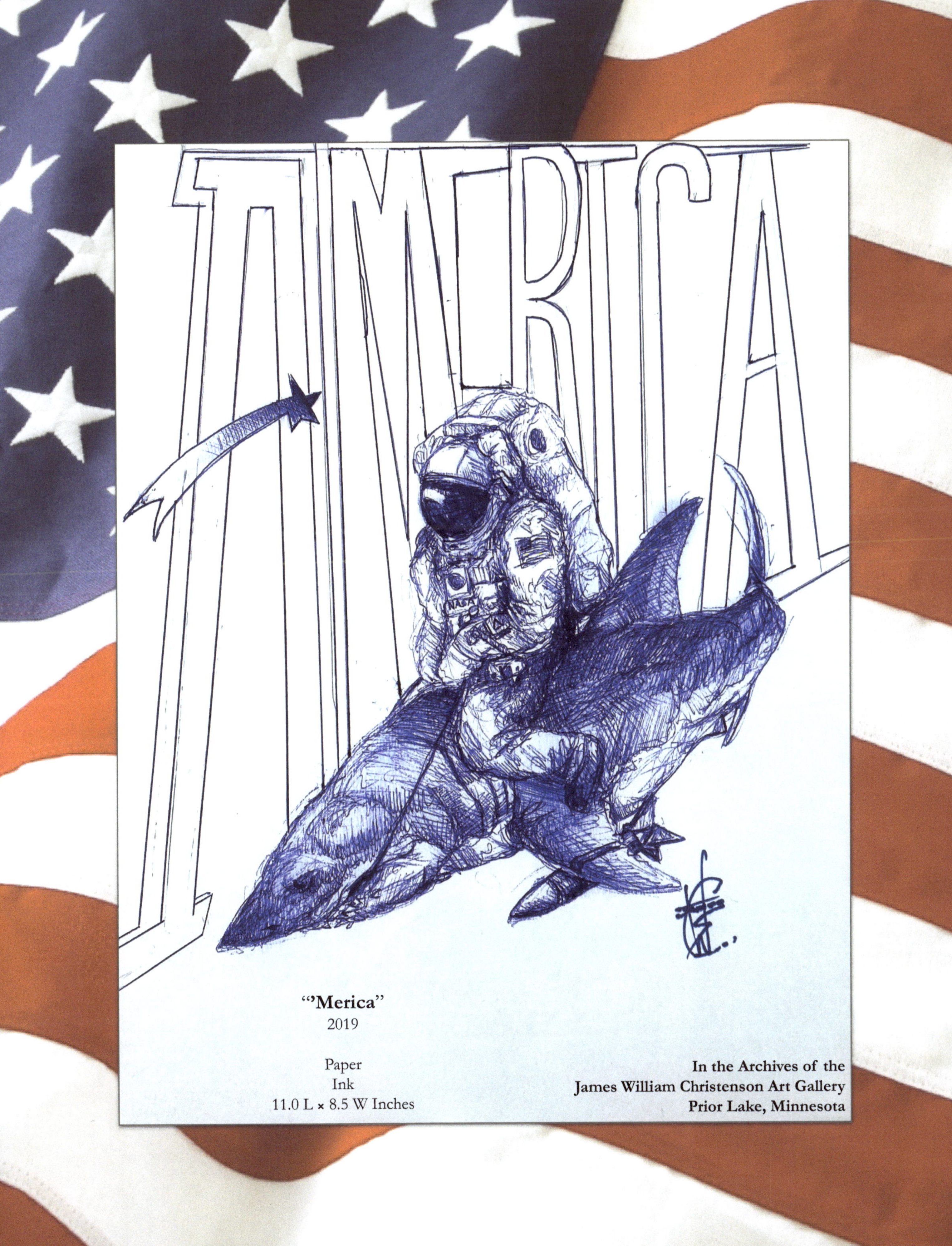

"'Merica"
2019

Paper
Ink
11.0 L × 8.5 W Inches

In the Archives of the
James William Christenson Art Gallery
Prior Lake, Minnesota

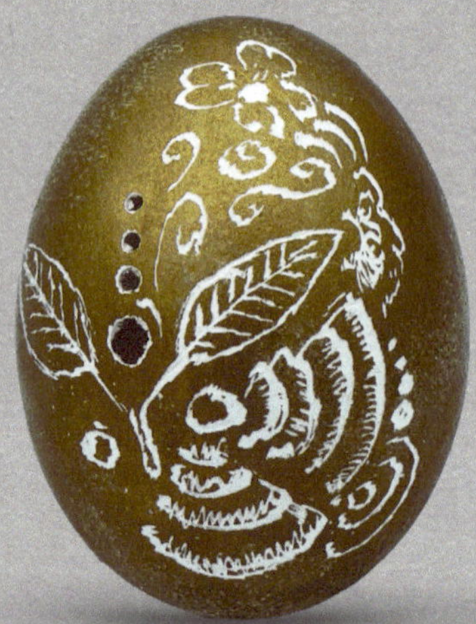

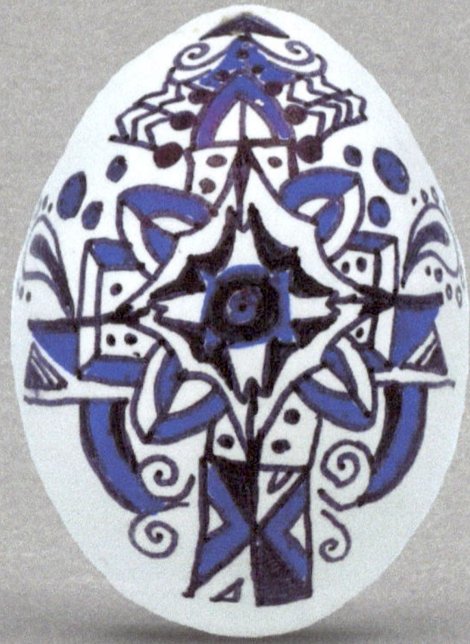

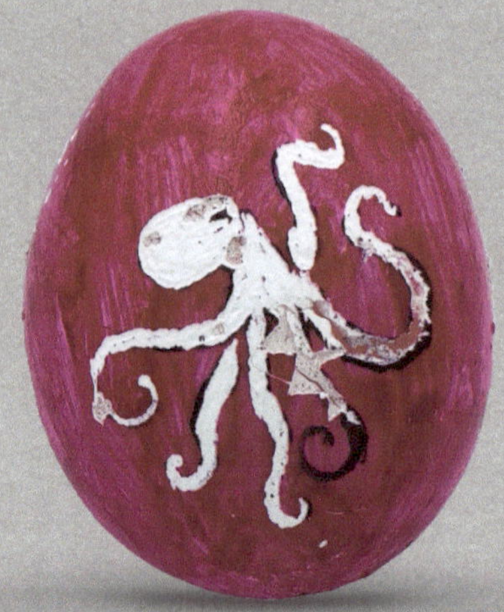

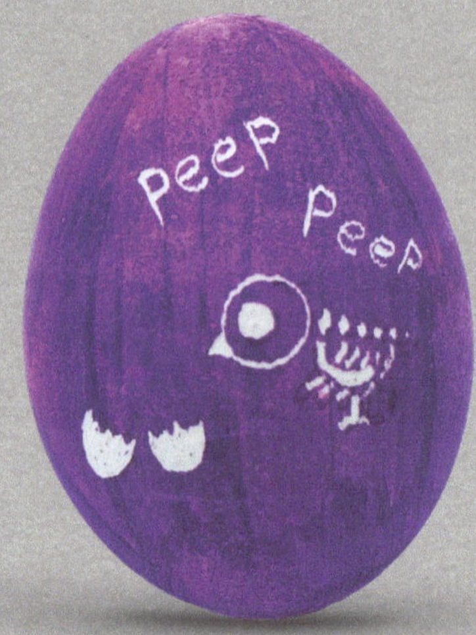

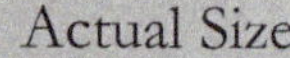

Actual Size

From the
Easter Egg
Series
2020

Blown Egg
Ink, Marker, Wax, Graphite,
Dremel
Approx. 2.25 L × 1.75 W Inches

In the Archives of the
James William Christenson Art Gallery
Prior Lake, Minnesota

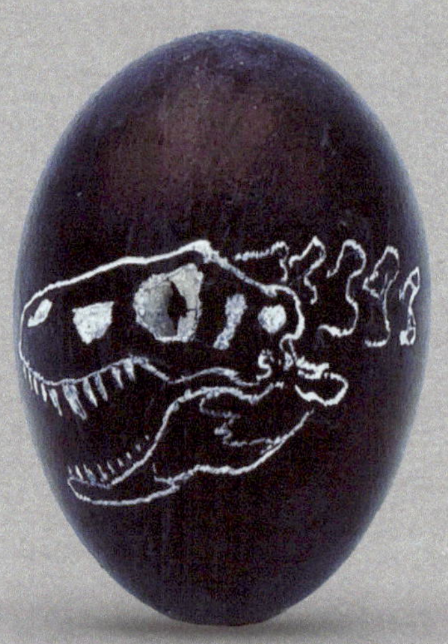

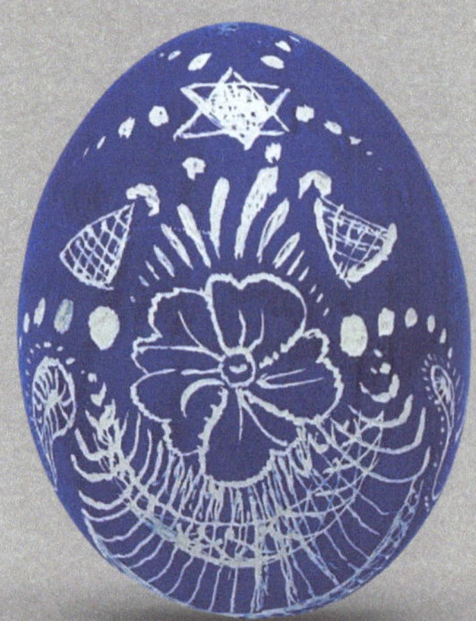

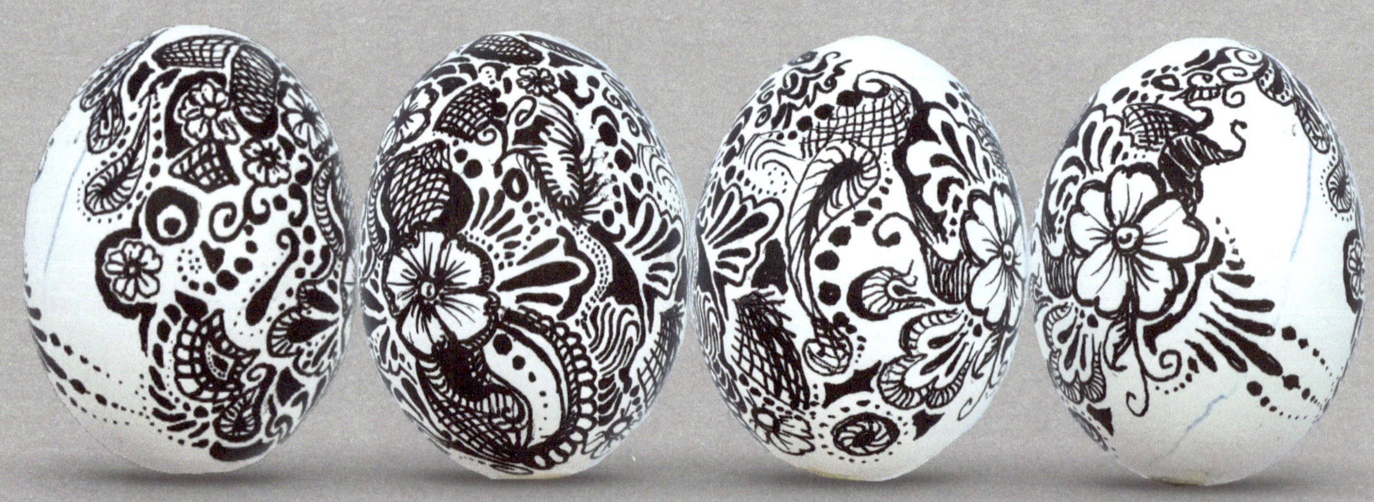

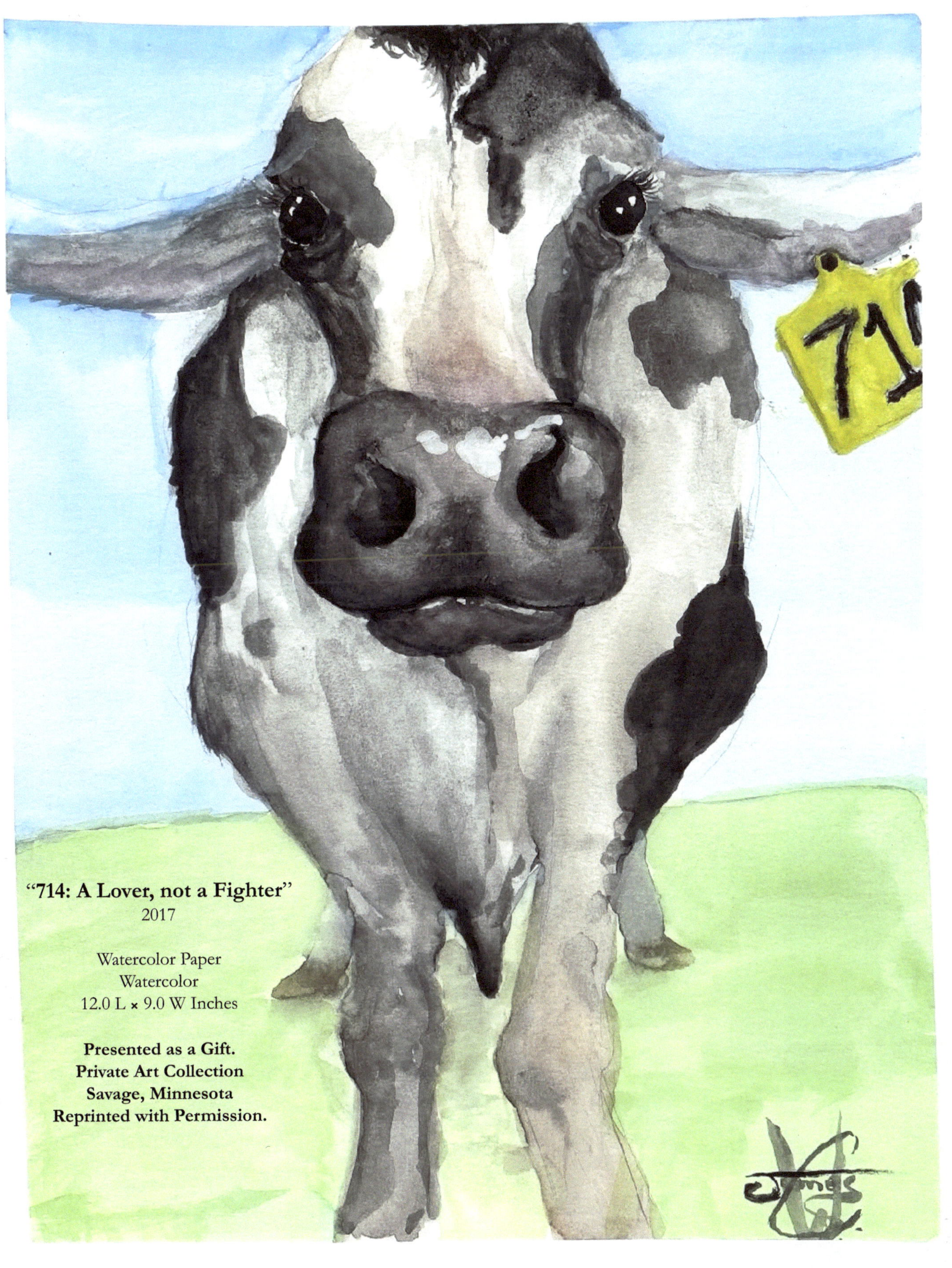

"714: A Lover, not a Fighter"
2017

Watercolor Paper
Watercolor
12.0 L × 9.0 W Inches

Presented as a Gift.
Private Art Collection
Savage, Minnesota
Reprinted with Permission.

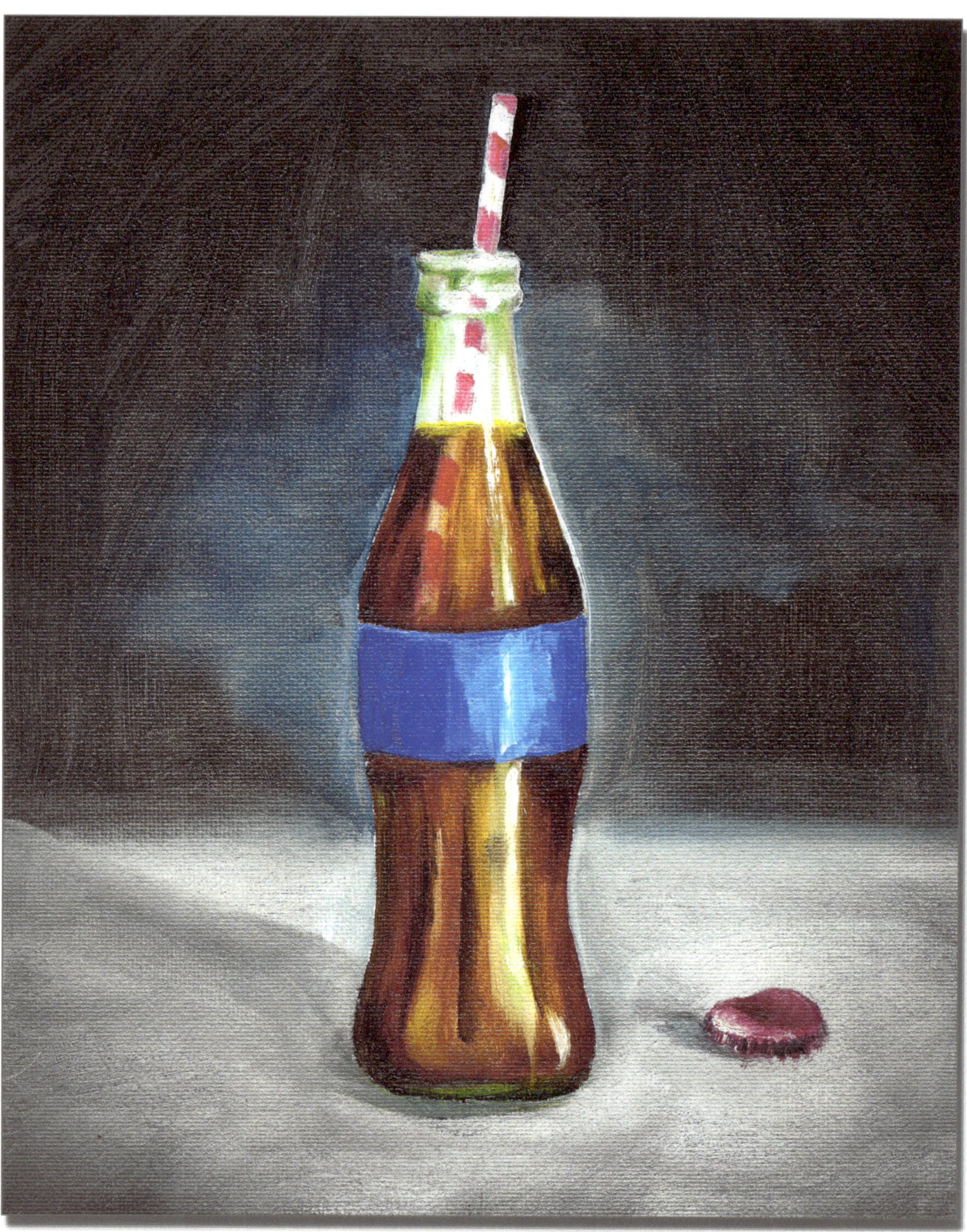

Cover Art for Book
2020

Canvas Board
Oil
16.0 L × 20.0 W Inches

Commissioned Artwork for
"The Bottlecap Score"
Published in 2020 by Kayto & Co. Publishing
Reprinted with Permission.

"Harker Brayton's End"

OR

"Tory's Nightmare"
2016

Canvas Board
Polymer Clay, Acrylic, Rubberband
12.0 L × 9.0 W Inches

Presented as a Gift.
Private Art Collection
Cedarville, Ohio
Reprinted with Permission.

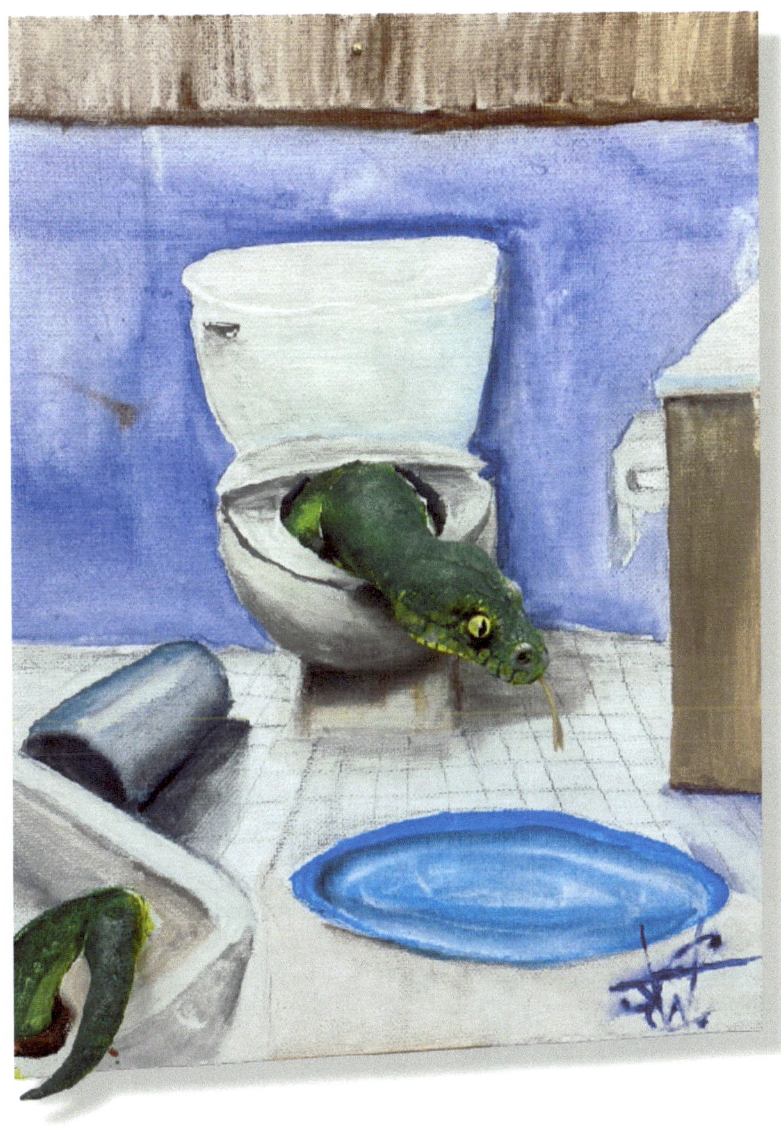

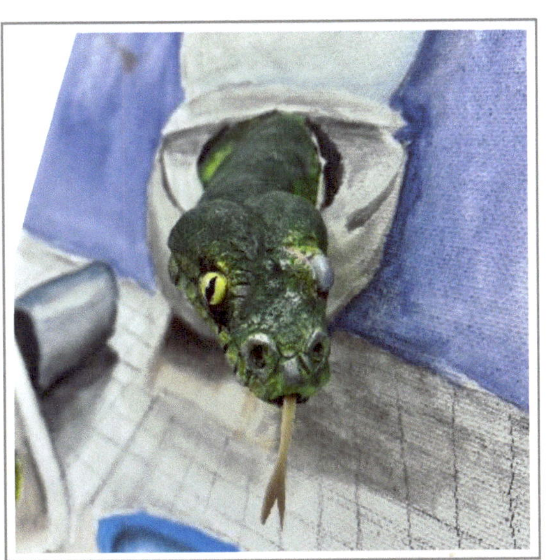

Snake Head Detail

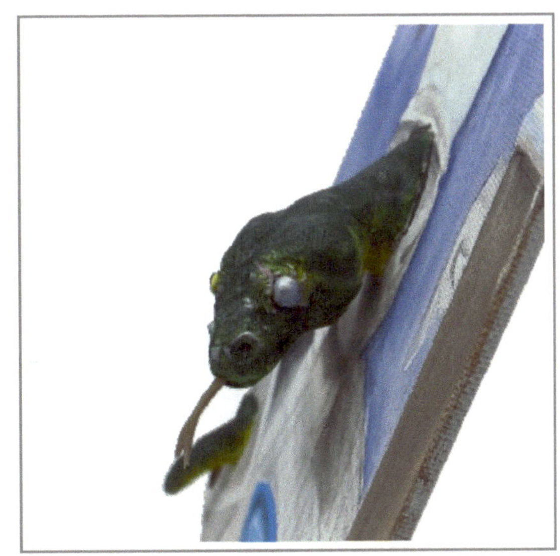

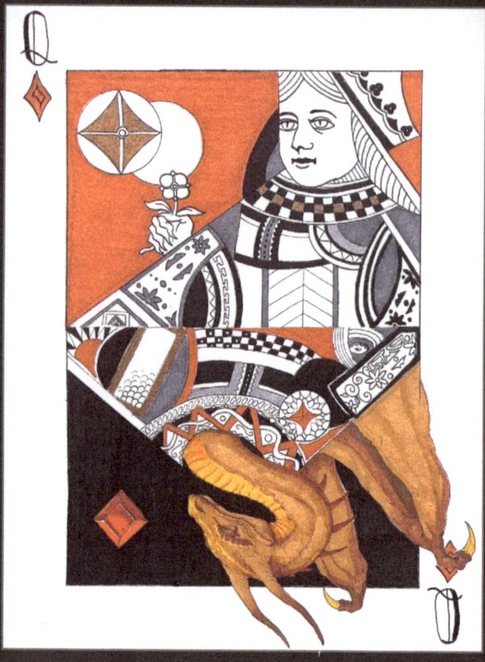

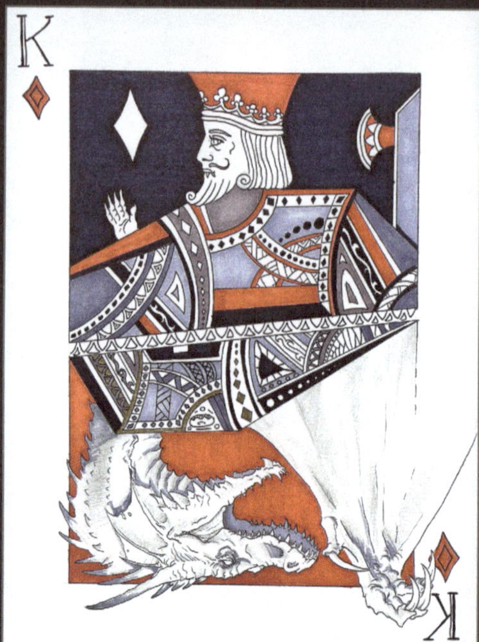

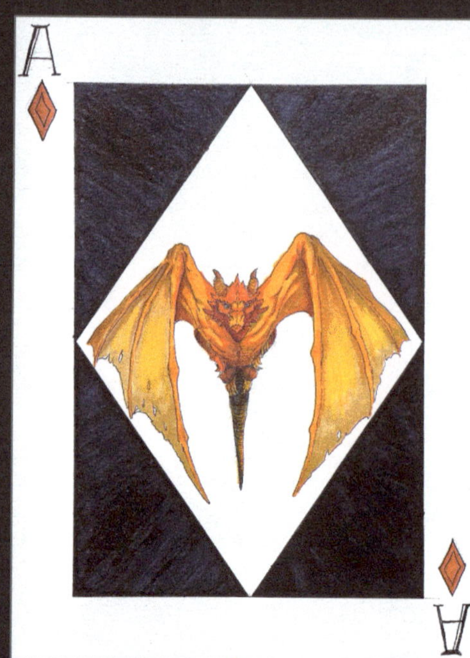

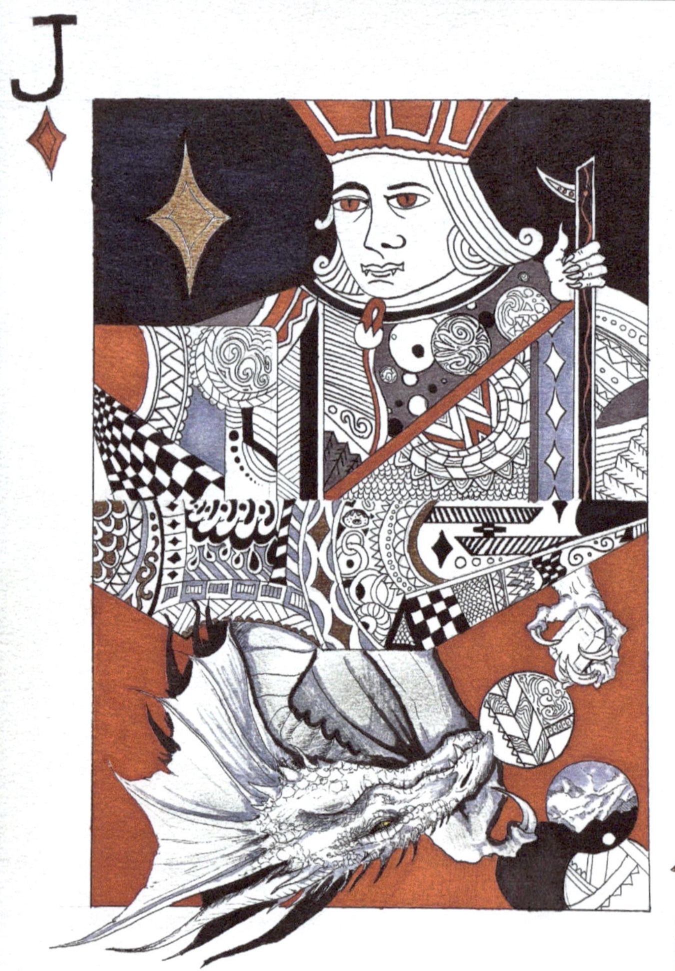

From the
Deck of Cards
Series
2019 - 2020

Watercolor Paper
Pen, Felt Marker, Ink, Watercolor
12.0 L × 9.0 W Inches

In the Archives of the
James William Christenson Art Gallery
Prior Lake, Minnesota

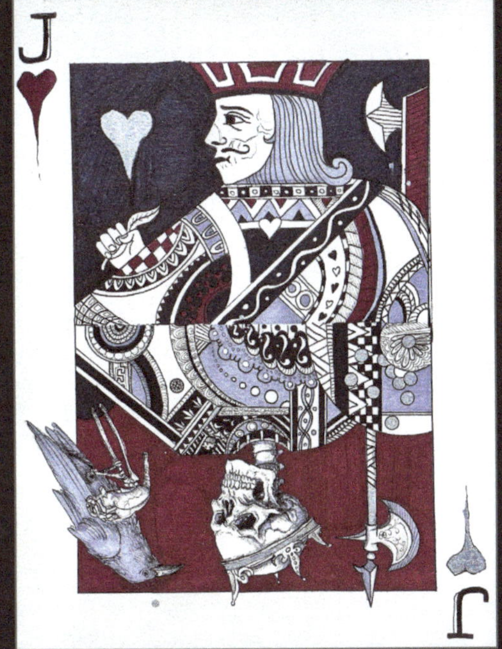

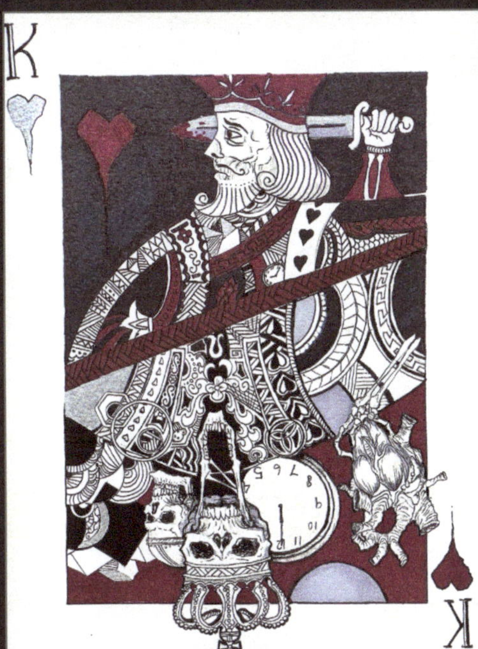

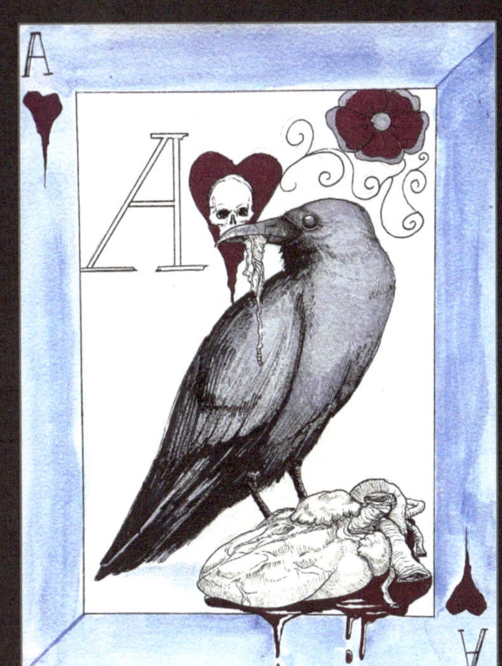

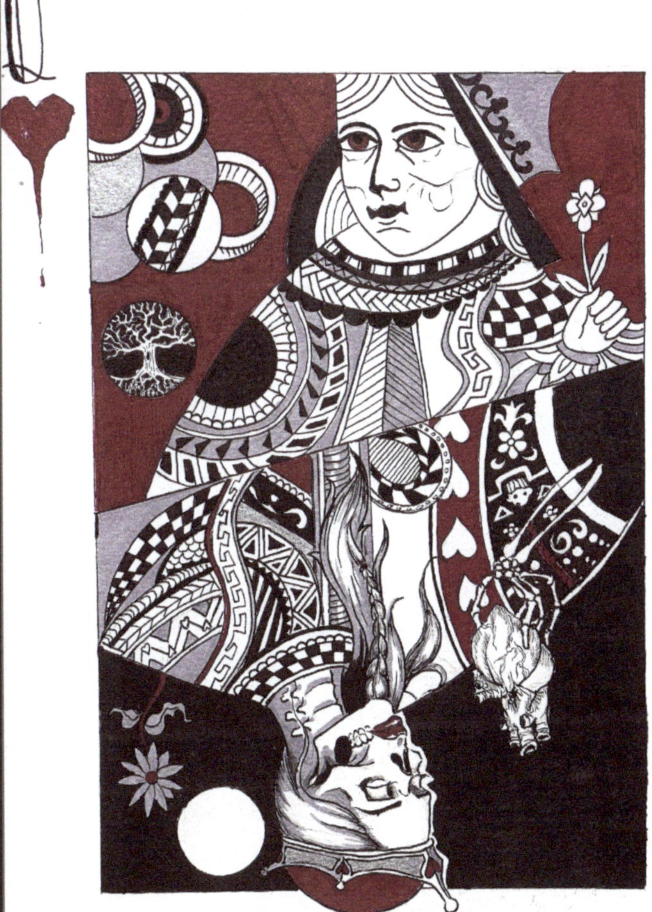

Look for the muffin in the Hearts.

Look for donuts in the Diamonds.

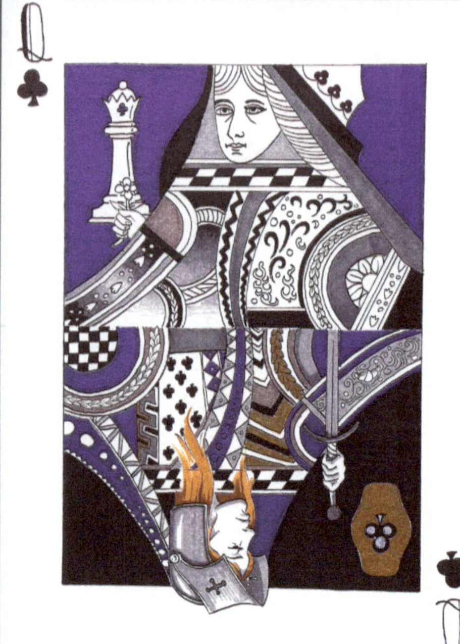

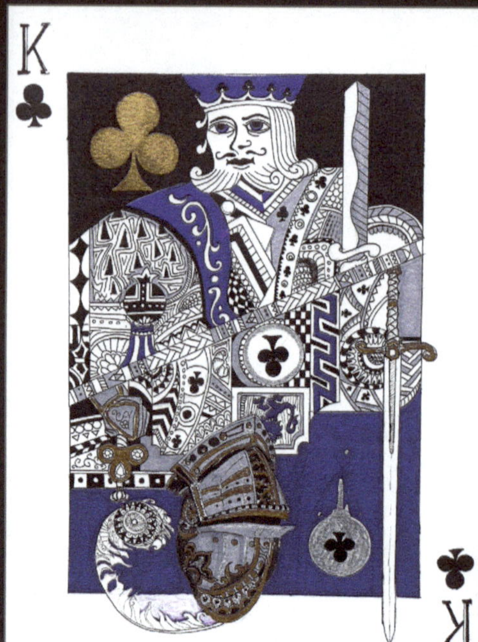

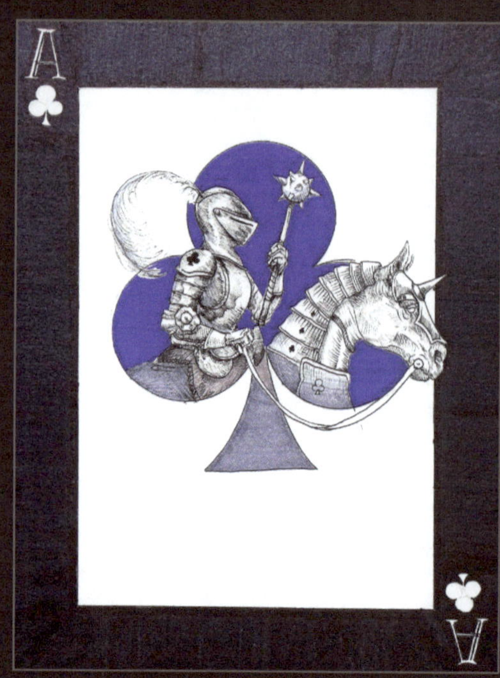

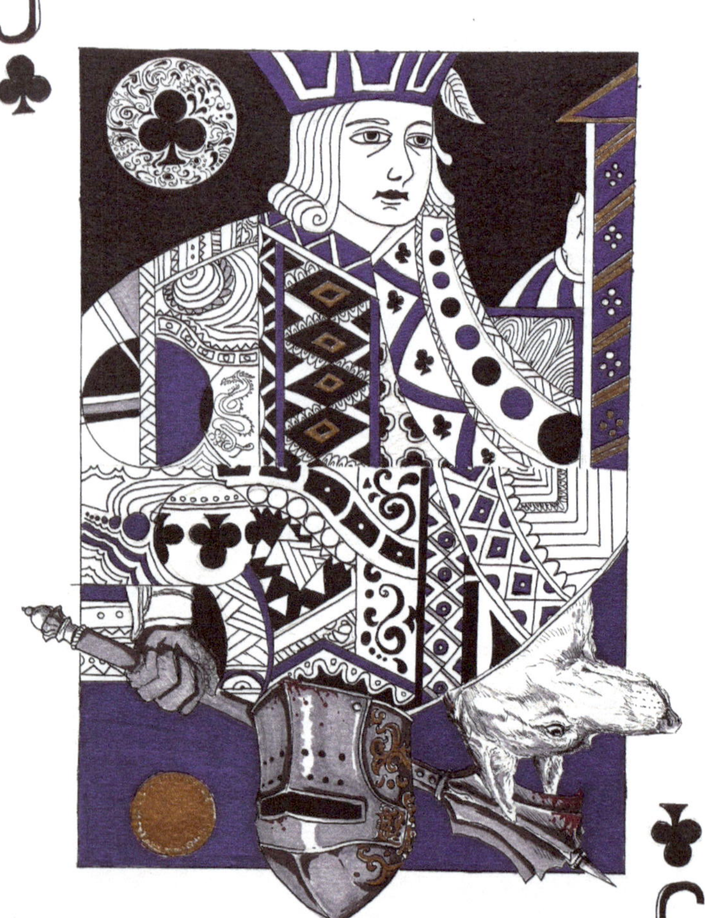

From the
Deck of Cards
Series
2019 - 2020

Watercolor Paper
Graphite, Pen, Felt Marker
12.0 L × 9.0 W Inches

In the Archives of the
James William Christenson Art Gallery
Prior Lake, Minnesota

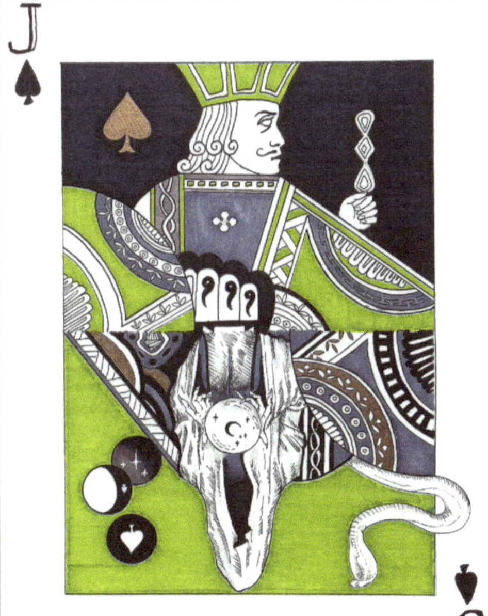

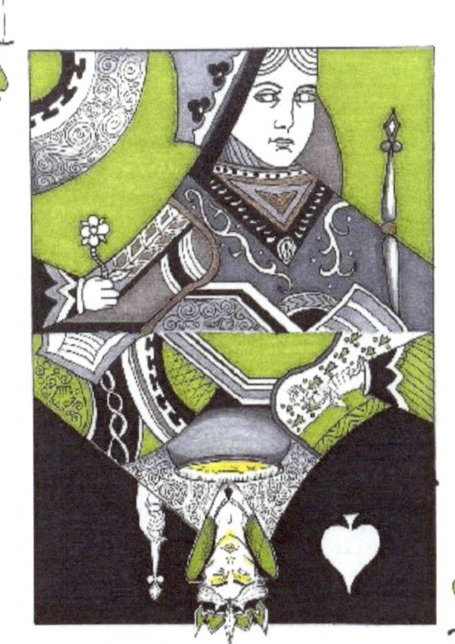

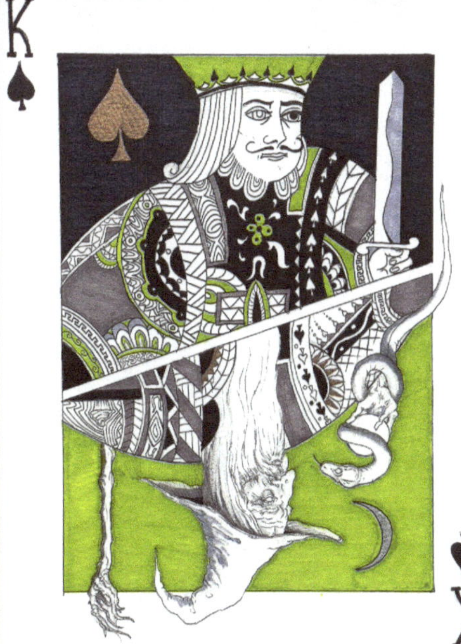

Look for the cupcake in the Spades.

Look for croissants in the Clubs.

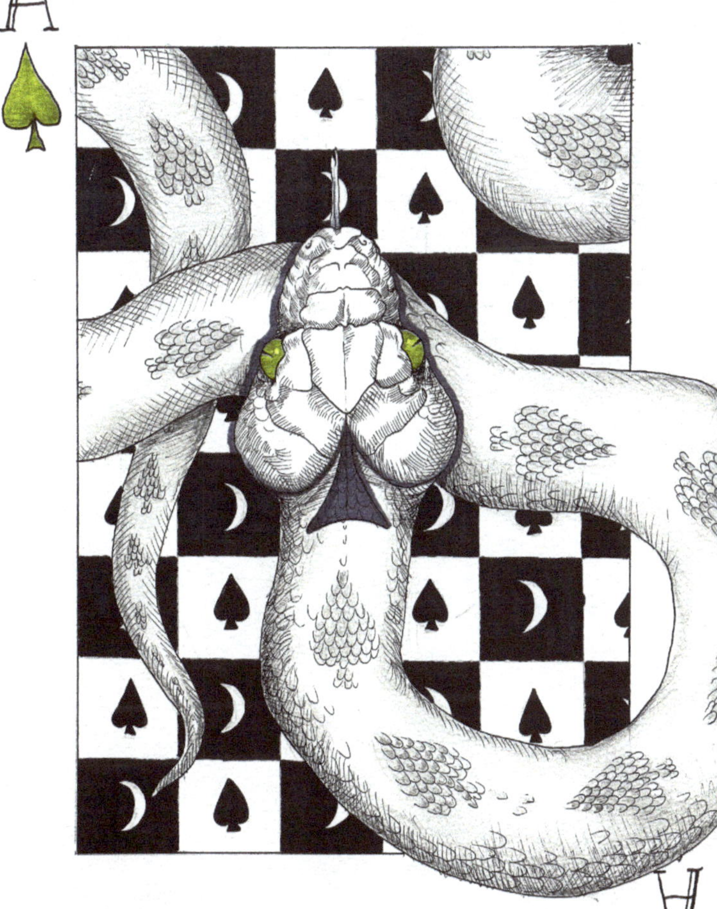

"Discerning Tastes"
A Pair of Portraits
2020

Paper
Graphite
12.0 L × 9.0 W Inches

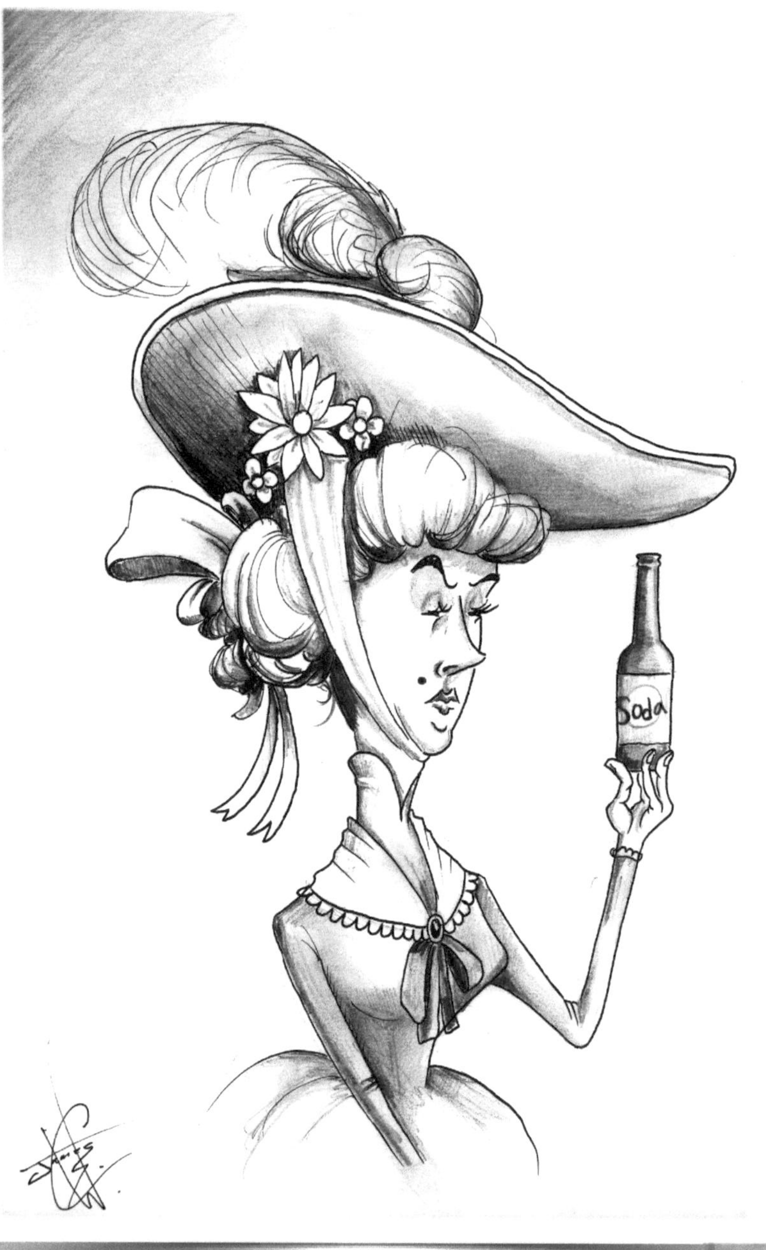

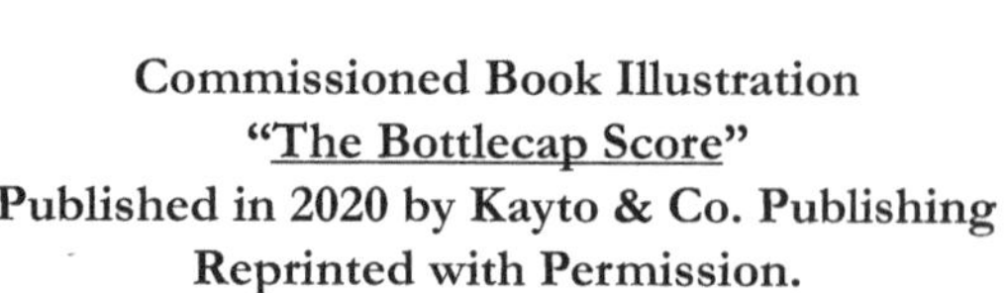
Commissioned Book Illustration
"<u>The Bottlecap Score</u>"
Published in 2020 by Kayto & Co. Publishing
Reprinted with Permission.

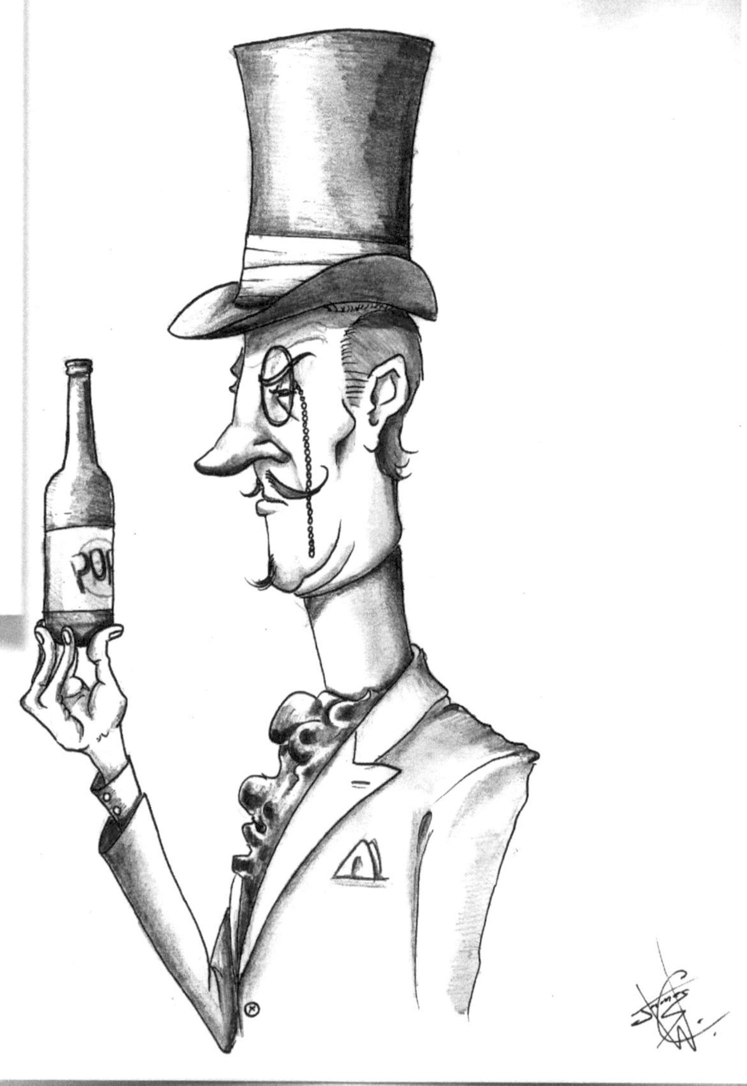

"Santa's Little Helper"
2020

Watercolor Paper
Oil
9.0 L × 12.0 W Inches

In the Archives of the
James William Christenson Art Gallery
Prior Lake, Minnesota

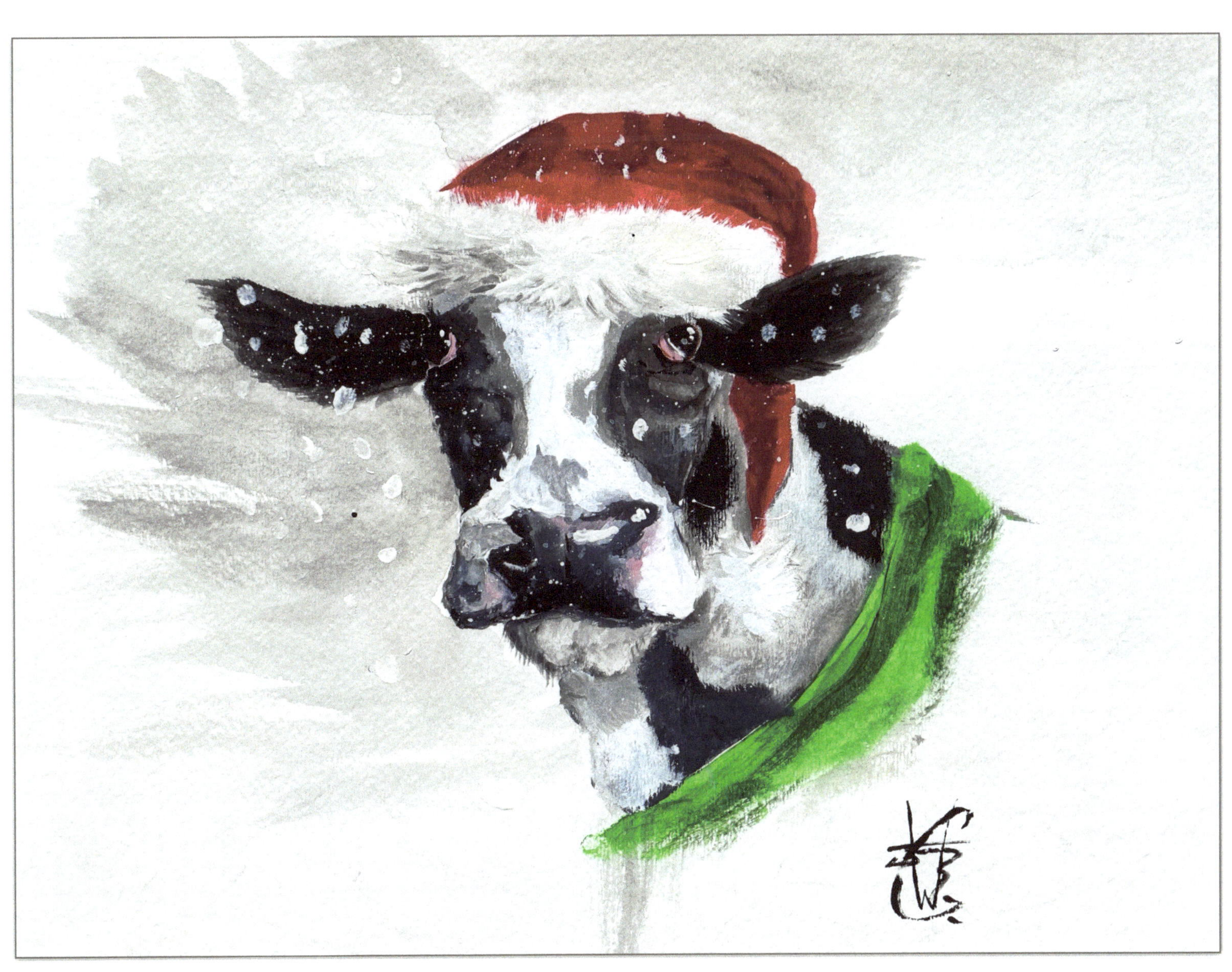

"Mail Bag"
2020

Leather, Suede Leather, Leather Cord,
Silver Dollar Coin, Nylon Strap

11.0 L × 16.0 W x 2.0 H Inches

**In the Archives of the
James William Christenson Art Gallery
Prior Lake, Minnesota**

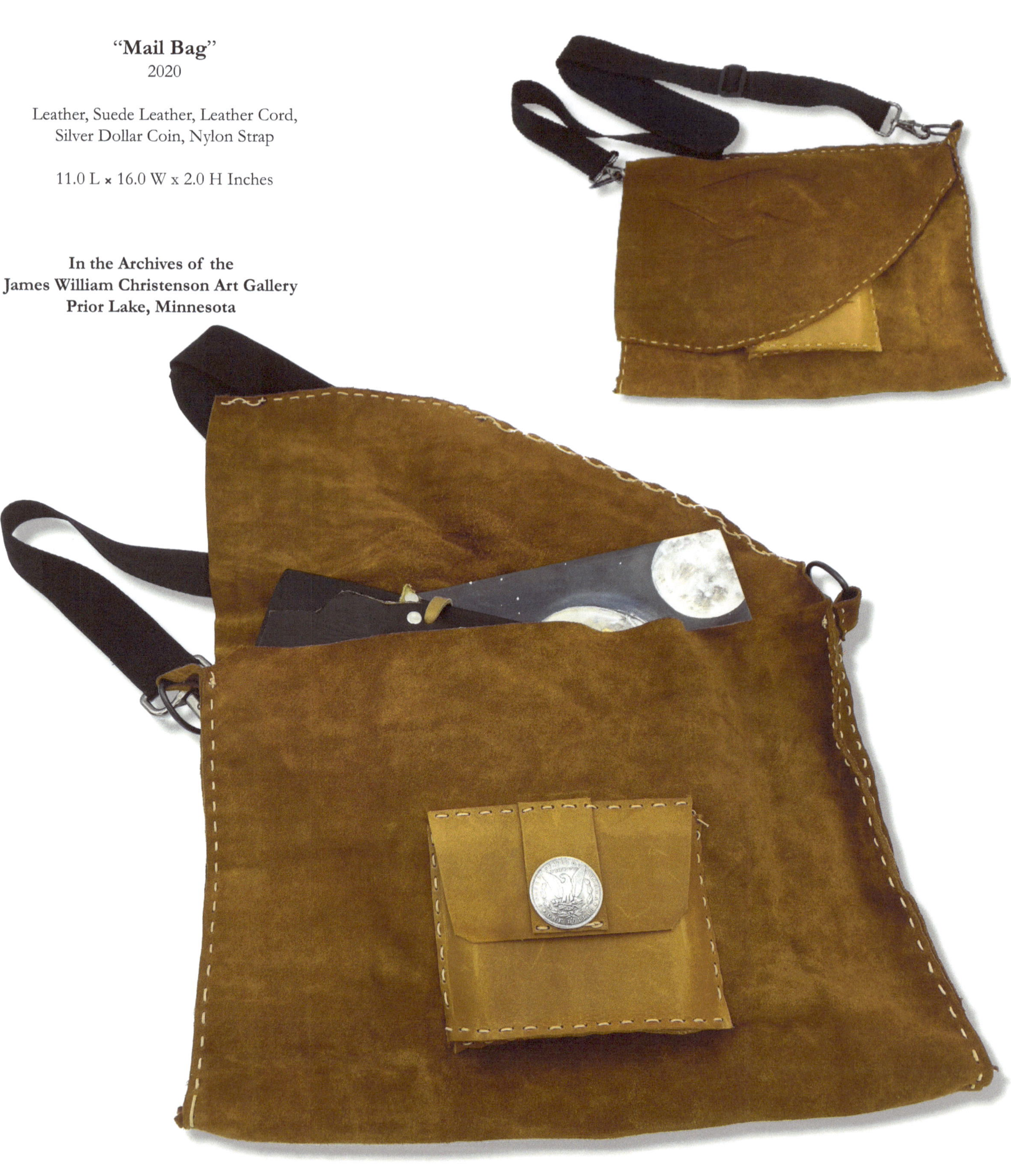

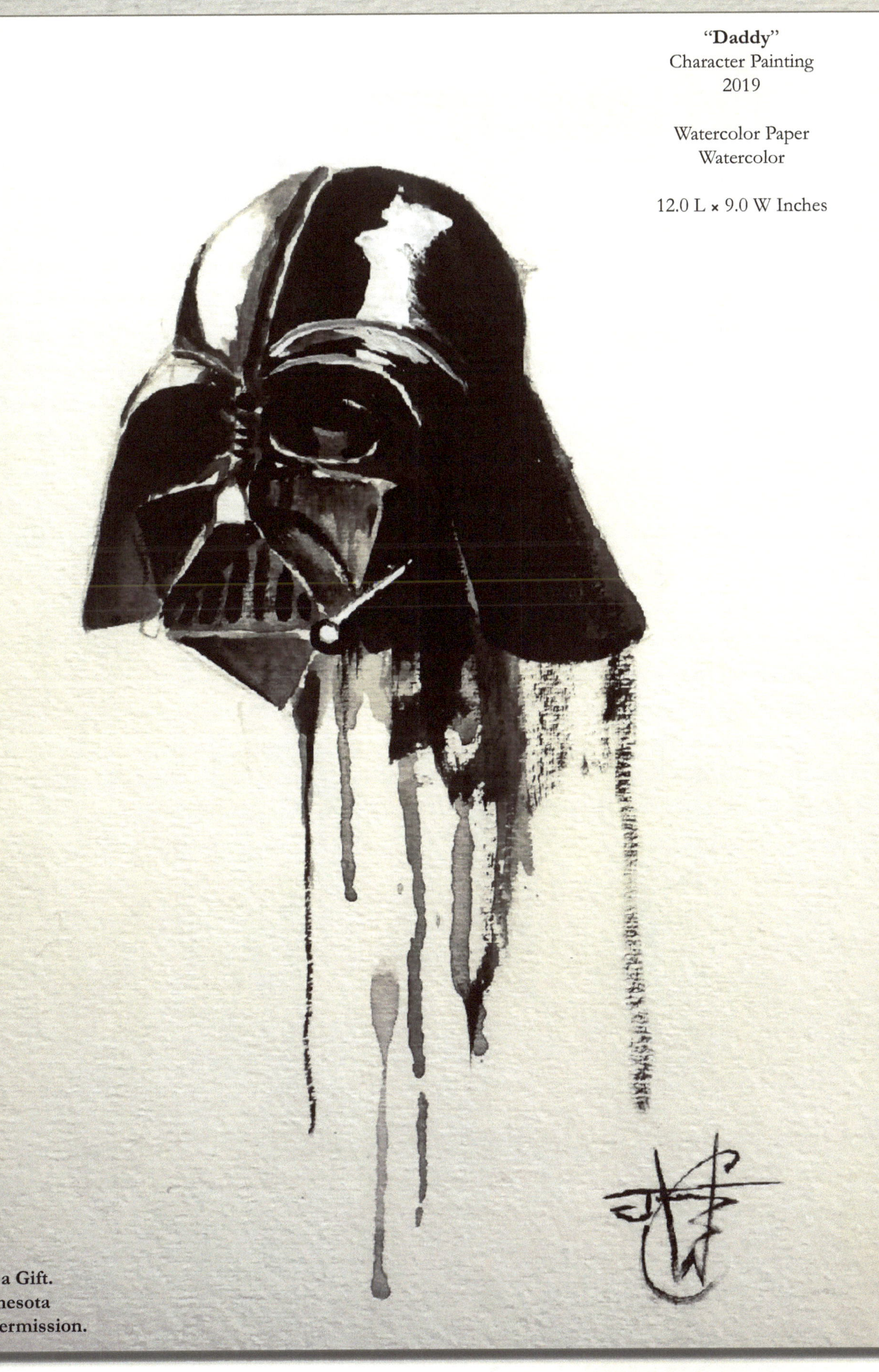

"**Daddy**"
Character Painting
2019

Watercolor Paper
Watercolor

12.0 L × 9.0 W Inches

Presented as a Gift.
Savage, Minnesota
Reprinted with Permission.

"Root Beer: The Preferred Drink of Sober & Underage Pirates"
2020

Paper
Graphite
12.0 L × 9.0 W Inches

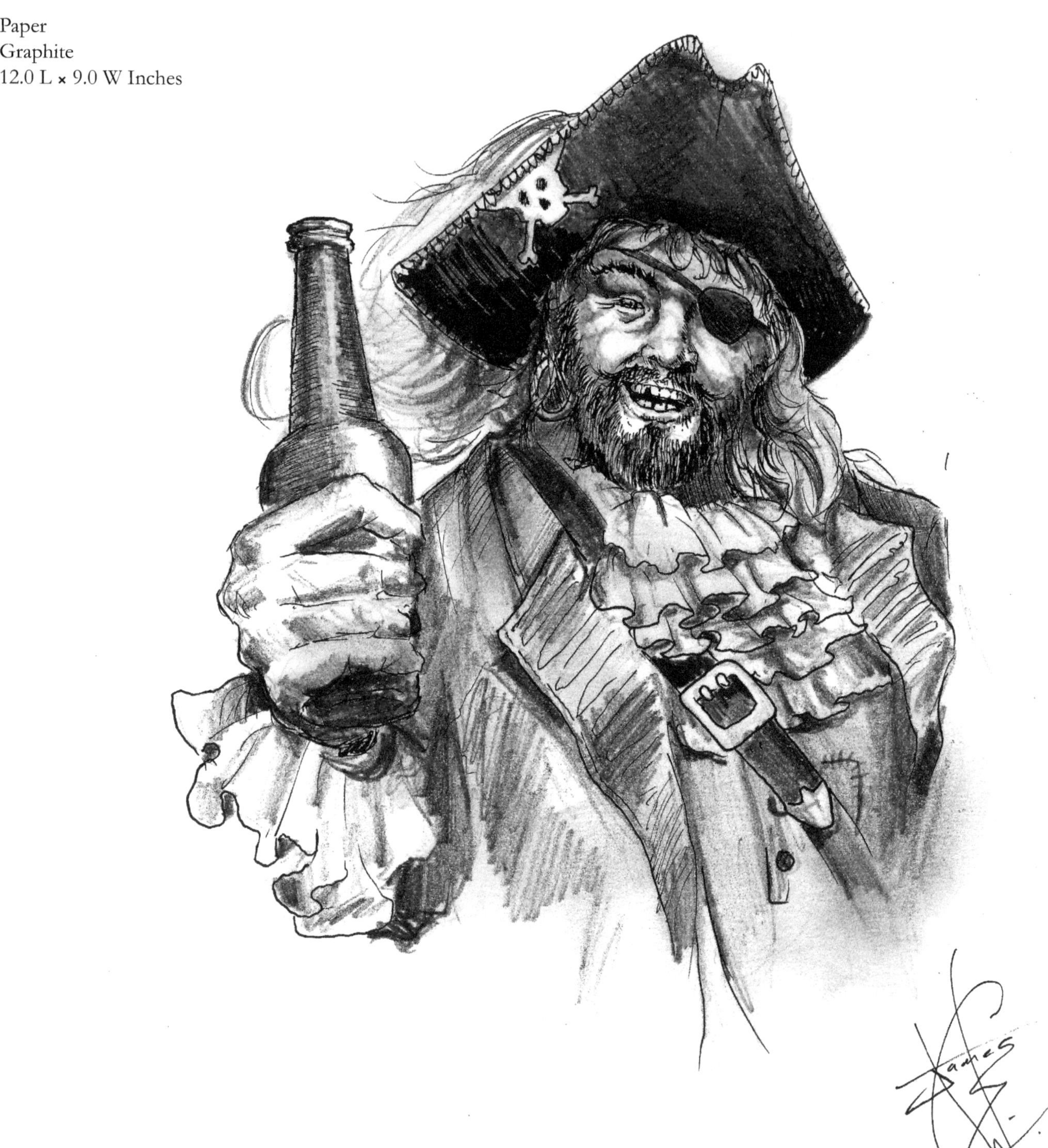

Commissioned Book Illustration
"<u>The Bottlecap Score</u>"
Published in 2020 by Kayto & Co. Publishing
Reprinted with Permission.

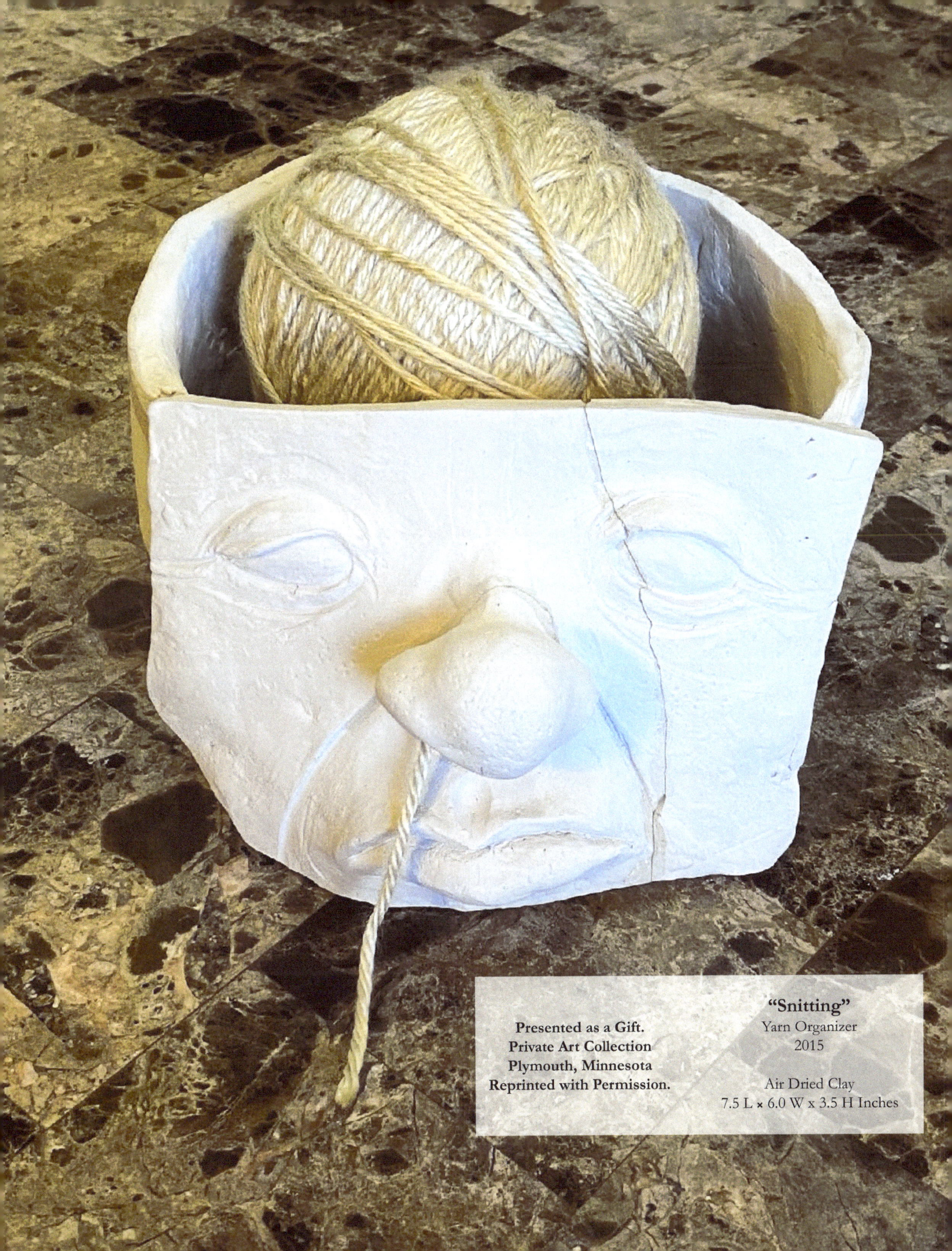

Presented as a Gift.
Private Art Collection
Plymouth, Minnesota
Reprinted with Permission.

"Snitting"
Yarn Organizer
2015

Air Dried Clay
7.5 L × 6.0 W x 3.5 H Inches

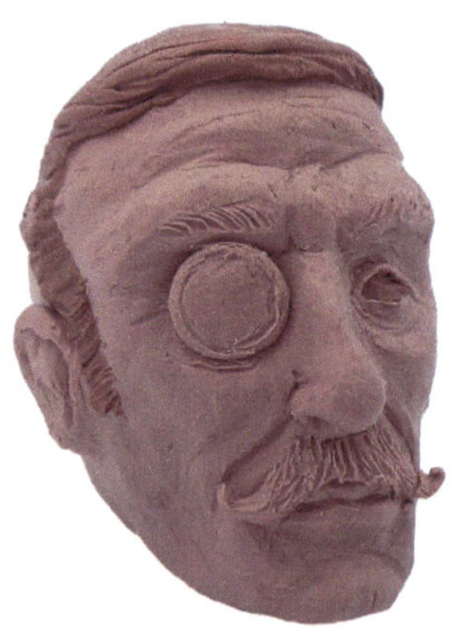

"Mono Perspective"
Actual Size
2020

Polymer Clay
2.0 L × 1.5 W x 1.5 H Inches

"Nolan's Forearms"
2019

Ink, Polymer Clay, Cork
3.0 L × 2.75 W x 3.75 H Inches

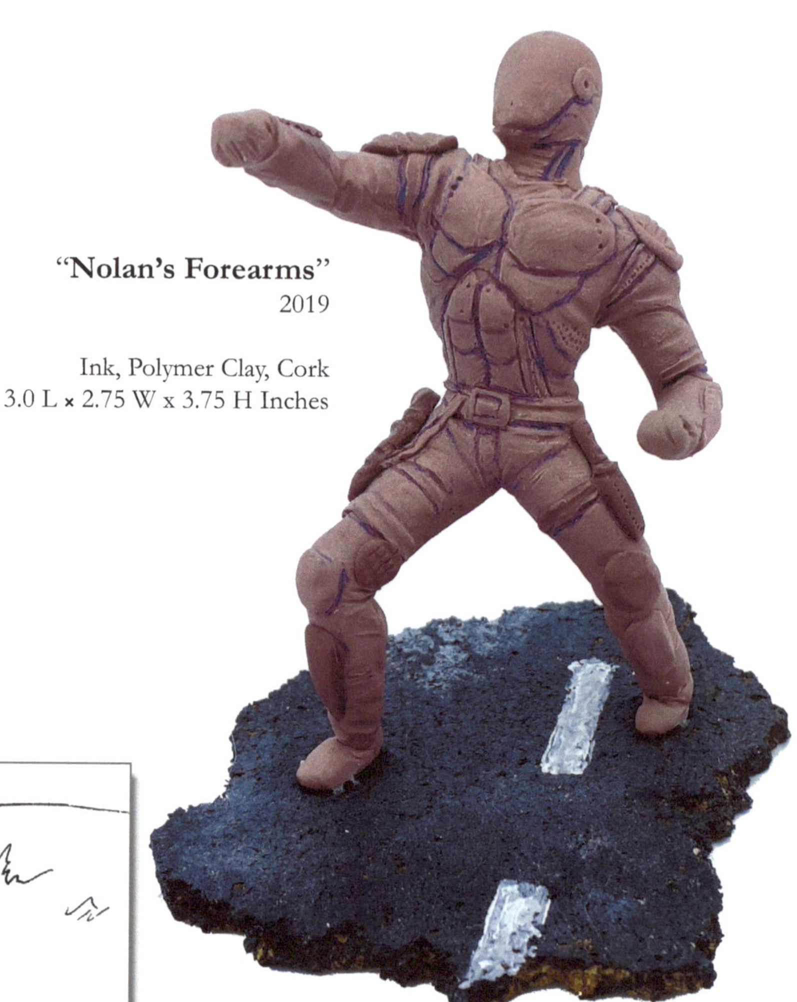

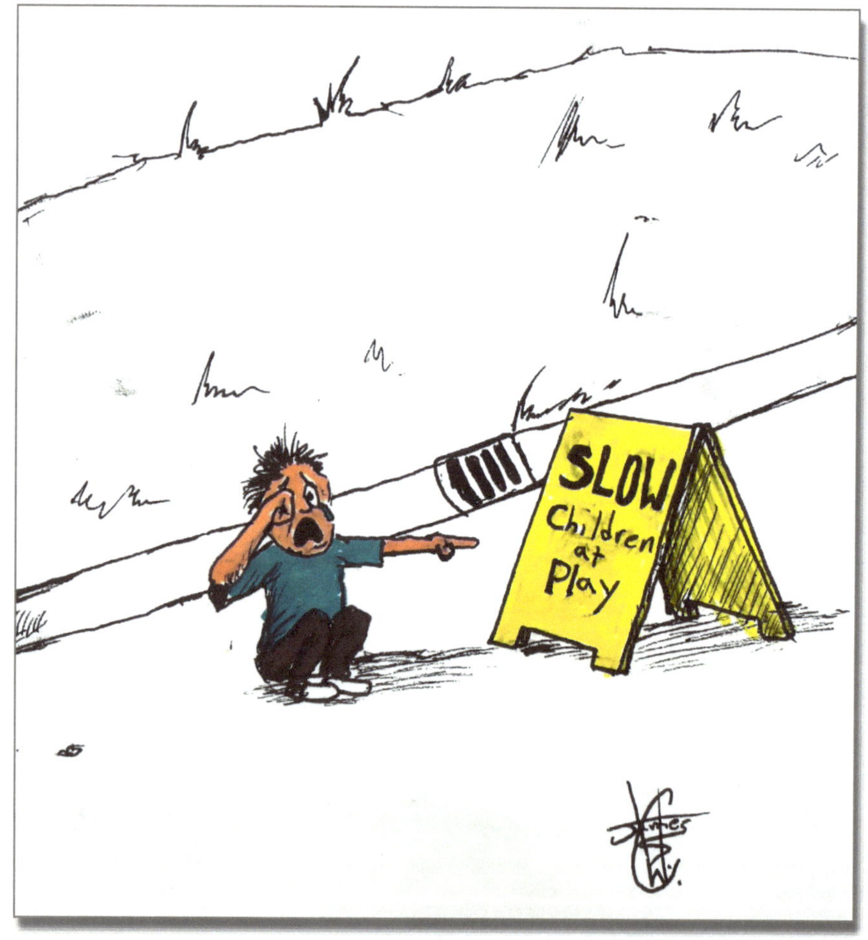

"Congratulations On Your Child"
Greeting Card
2010

Cardstock
Ink, Felt Marker
6.0 L × 4.0 W Inches

In the Archives of the
James William Christenson Art Gallery
Prior Lake, Minnesota

"Great Blue Coaster"
Actual Size
2019

Basswood
Woodburn
4.0 L × 4.0 W Inches

Commissioned for Display in the Private Art Collection of Casa del Flamingo, Minnesota Reprinted with Permission

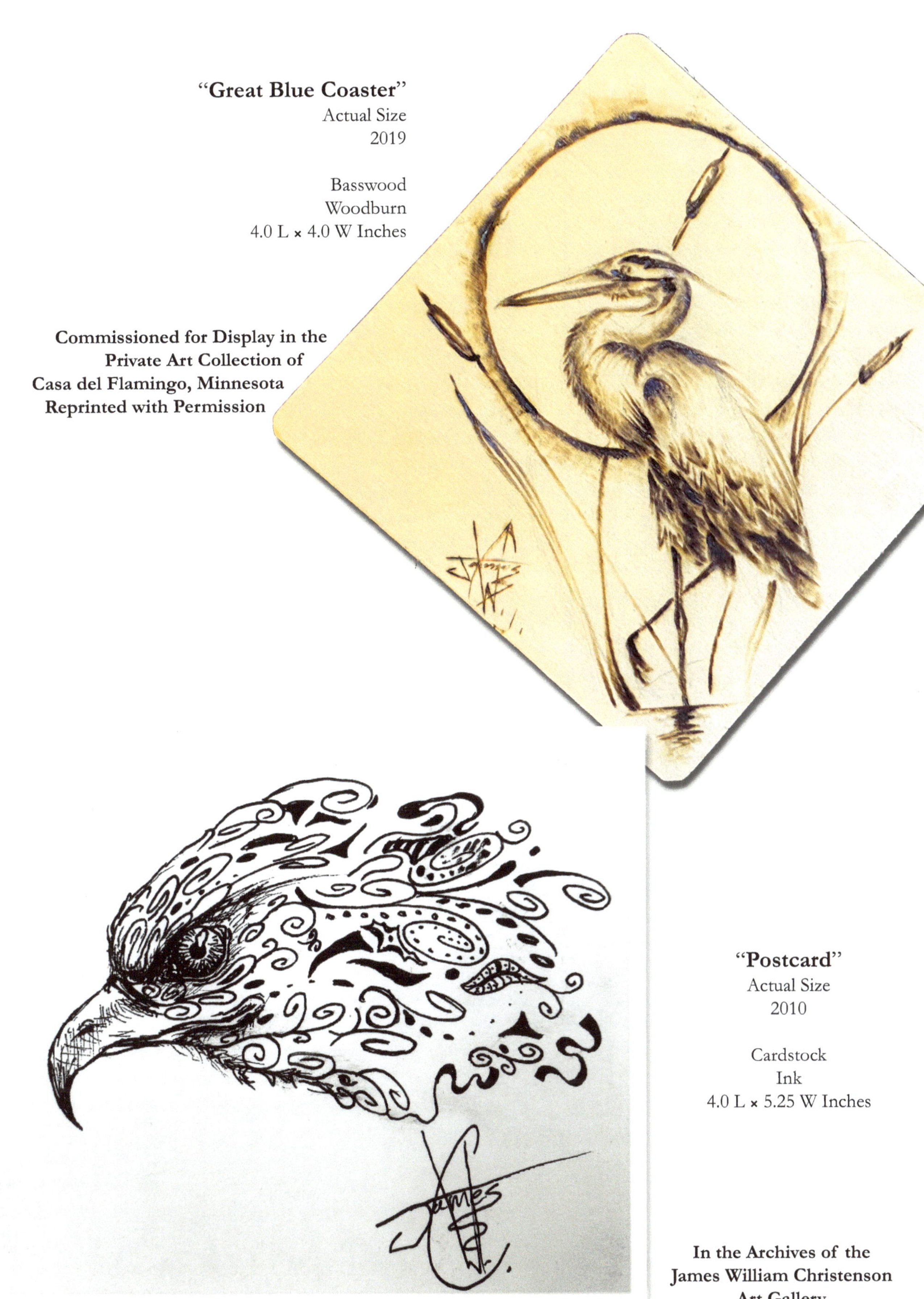

"Postcard"
Actual Size
2010

Cardstock
Ink
4.0 L × 5.25 W Inches

In the Archives of the James William Christenson Art Gallery Prior Lake, Minnesota

"Chad"
2019

Paper
Color Pencil
9.0 L × 12.0 W Inches

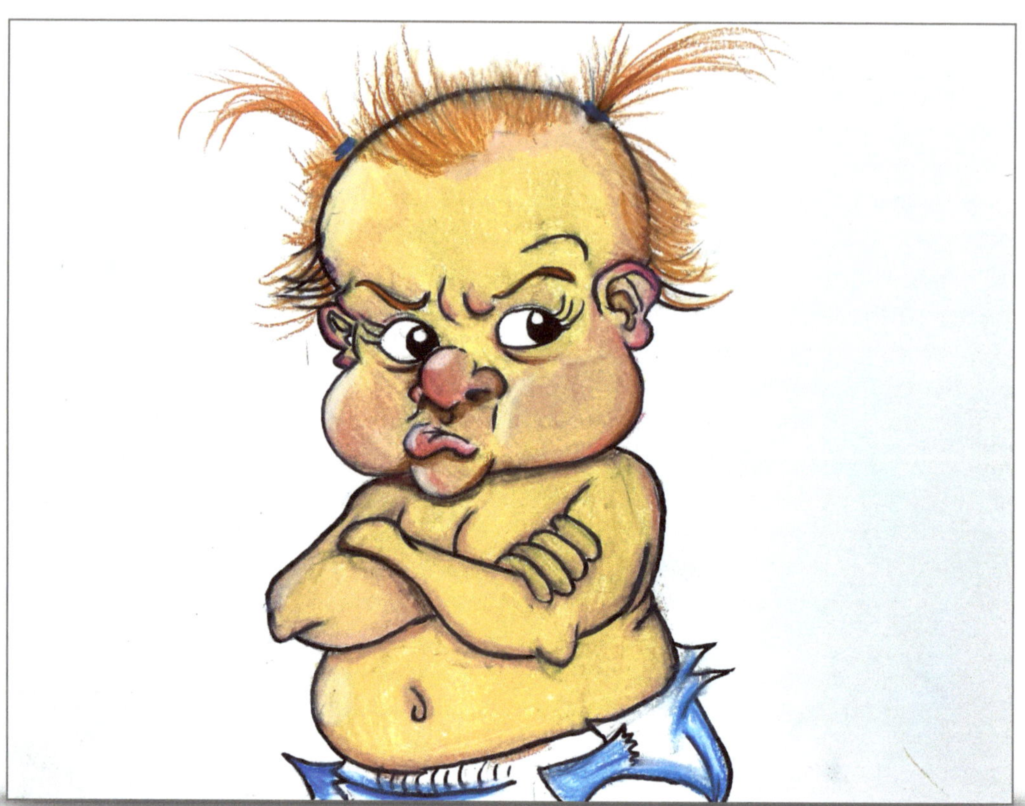

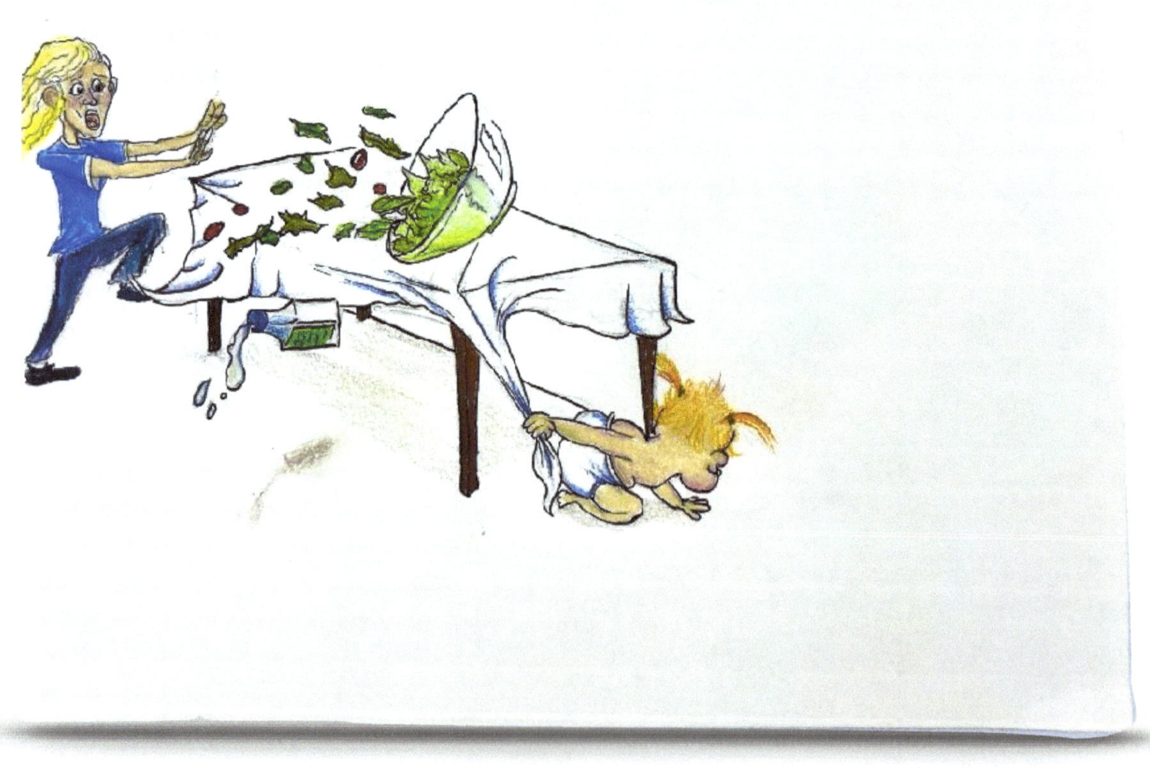

"Contraceptives"
2019

Paper
Color Pencil
9.0 L × 12.0 W Inches

In the Archives of the
James William Christenson
Art Gallery
Prior Lake, Minnesota

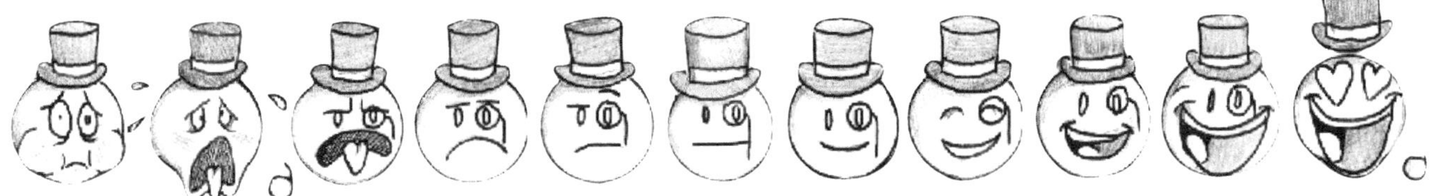

"Custom Emoji Scales"
2020

Paper
Graphite, Ink
12.0 L × 4.0 W Inches

Commissioned Book Illustration
"The Bottlecap Score"
Published in 2020 by
Kayto & Co. Publishing
Reprinted with Permission.

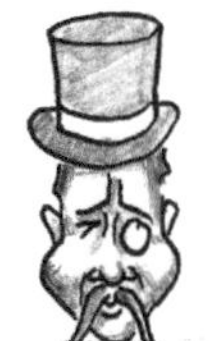
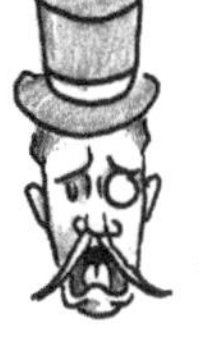
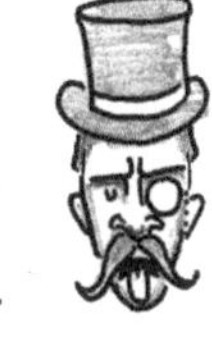
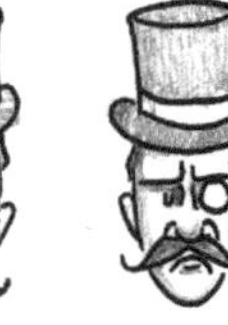
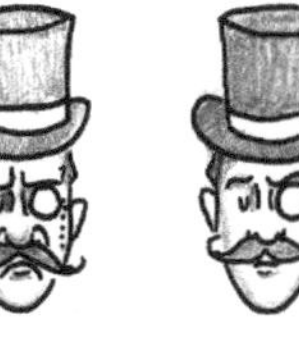
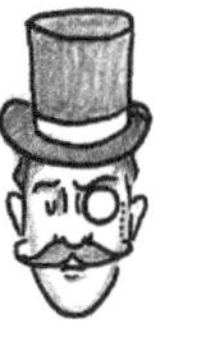
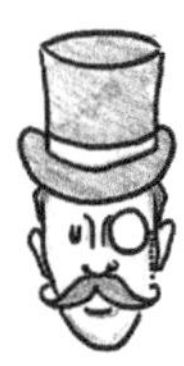
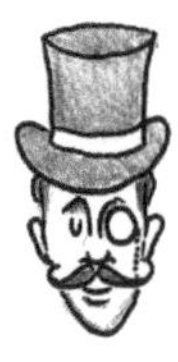
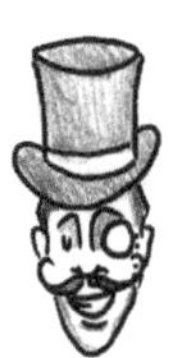
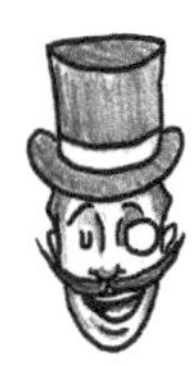
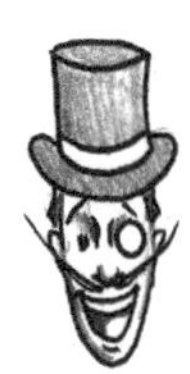
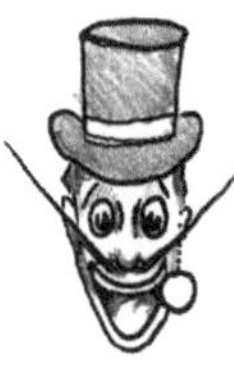

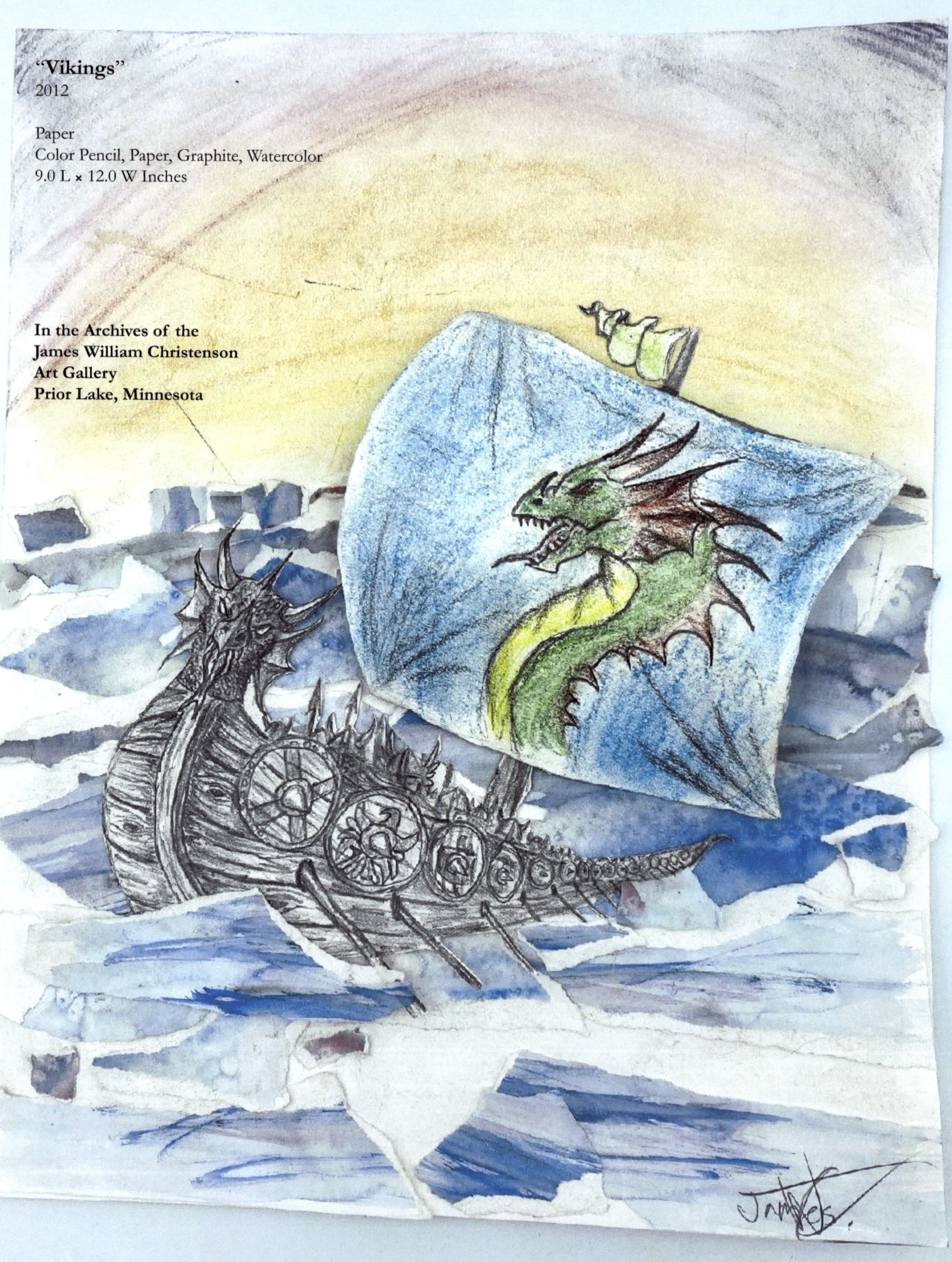

"Vikings"
2012

Paper
Color Pencil, Paper, Graphite, Watercolor
9.0 L × 12.0 W Inches

In the Archives of the
James William Christenson
Art Gallery
Prior Lake, Minnesota

"I Don't Like This One, Actually"
2015

Mat Board
Watercolor
12.0 L × 9.0 W Inches

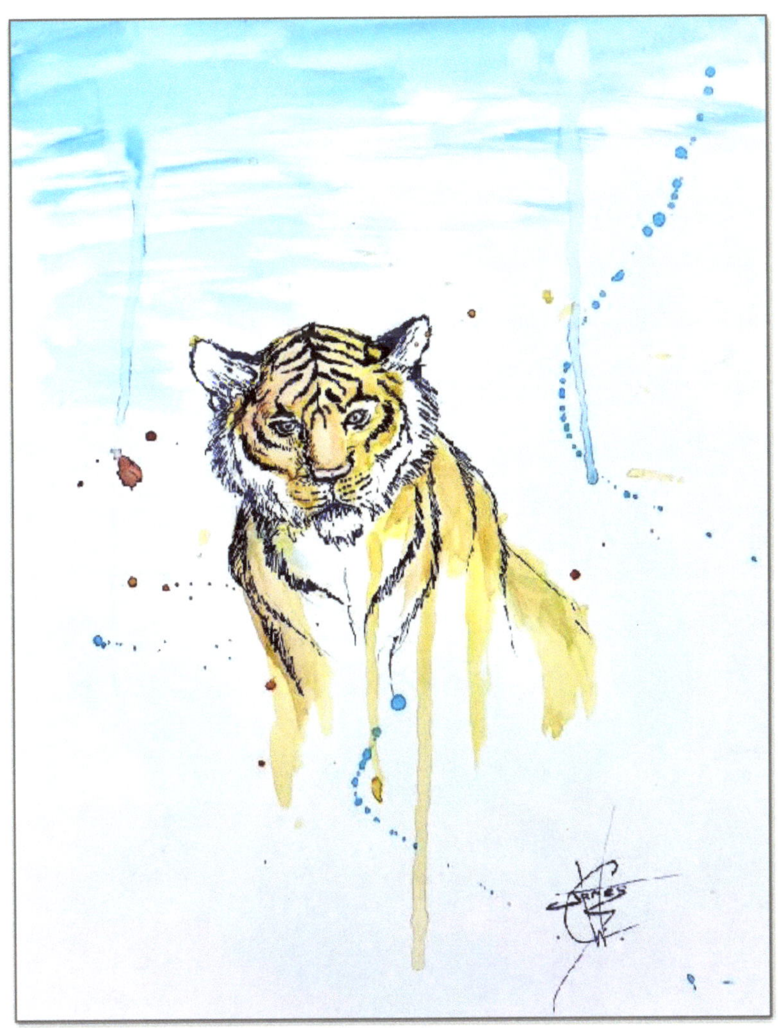

Hidden in the Archives of the
James William Christenson Art Gallery
Prior Lake, Minnesota

"Sir Lance Builds Character"
Unfinished
2015

Canvas Board
Acrylic
18.0 L × 24.0 W Inches

In the Archives of the
James William Christenson Art Gallery
Prior Lake, Minnesota

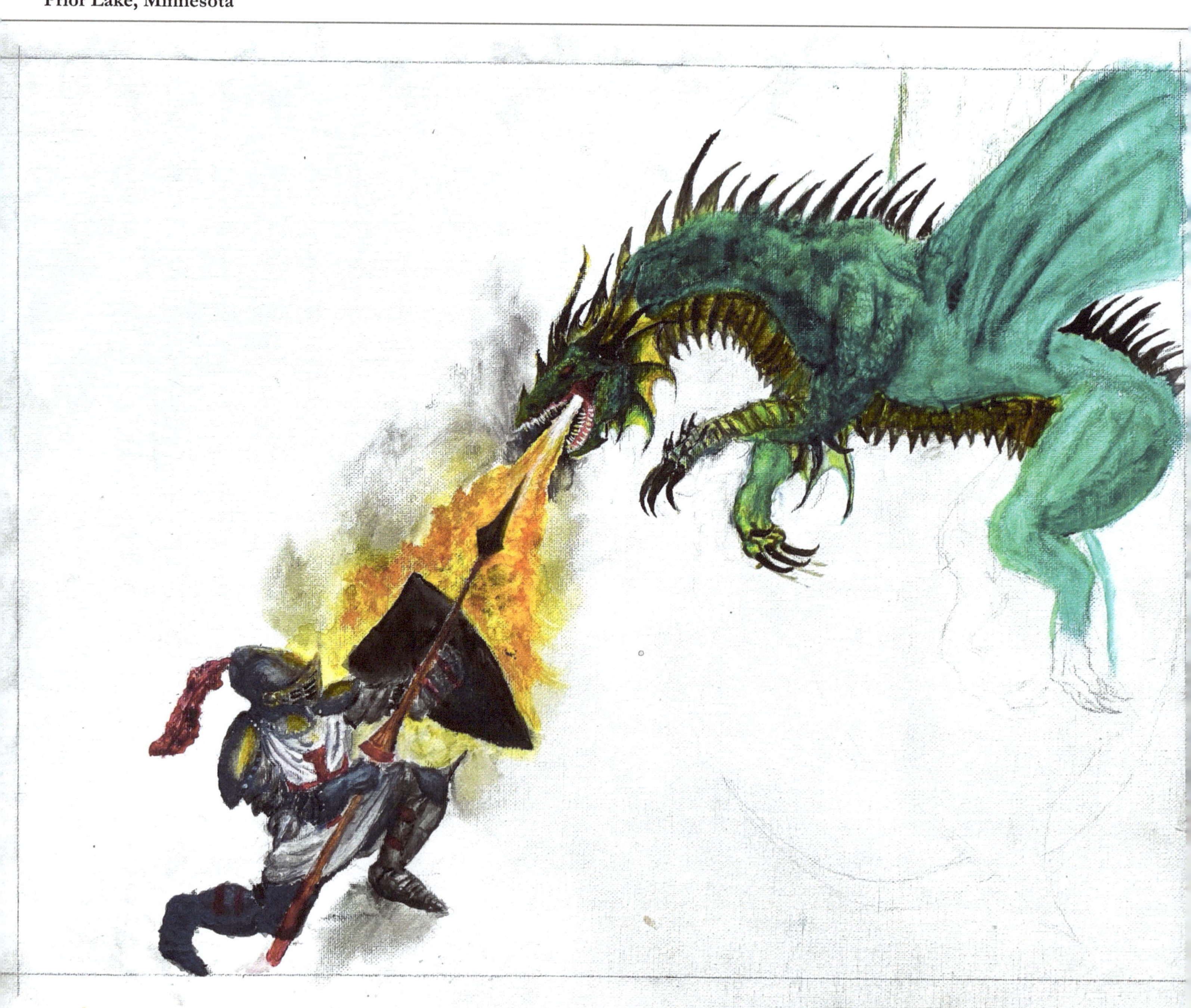

“Run & Hyde”
Unfinished Character Sketch
2019

Paper
Graphite
12.0 L × 9.0 W Inches

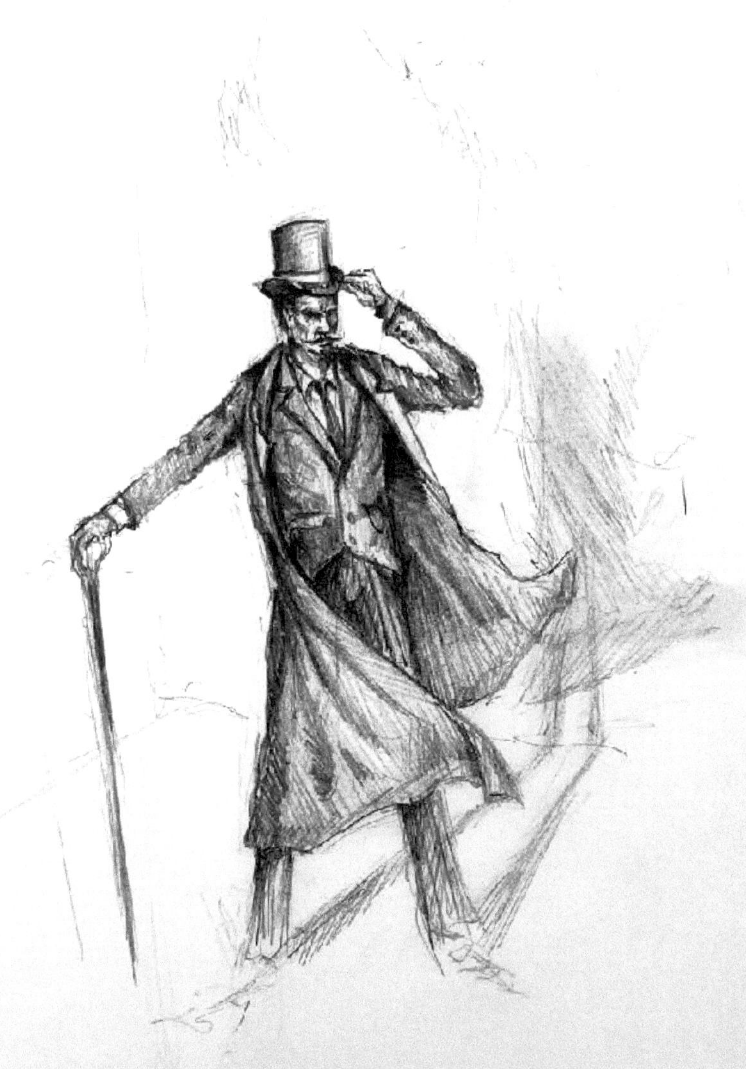

In the Archives of the
James William Christenson Art Gallery
Prior Lake, Minnesota

"Jack-o'-Lantern"
2017

Pumpkin Carving
9.0 L × 12.0 W Inches

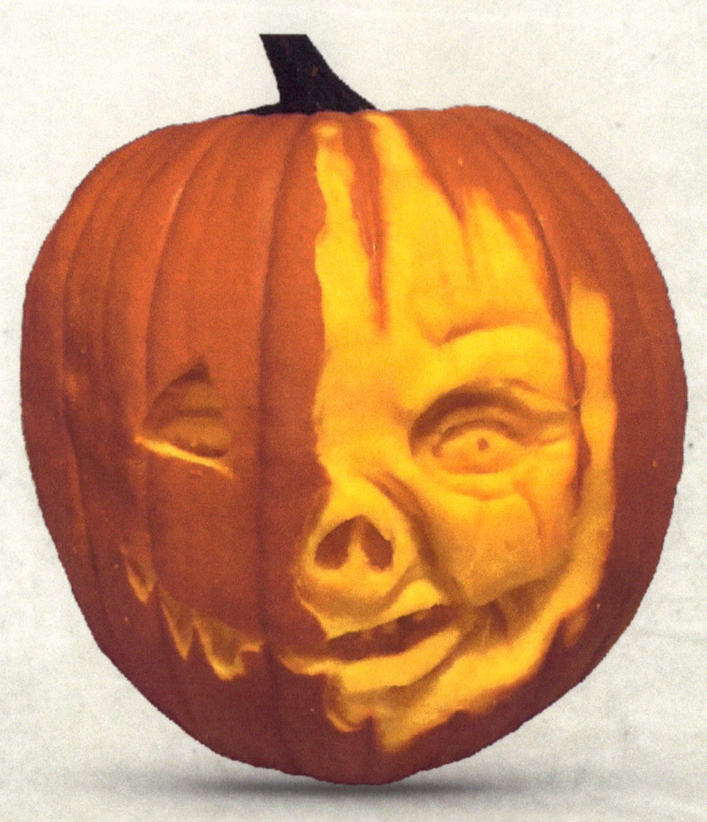

Perishable
Prior Lake, Minnesota

In the Archives of the
James William Christenson Art Gallery
Prior Lake, Minnesota

"Pentimento"
Sketch
2019

Paper
Color Pencil
9.0 L × 12.0 W Inches

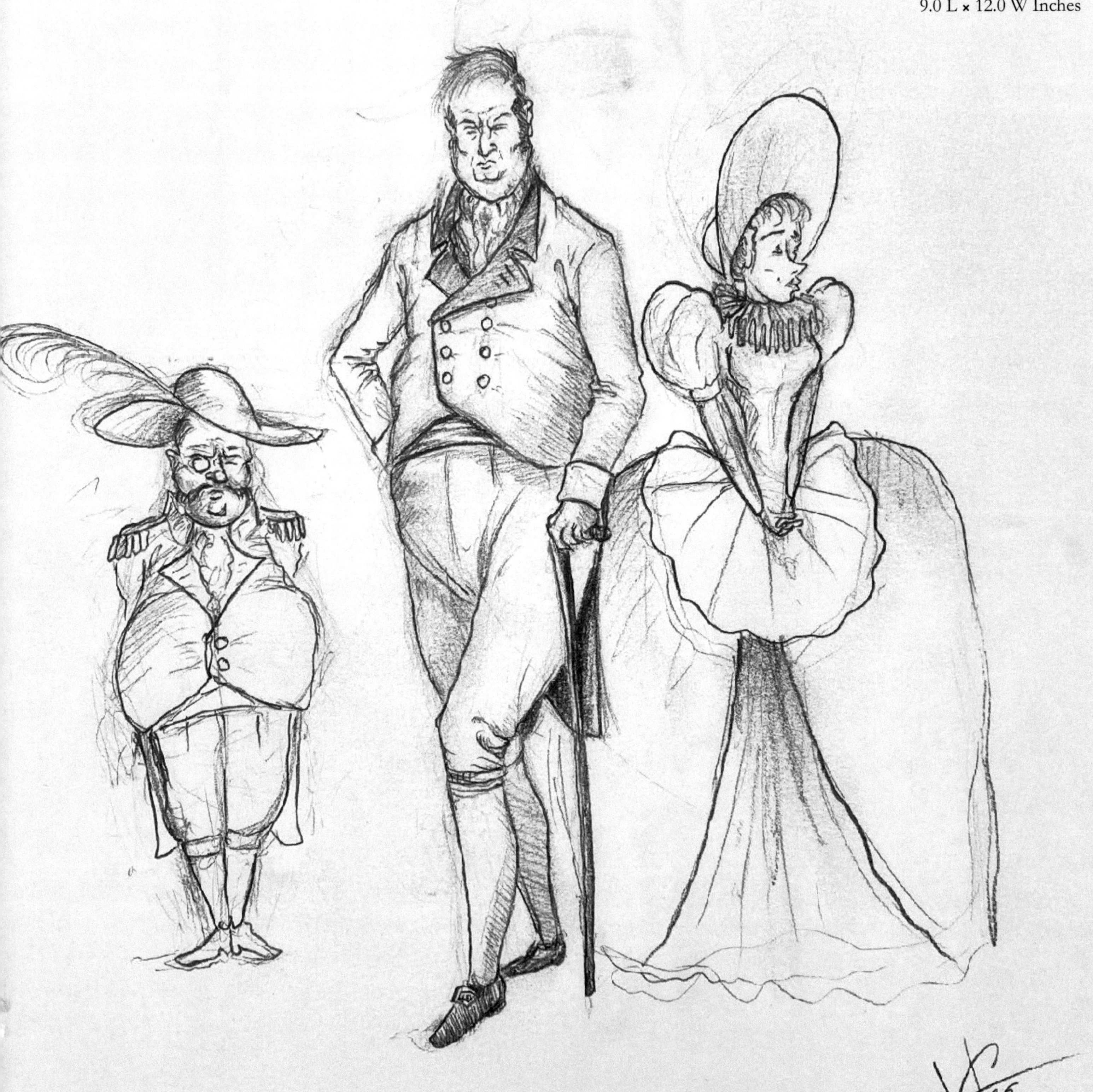

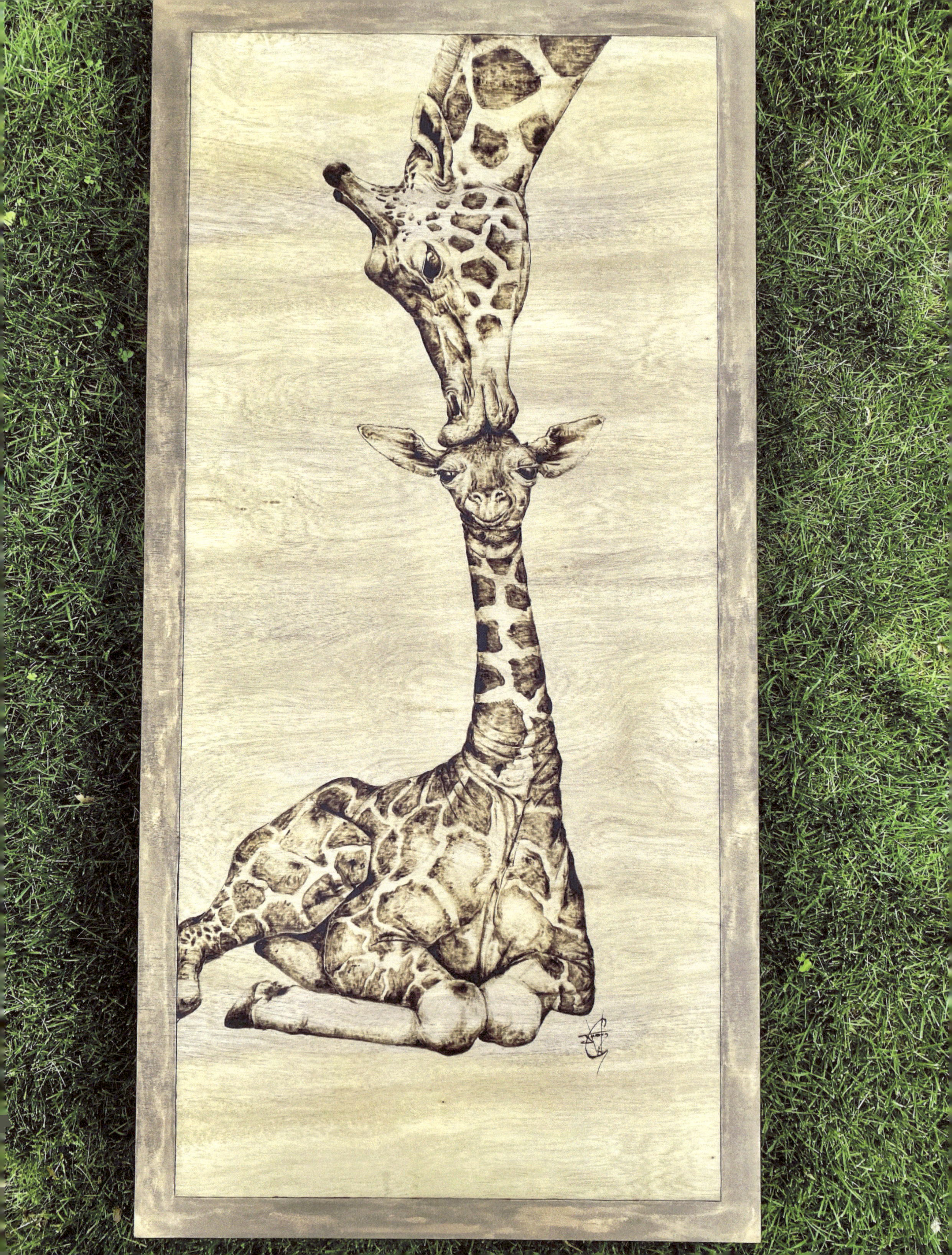

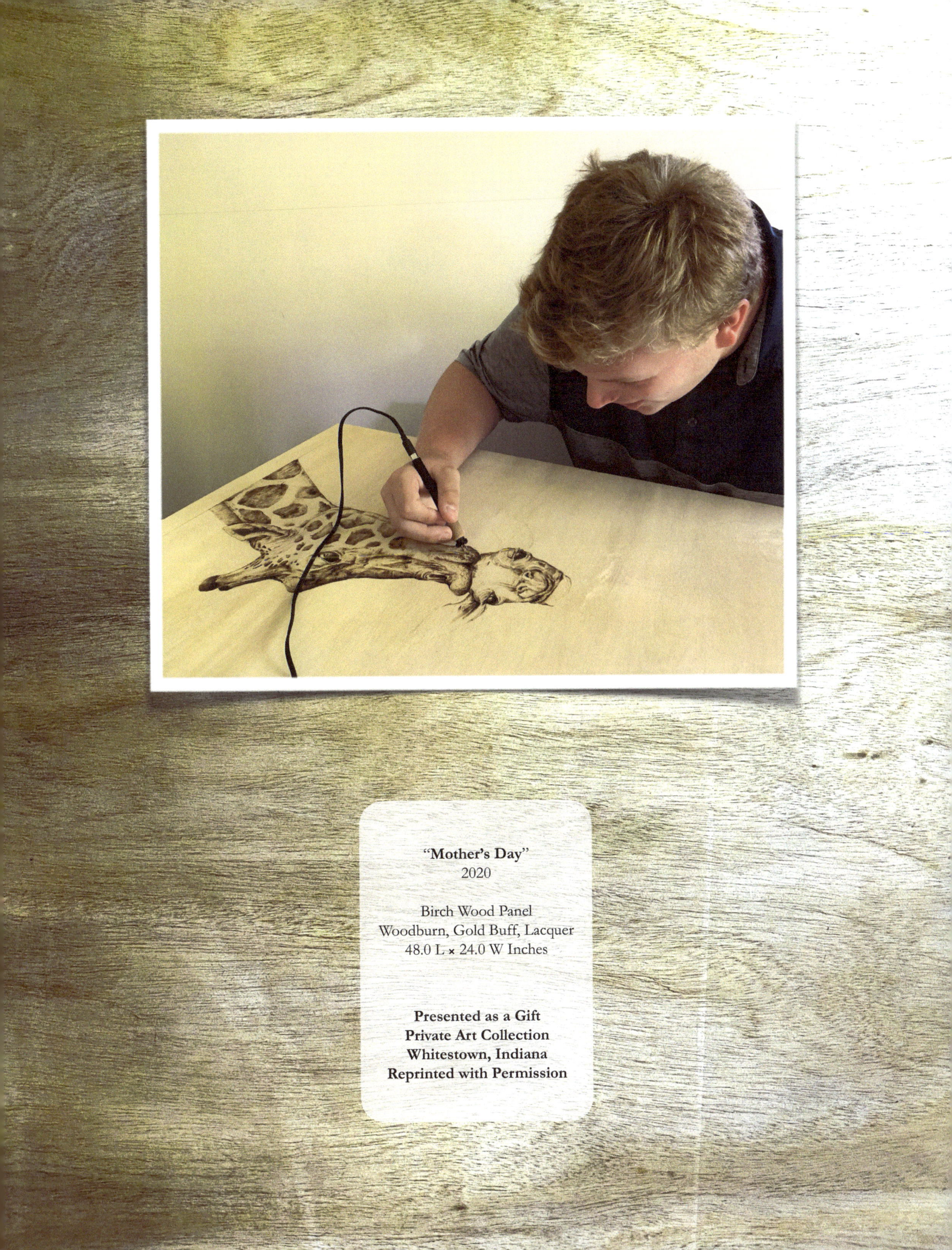

"Mother's Day"
2020

Birch Wood Panel
Woodburn, Gold Buff, Lacquer
48.0 L × 24.0 W Inches

Presented as a Gift
Private Art Collection
Whitestown, Indiana
Reprinted with Permission

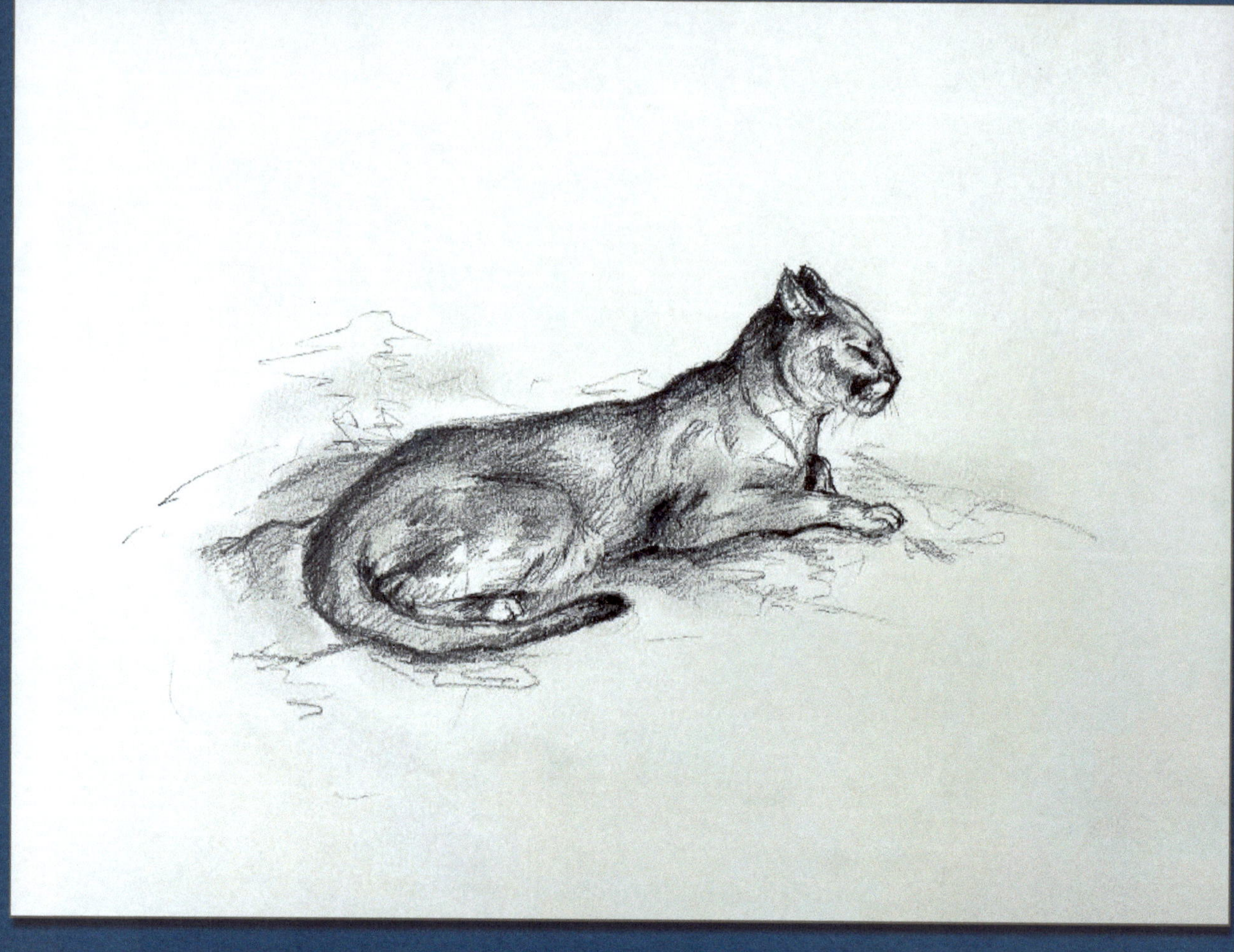

"Landslide"
Sketch
Medtronic Minnesota Trail Exhibit
Minnesota Zoo
2019

Paper
Graphite
9.0 L × 12.0 W Inches

In the Archives of the
James William Christenson Art Gallery
Prior Lake, Minnesota

From the
Fearsome Tie Collection
2020

Necktie
Ink, Fabric Marker

Presented as a Gift.
Private Art Collection
Prior Lake, Minnesota
Reprinted with Permission.

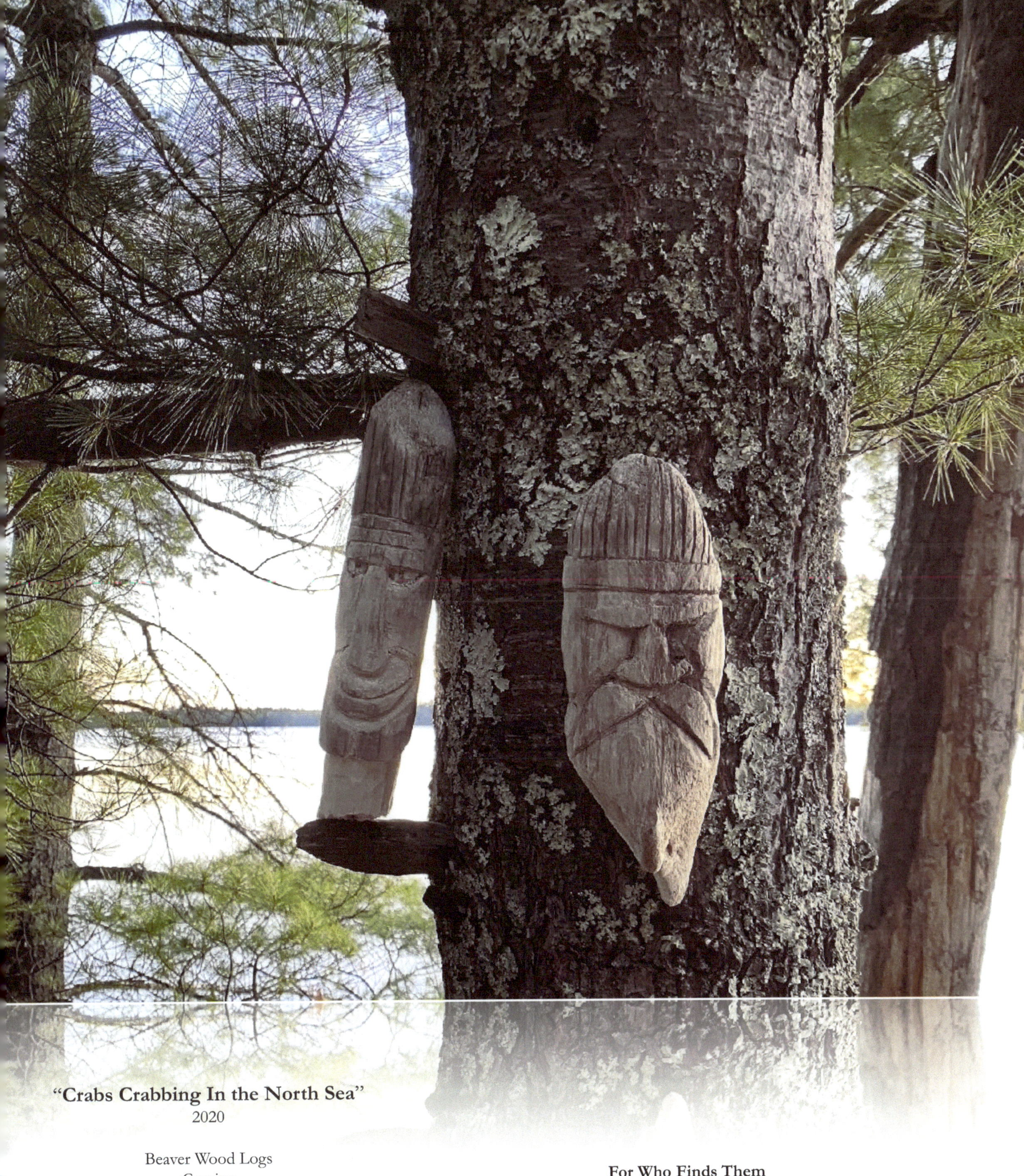

"Crabs Crabbing In the North Sea"
2020

Beaver Wood Logs
Carving
13.5 L × 4.25 W & 12.5 L × 6.0 W Inches

For Who Finds Them
Boundary Water Canoe Area Wilderness, Minnesota

"Tonsil"
Color Study
2020

Linen Paper
Oil
5.5 L × 8.5 W Inches

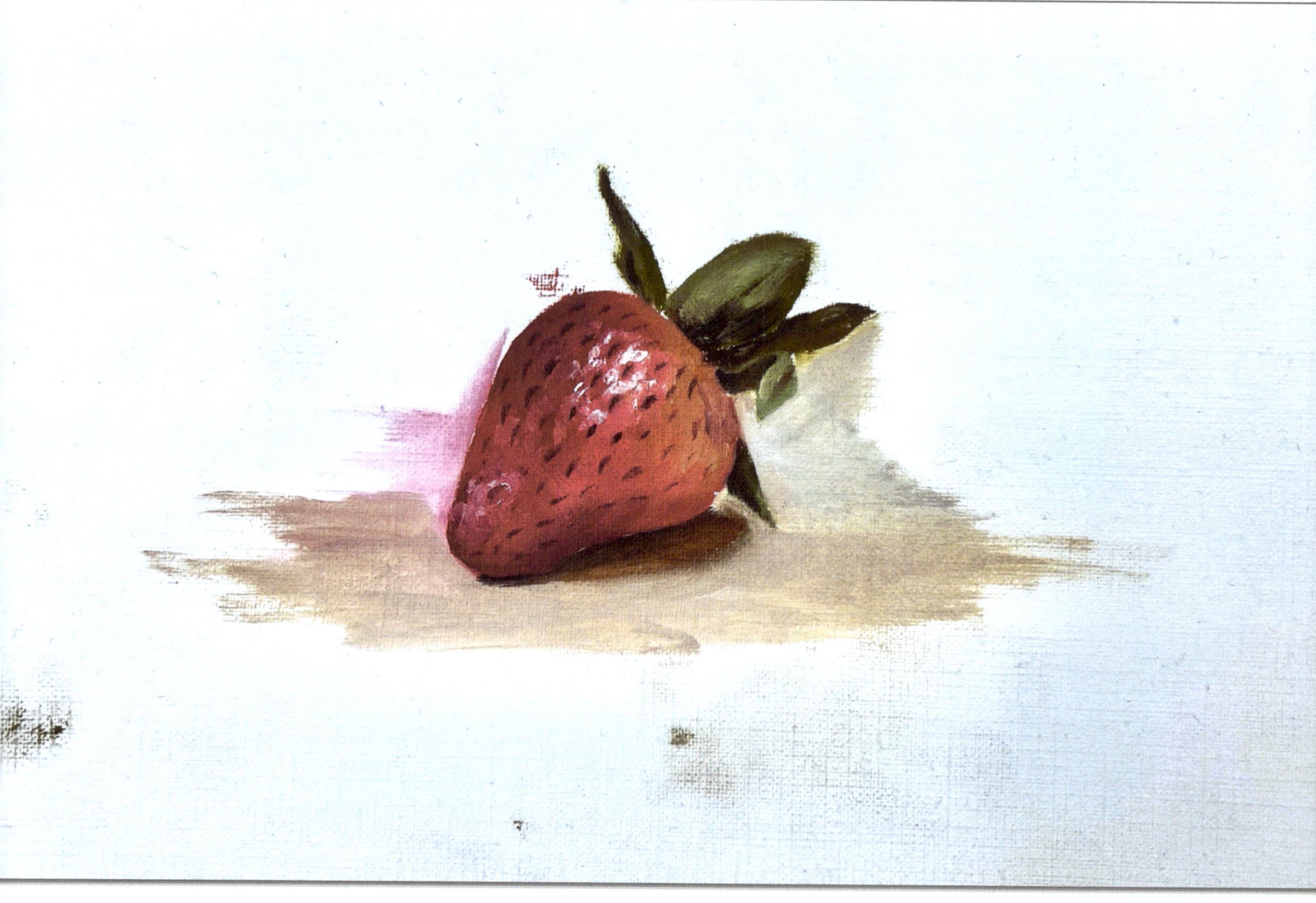

In the Archives of the
James William Christenson Art Gallery
Prior Lake, Minnesota

“Etherial”
2014

Paper
Watercolor, Pen
4.0 L × 6.0 W Inches

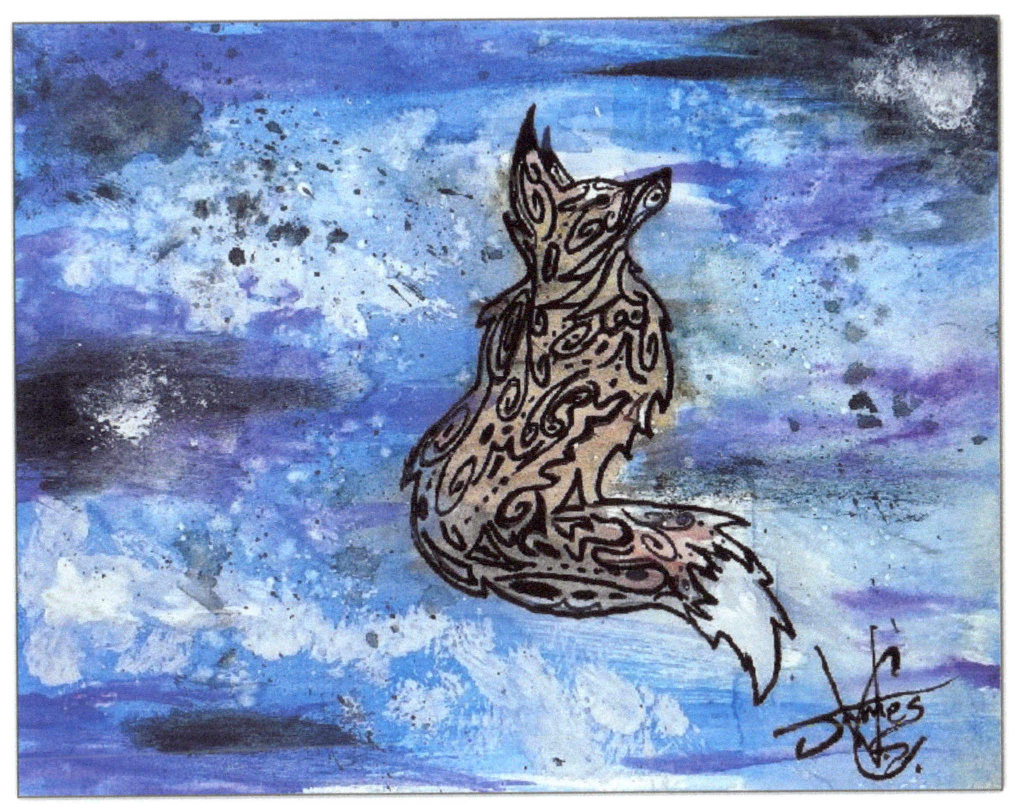

“Hmmmm!”
2014

Paper
Watercolor, Pen
4.0 L × 6.0 W Inches

In the Archives of the
James William Christenson Art Gallery
Prior Lake, Minnesota

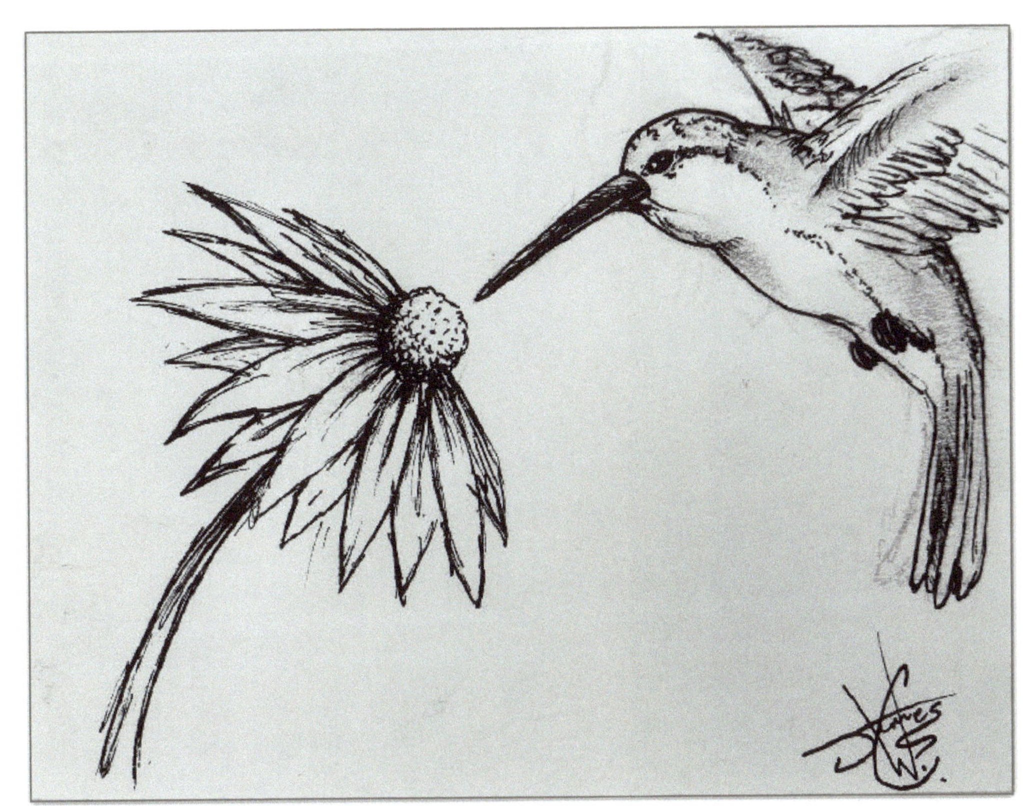

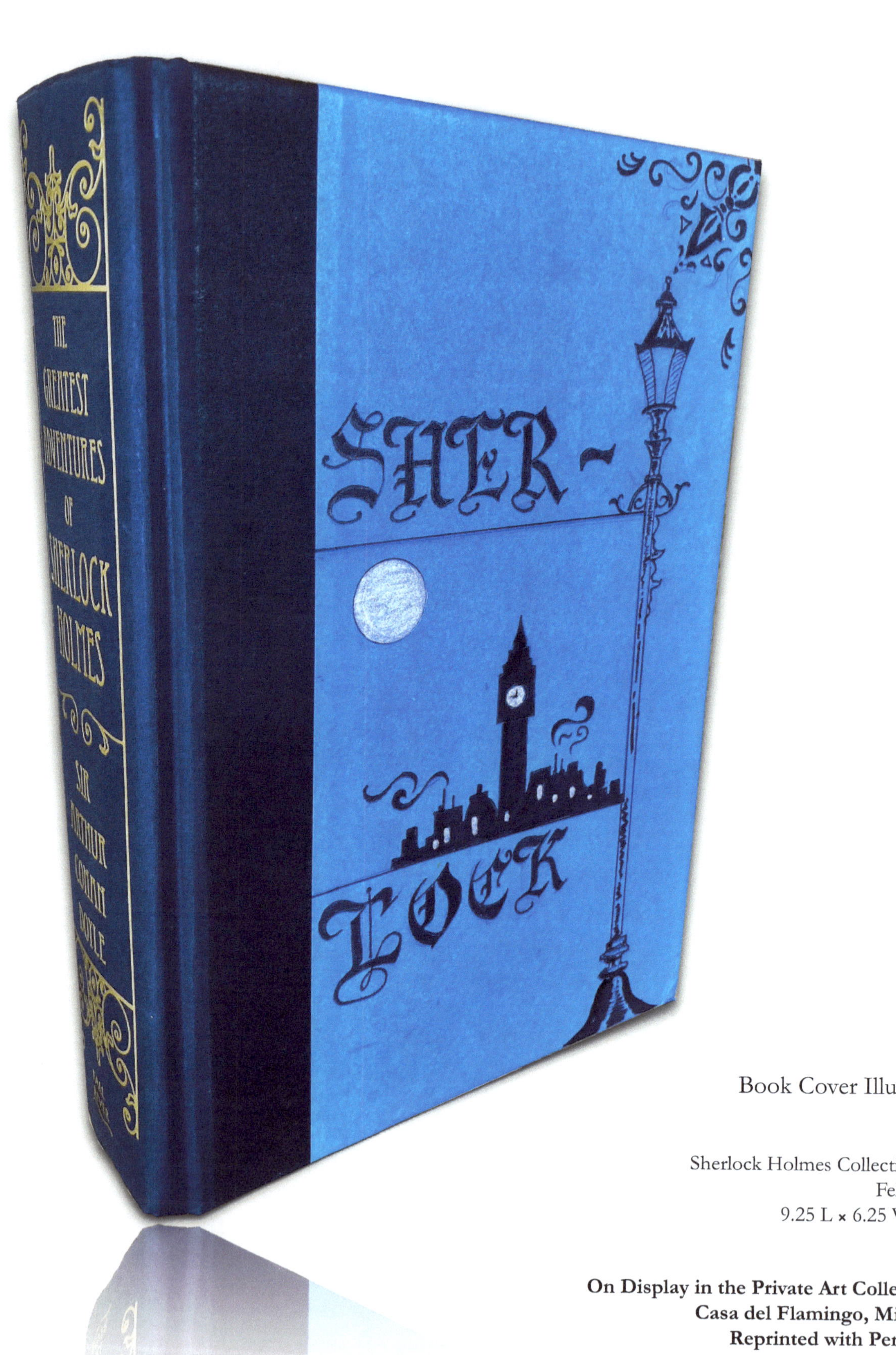

Book Cover Illustration
2020

Sherlock Holmes Collection Book
Felt Marker
9.25 L × 6.25 W Inches

On Display in the Private Art Collection of
Casa del Flamingo, Minnesota
Reprinted with Permission

"Hook & Smee"
2017

Paper
Graphite
9.0 L × 12.0 W Inches

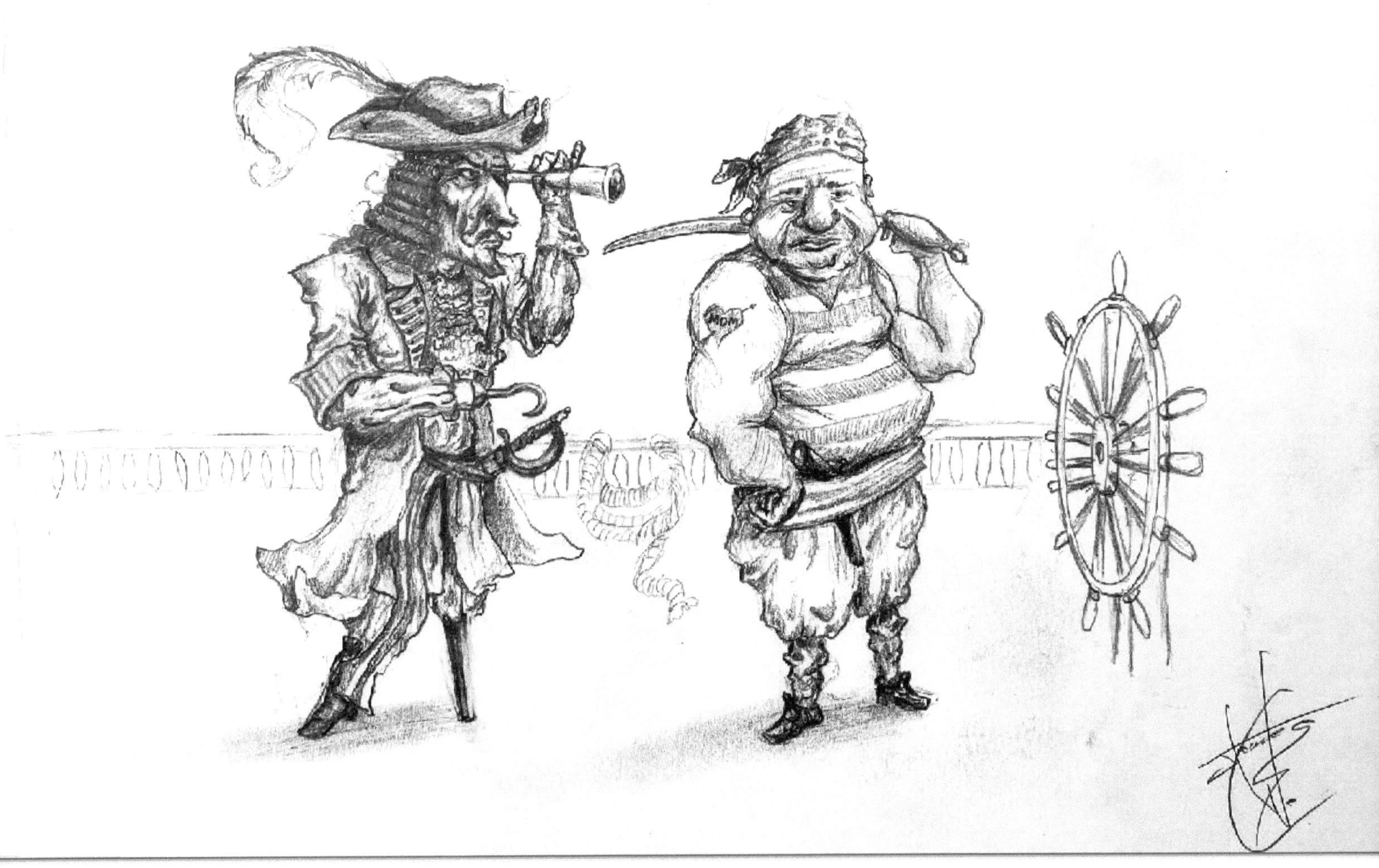

In the Archives of the
James William Christenson Art Gallery
Prior Lake, Minnesota

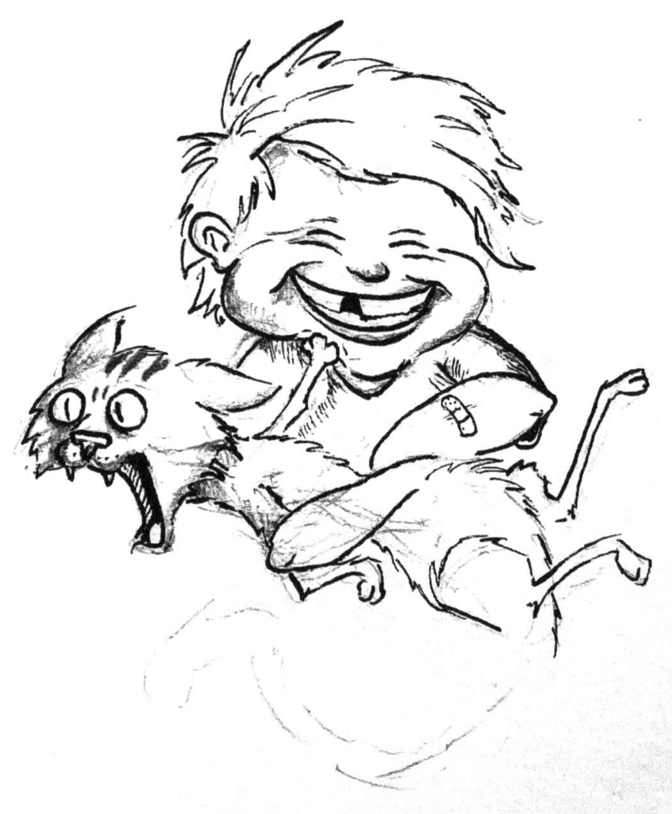

"Darla's Brother"
Unfinished Sketch
2018

Paper
Graphite
9.0 L × 12.0 W Inches

In the Archives of the
James William Christenson Art Gallery
Prior Lake, Minnesota

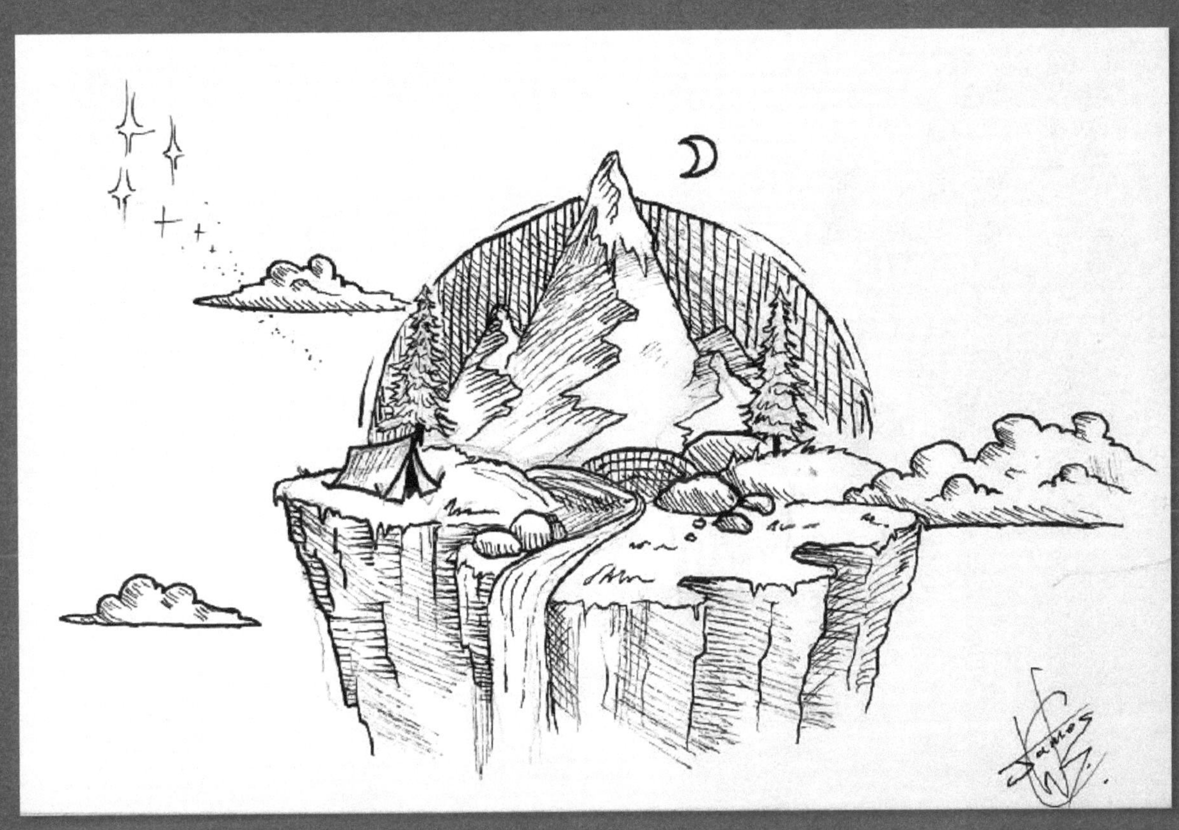

"Camping"
Postcard, Actual Size
2018

Watercolor Paper
Graphite, Pen
4.0 L × 6.0 W Inches

In the Archives of the
James William Christenson Art Gallery
Prior Lake, Minnesota

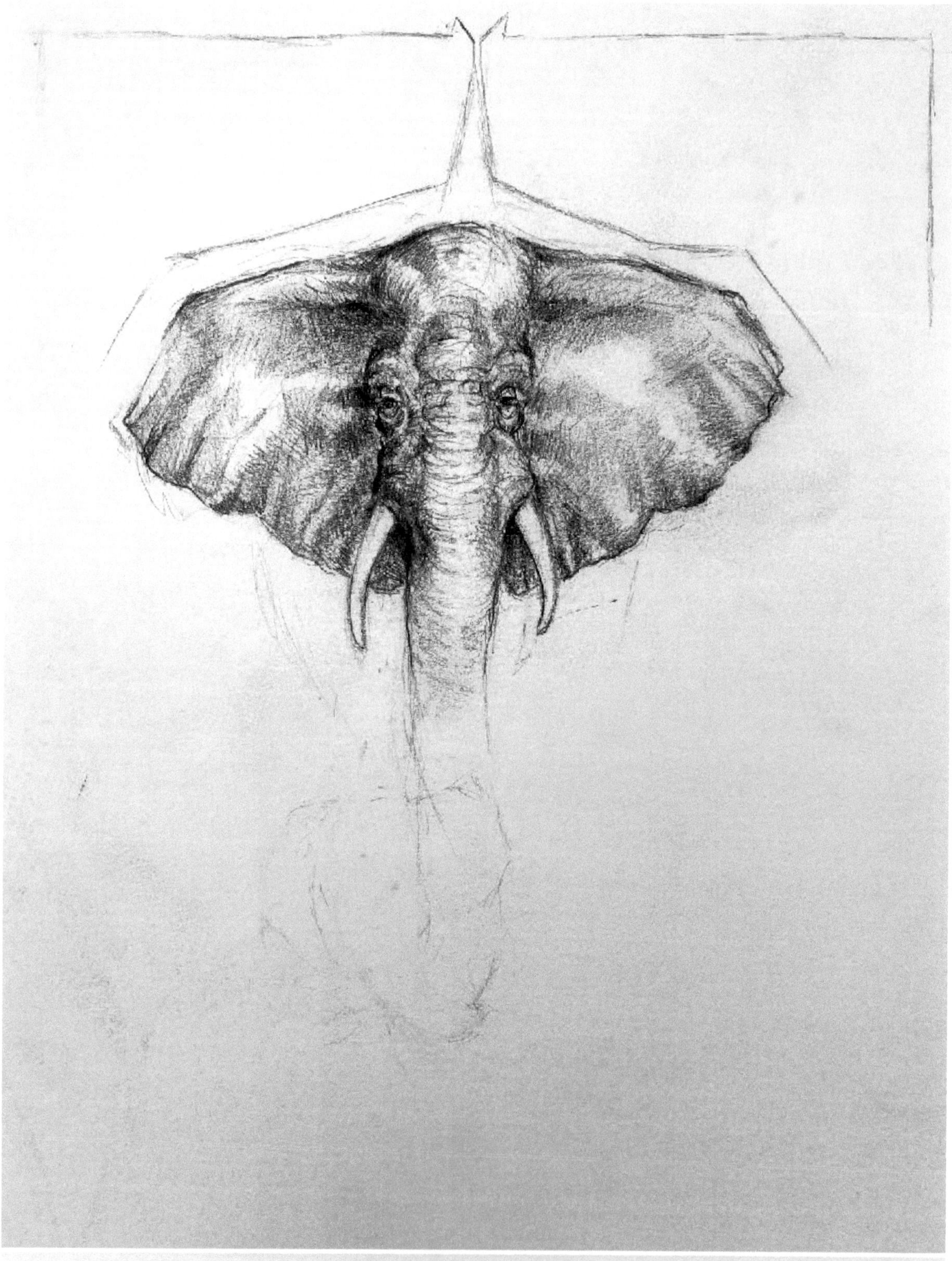

Untitled
Unfinished Sketch
2018

Paper
Graphite
12.0 L × 9.0 W Inches

In the Archives of the
James William Christenson
Art Gallery
Prior Lake, Minnesota

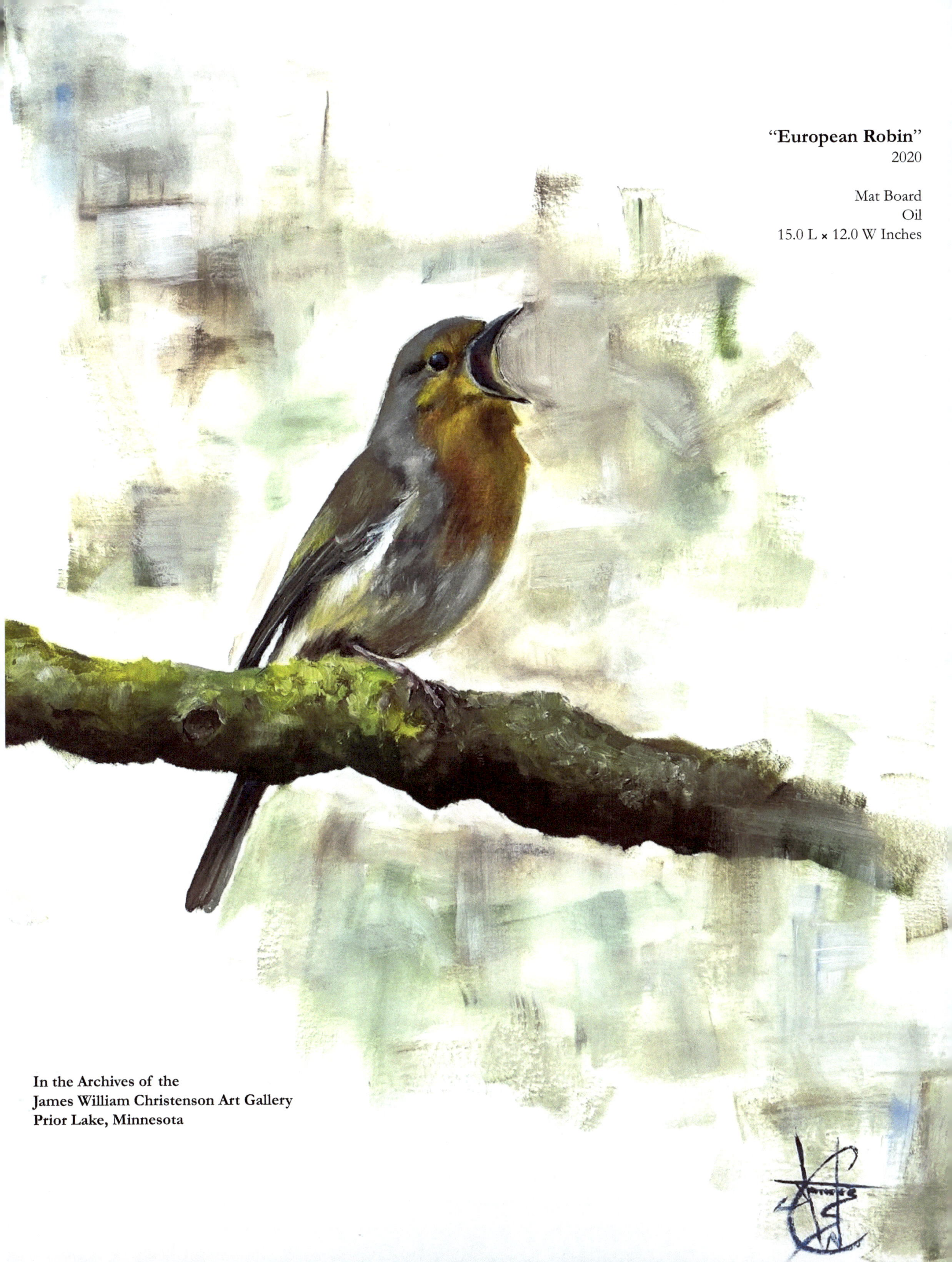

"European Robin"
2020

Mat Board
Oil
15.0 L × 12.0 W Inches

In the Archives of the
James William Christenson Art Gallery
Prior Lake, Minnesota

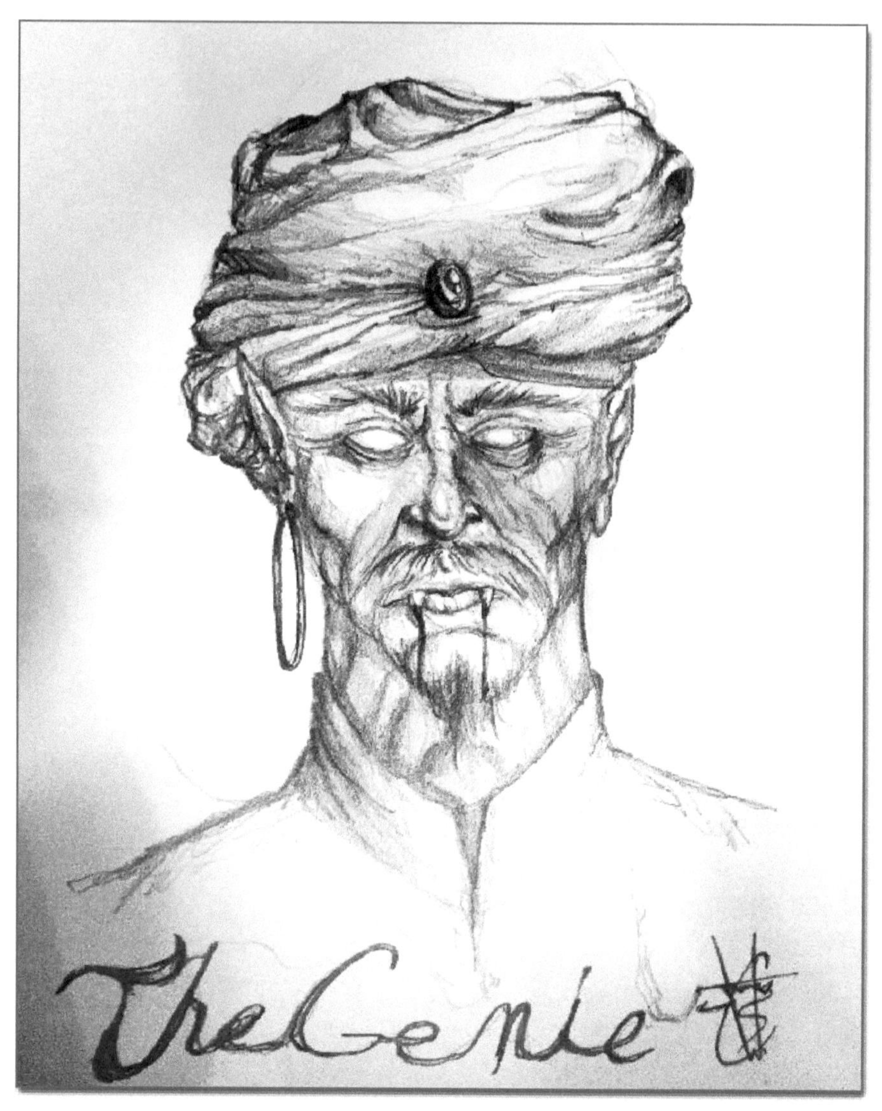

"The Genie"
Single Line Drawing
2016

Paper
Graphite
12.0 L × 9.0 W Inches

In the Archives of the
James William Christenson Art Gallery
Prior Lake, Minnesota

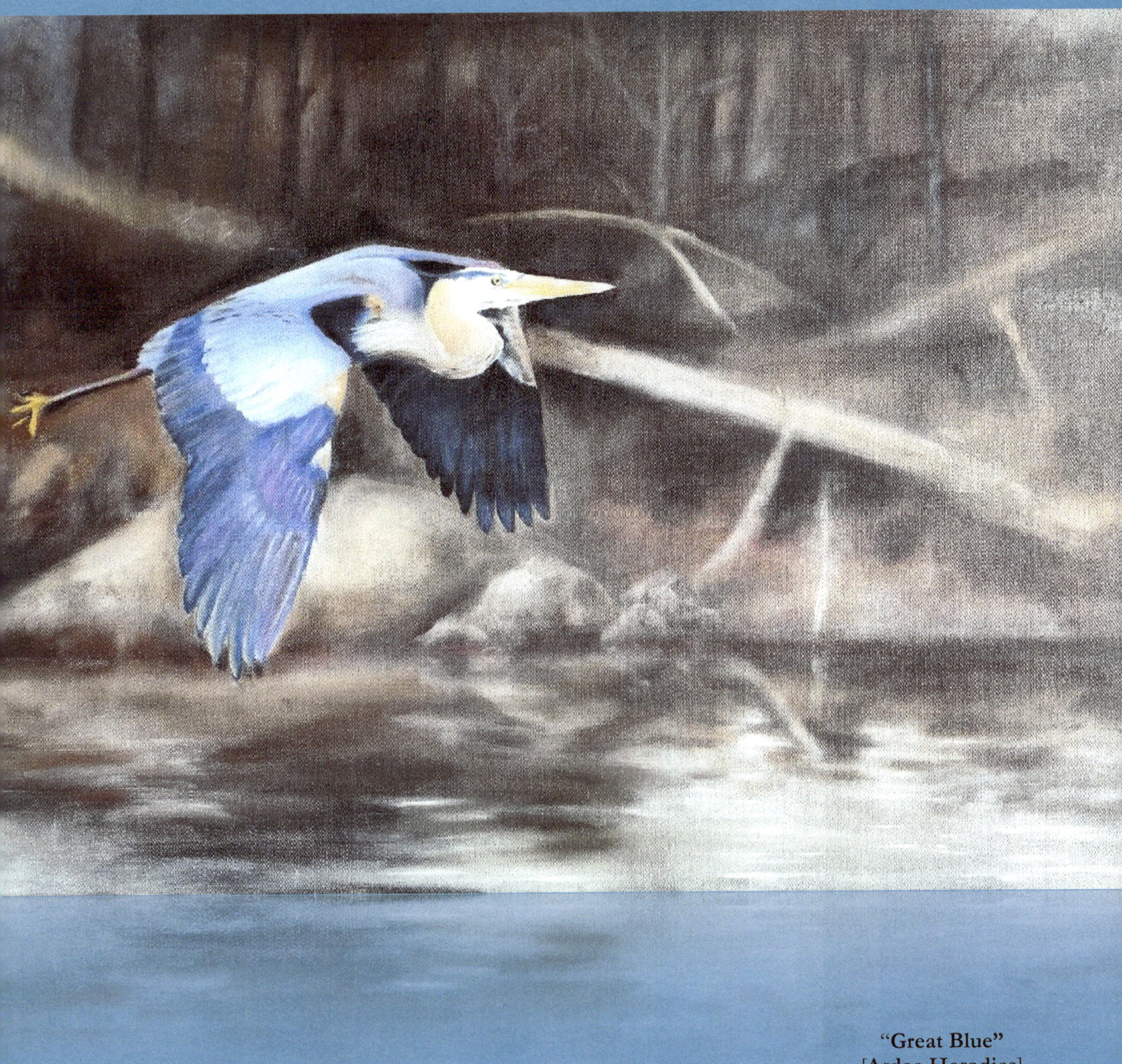

"Great Blue"
[Ardea Herodias]
2020

Canvas Stretched Over Wooden Frame
Oil
16.0 L × 20.0 W Inches

In the Archives of the
James William Christenson
Art Gallery
Prior Lake, Minnesota

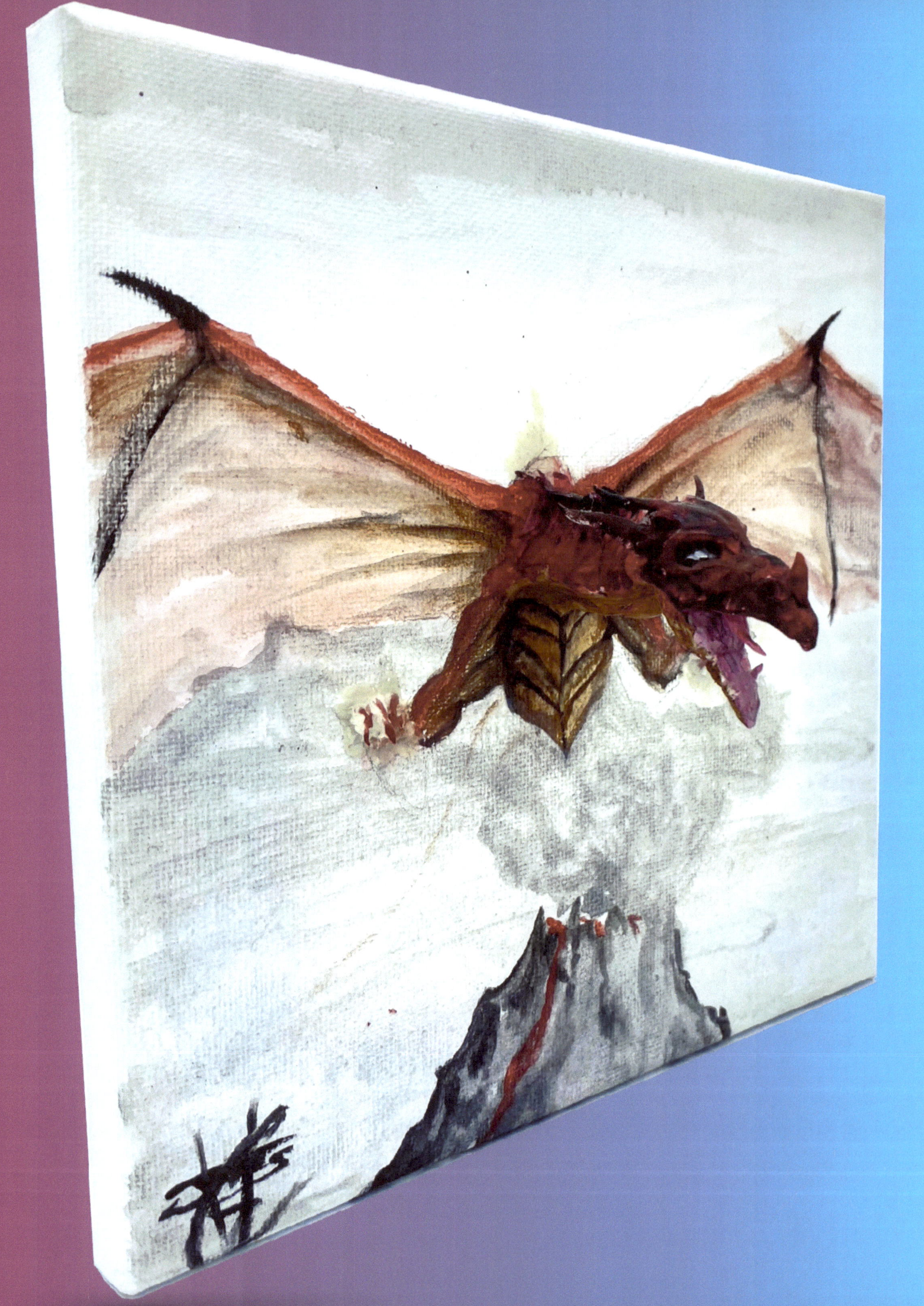

FACING PAGE

"Smaug"
2014

Canvas Over Wooden Frame
Acrylic, Polymer Clay
9.0 L × 9.0 W Inches

RIGHT

"Year of the Dragon"
2018

Paper
Ink
12.0 L × 9.0 W Inches

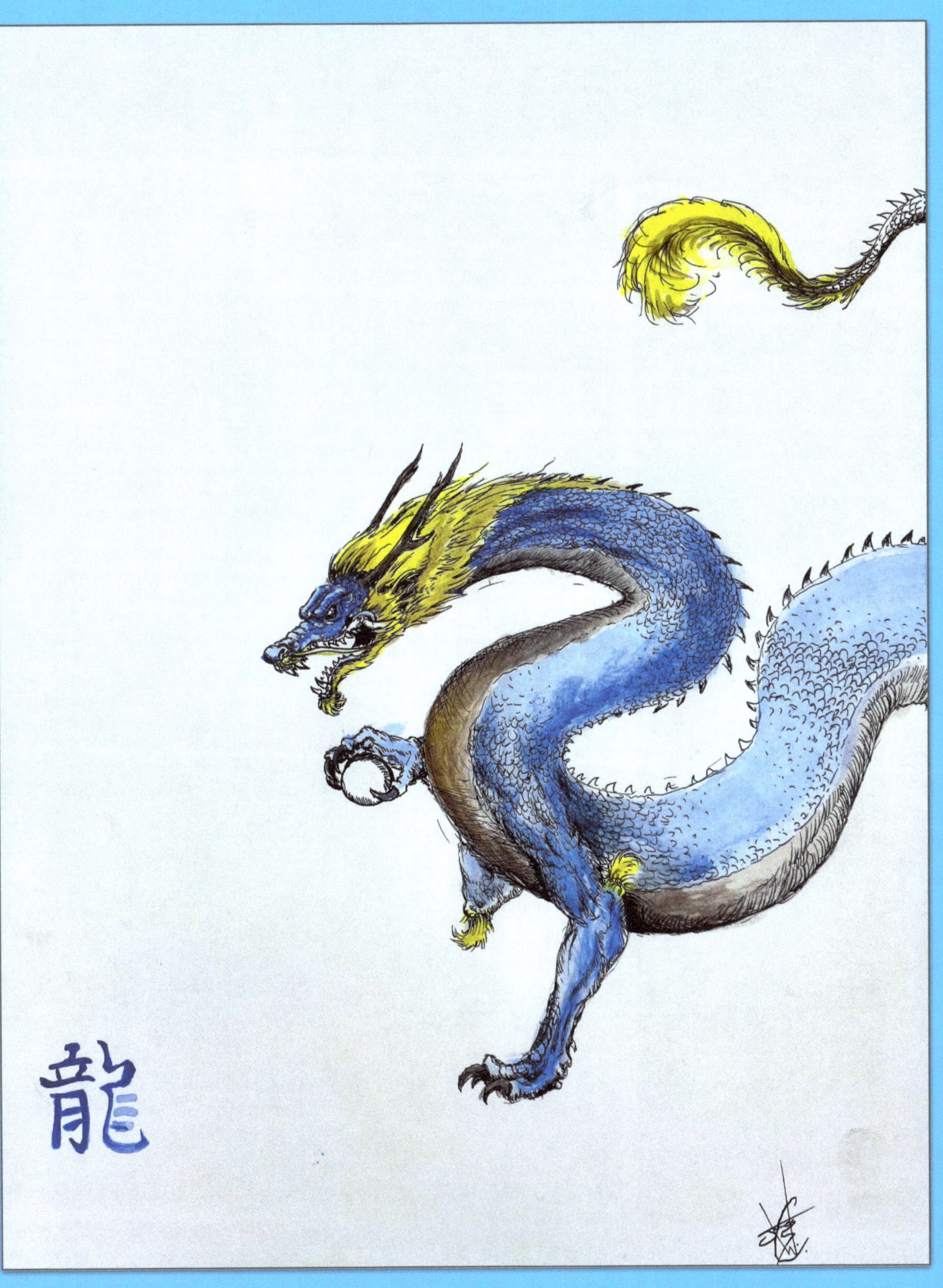

In the Archives of the
James William Christenson
Art Gallery
Prior Lake, Minnesota

"He Counts the Stars & Calls Them By Name"
2019

Mat Board
Oil
20.0 L × 16.0 W Inches

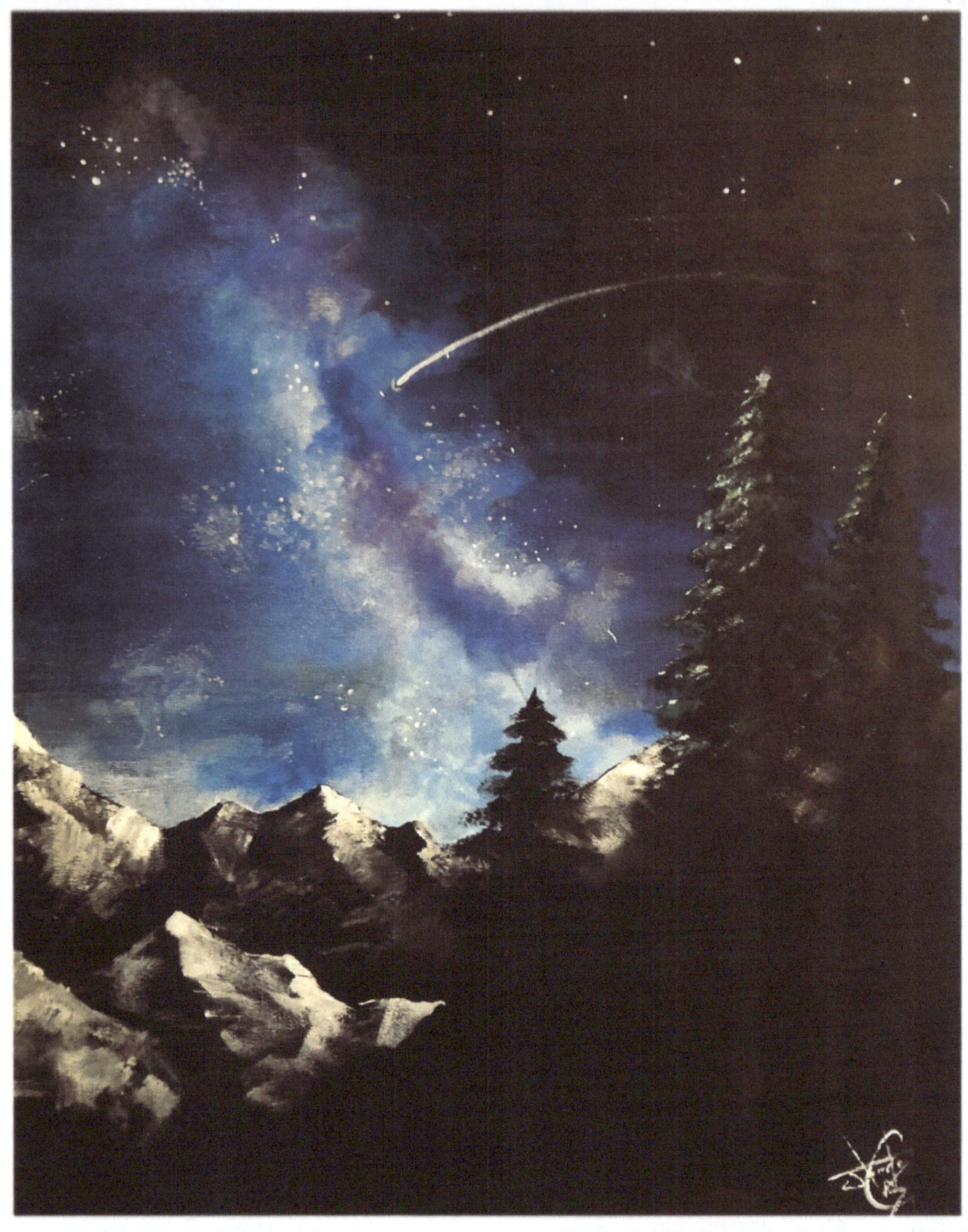

Presented as a Gift. Private Art Collection Cincinnati, Ohio Reprinted with Permission.

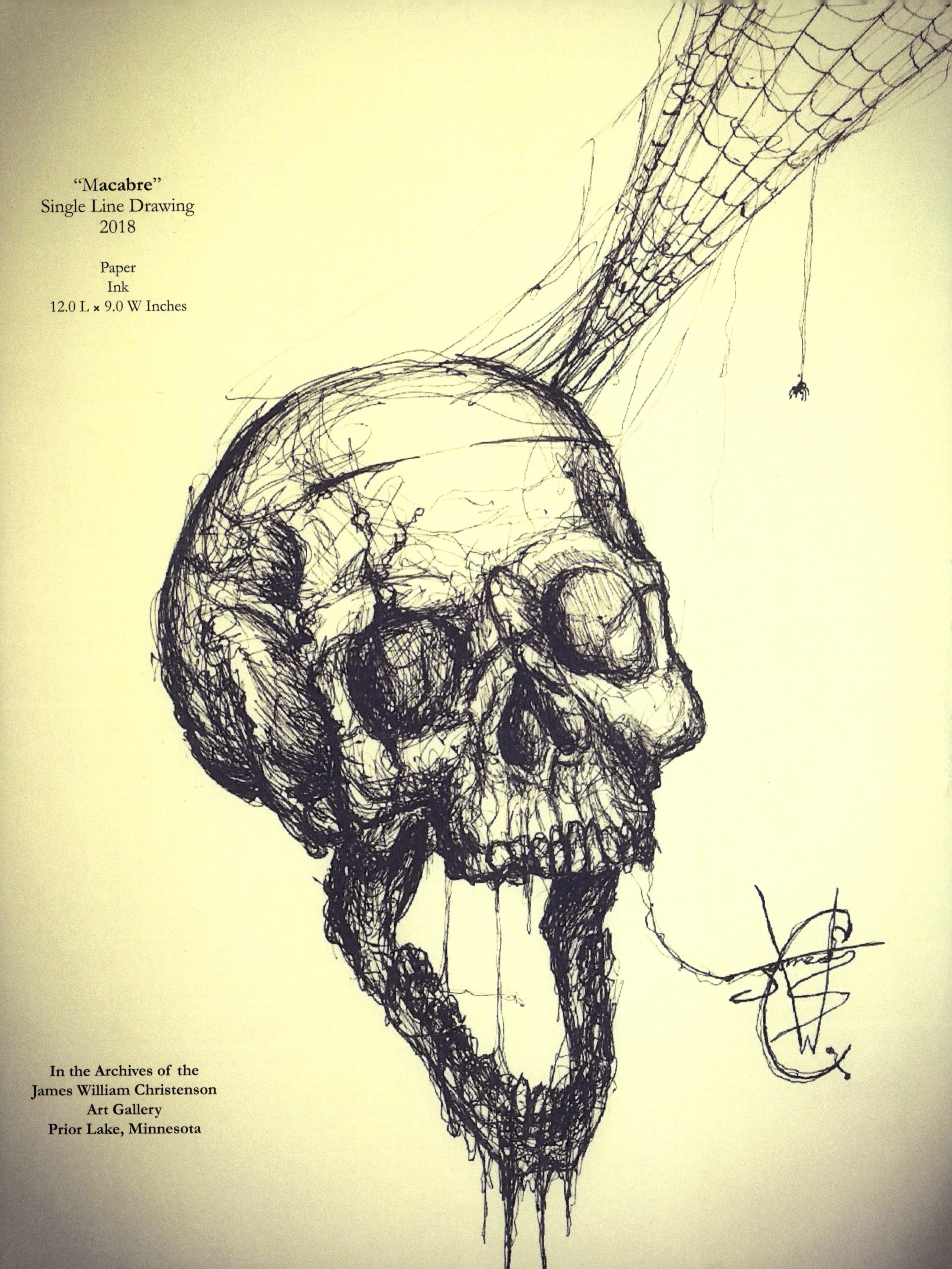
"Macabre"
Single Line Drawing
2018
Paper
Ink
12.0 L × 9.0 W Inches
In the Archives of the
James William Christenson
Art Gallery
Prior Lake, Minnesota

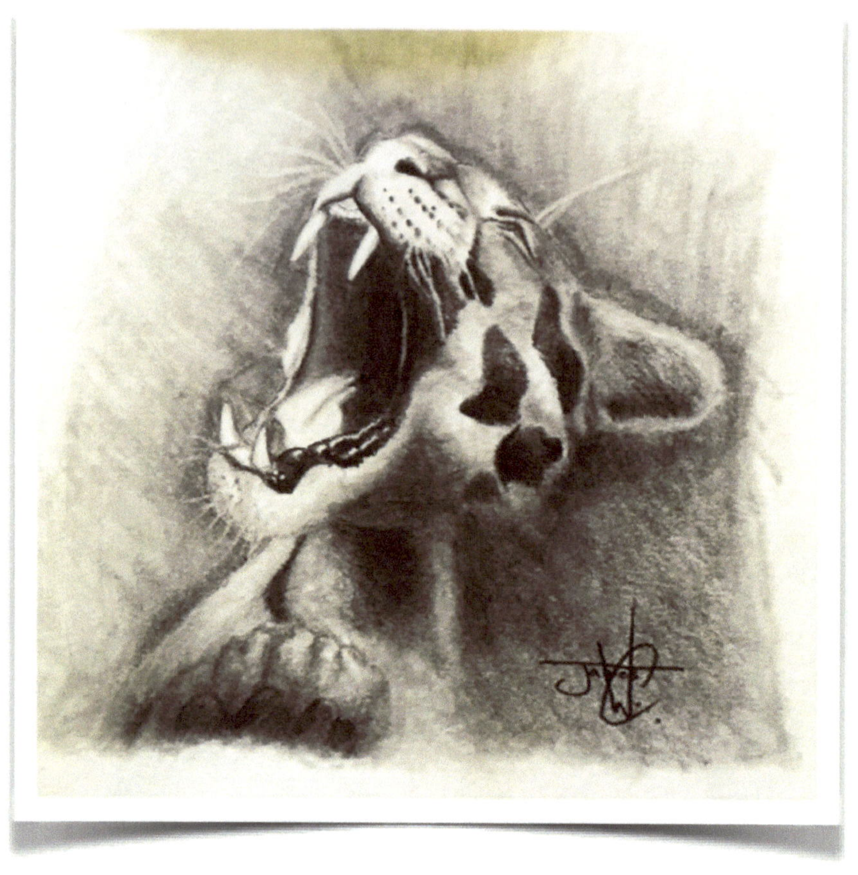

"Bengal Kitten"
2017

Paper
Graphite
6.0 L × 6.0 W Inches

In the Archives of the
James William Christenson
Art Gallery
Prior Lake, Minnesota

"Fireball"
2017

Watercolor Paper
Watercolor
9Fir.0 L × 12.0 W Inches

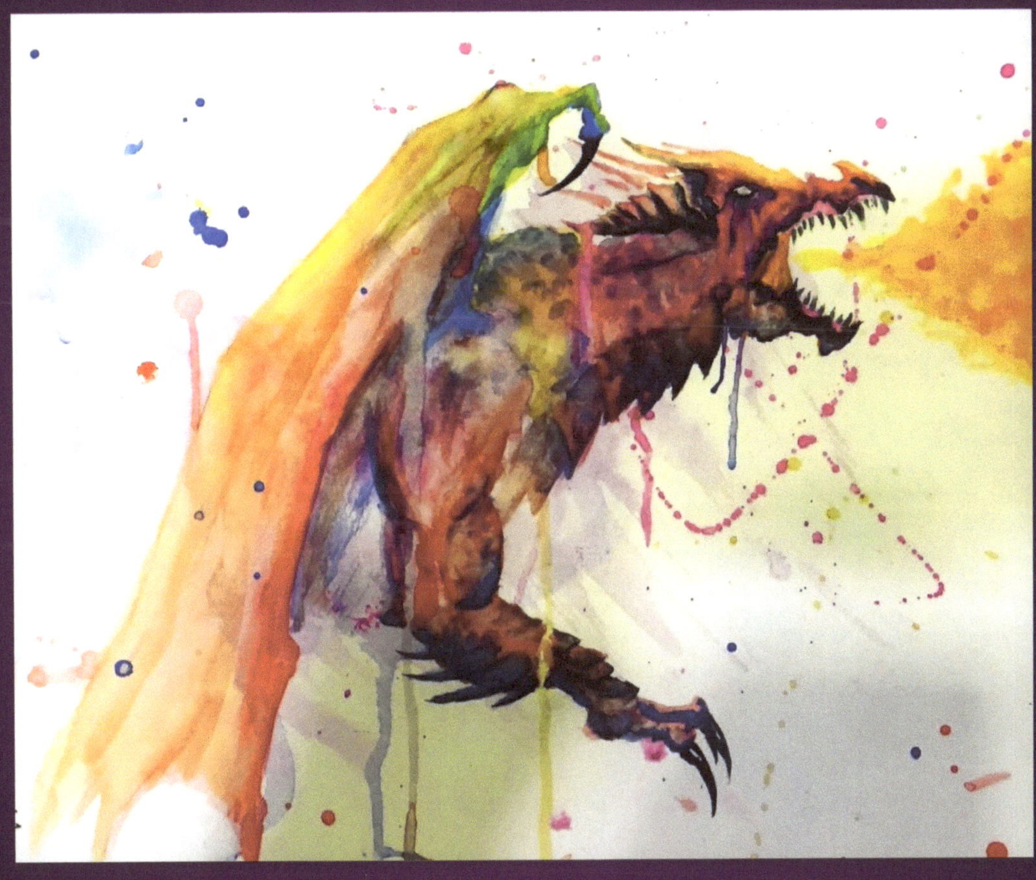

In the Archives of the
James William Christenson
Art Gallery
Prior Lake, Minnesota

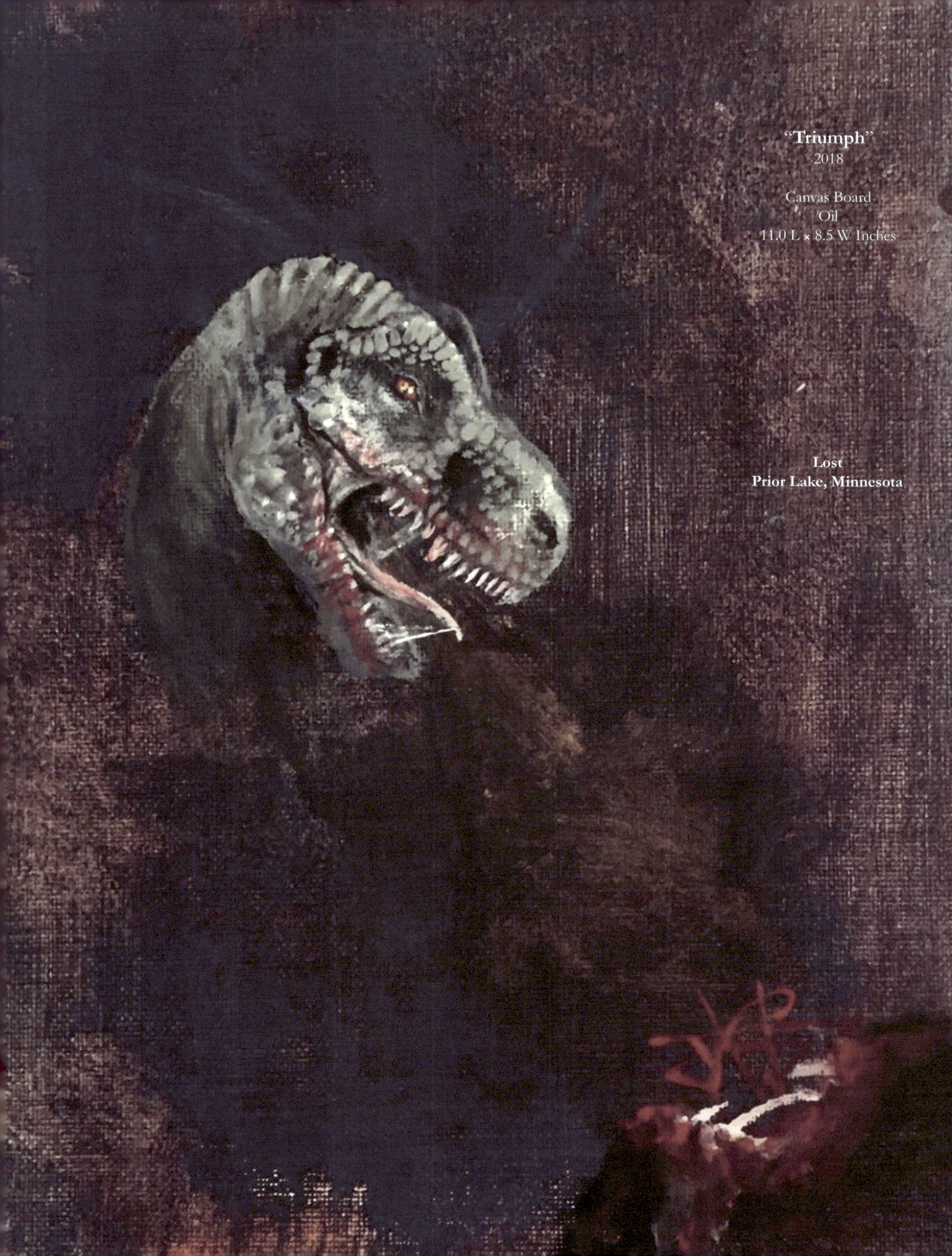

"Triumph"
2018

Canvas Board
Oil
11.0 L × 8.5 W Inches

Lost
Prior Lake, Minnesota

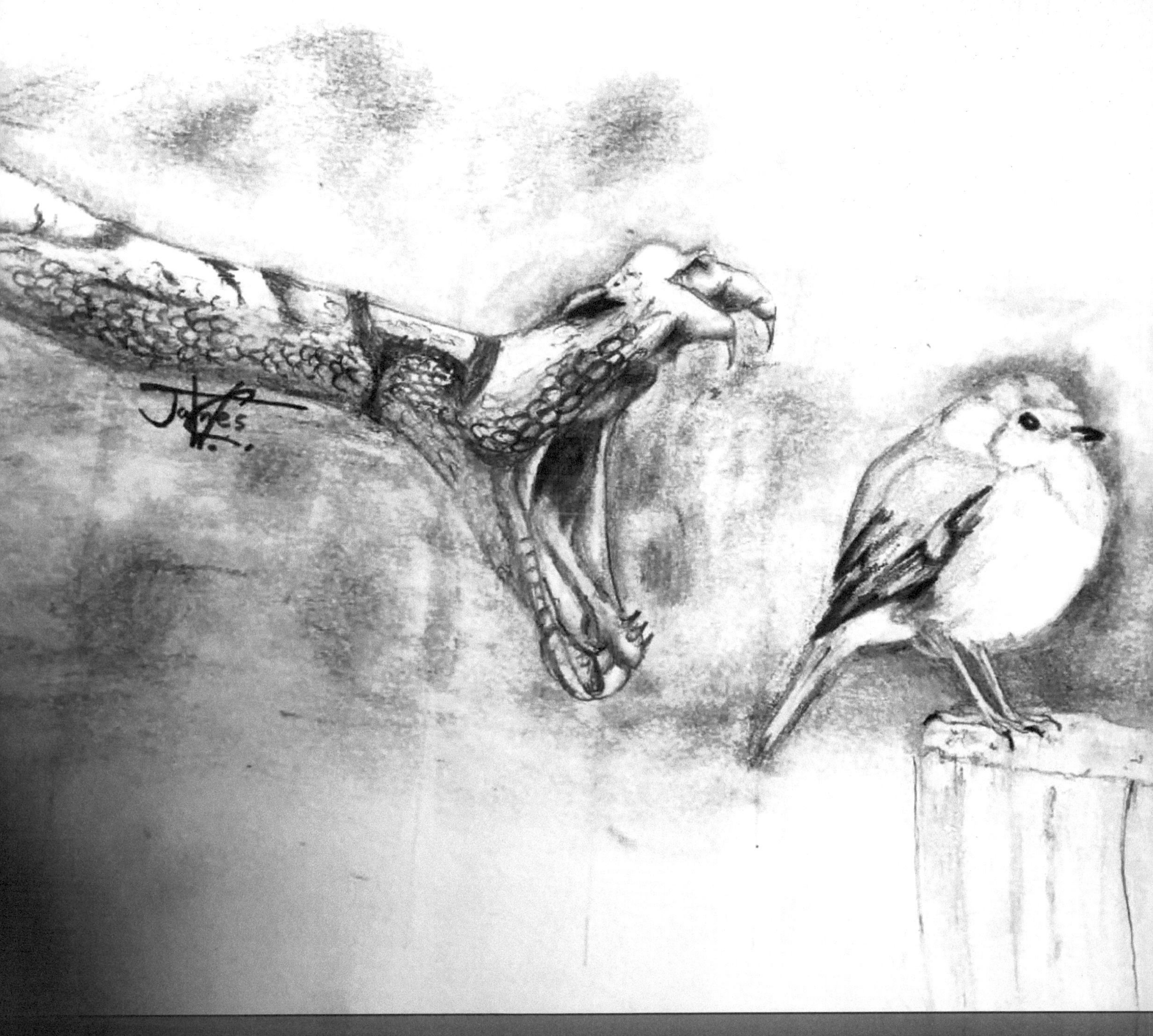

In the Archives of the
James William Christenson
Art Gallery
Prior Lake, Minnesota

"Ignorance is Bliss"
2014

Paper
Graphite
9.0 L × 12.0 W Inches

"The Zoo Visits Ellie"
2019

Watercolor Paper
Graphite
9.0 L × 12.0 W Inches

Commissioned for Display
Private Art Collection
Whitestown, Indiana
Reprinted with Permission

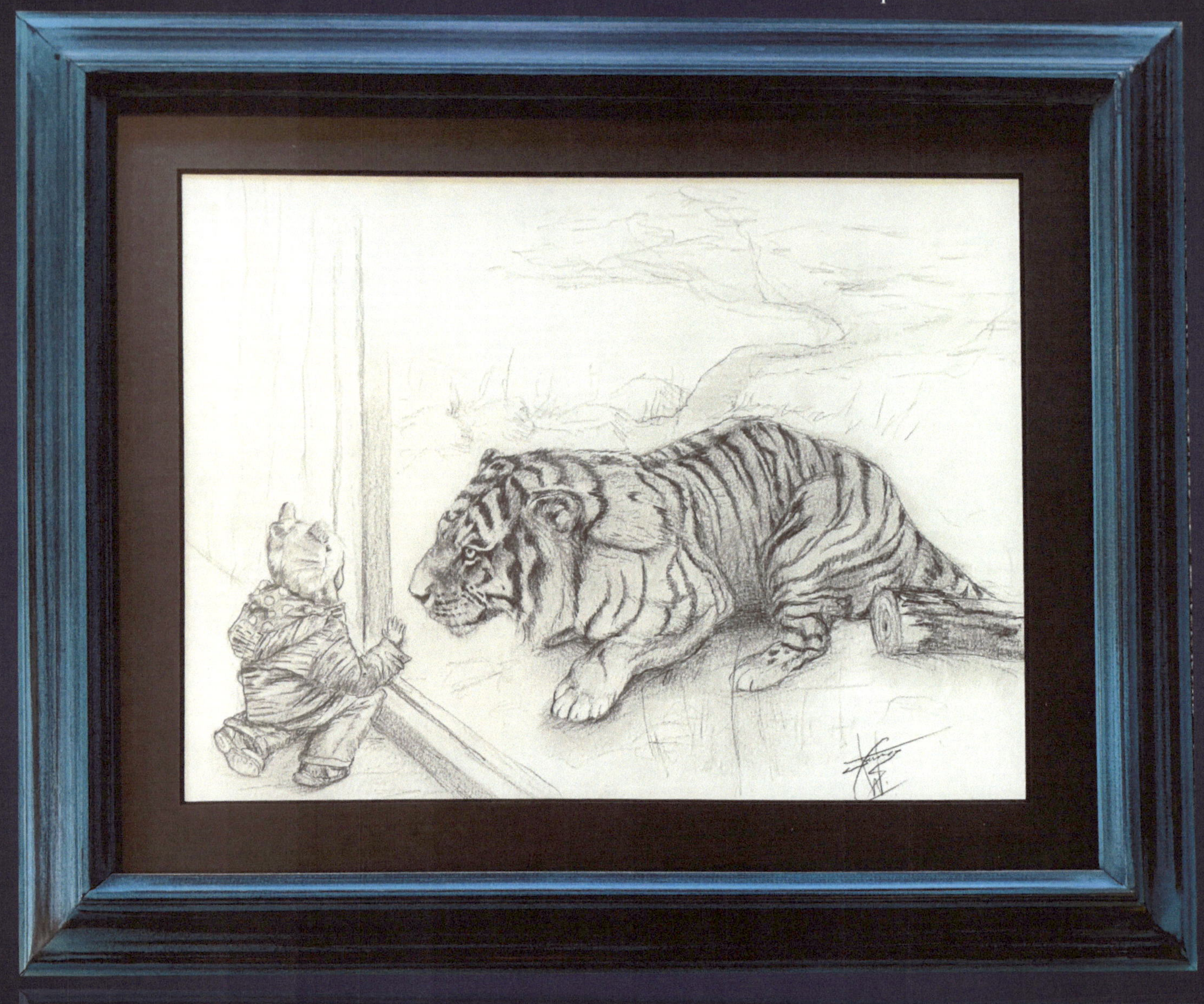

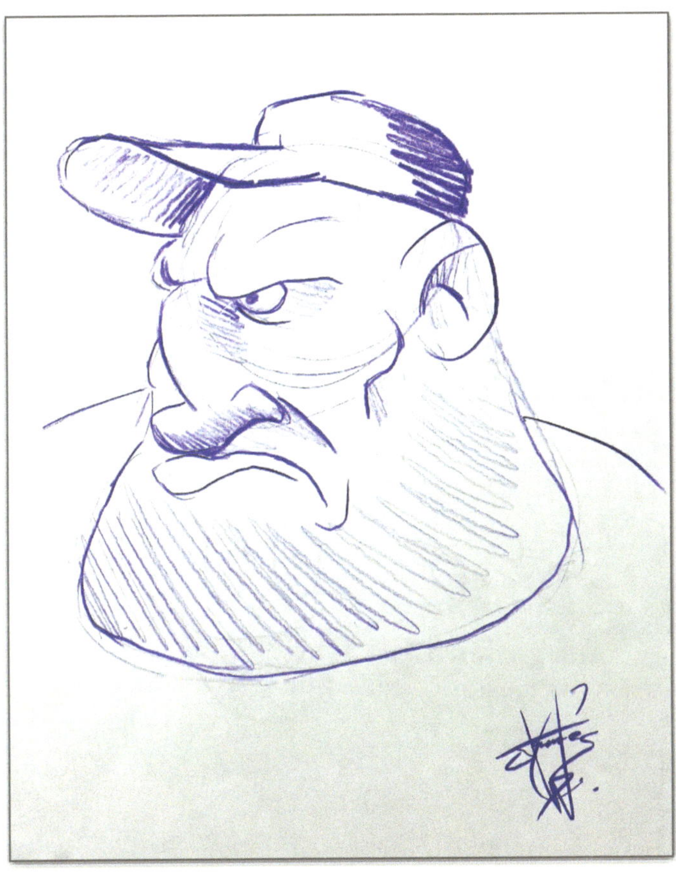

"Heartburn"
Quick Character Sketch
2019

Paper
Colored Pencil
11.0 L × 8.5 W Inches

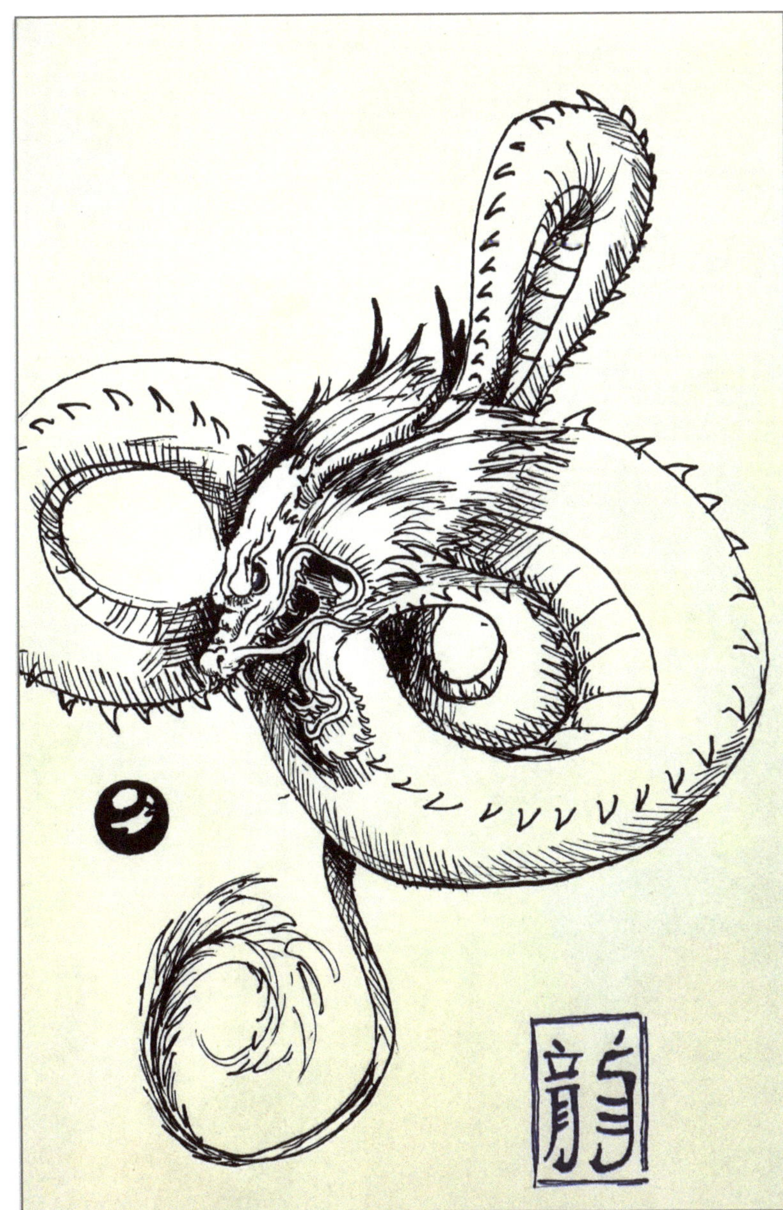

"Twisted"
2016

Paper
Ink, Marker
6.25 L × 4.0 W Inches

In the Archives of the
James William Christenson Art Gallery
Prior Lake, Minnesota

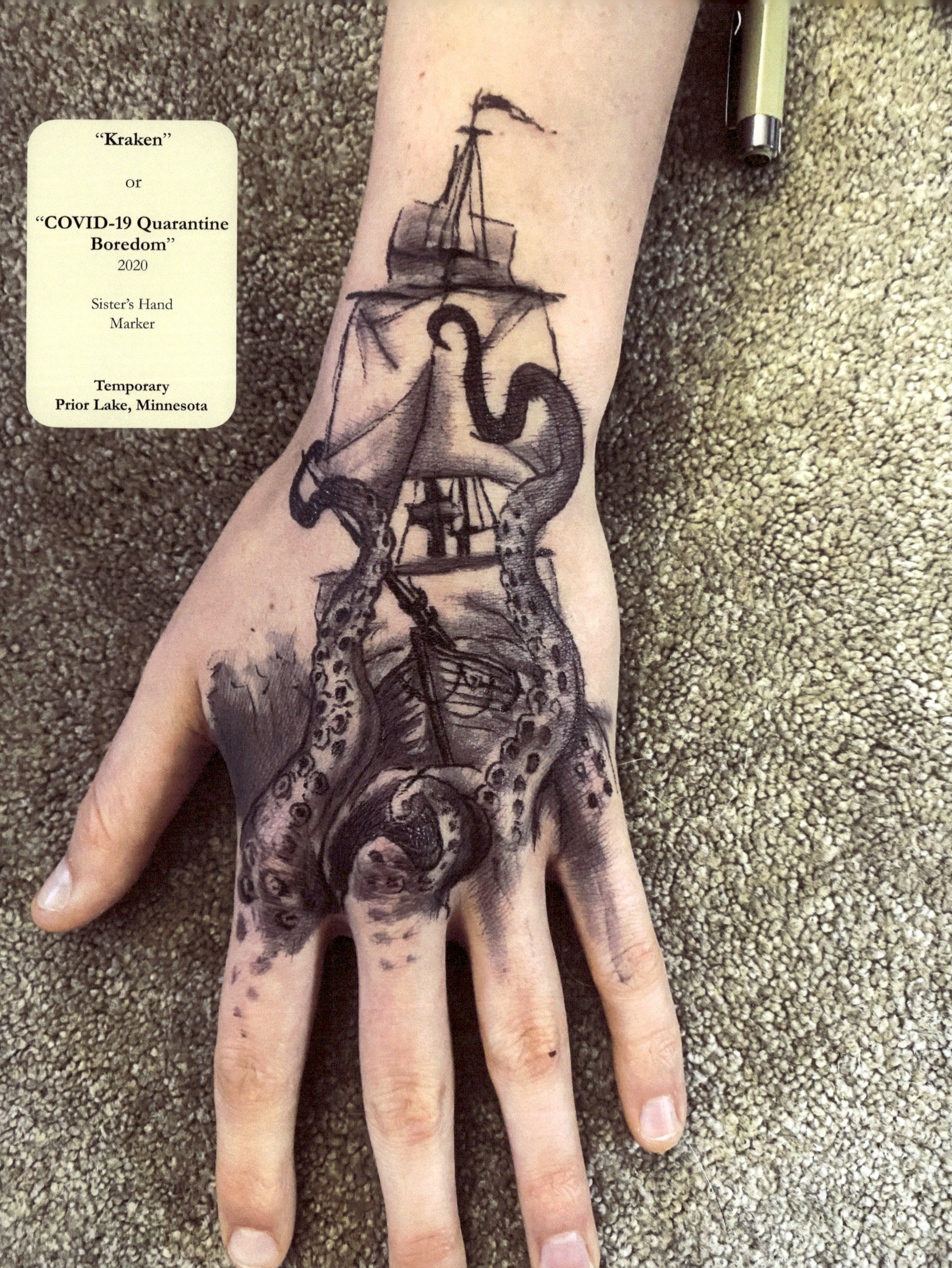

"Kraken"

or

"COVID-19 Quarantine Boredom"
2020

Sister's Hand
Marker

Temporary
Prior Lake, Minnesota

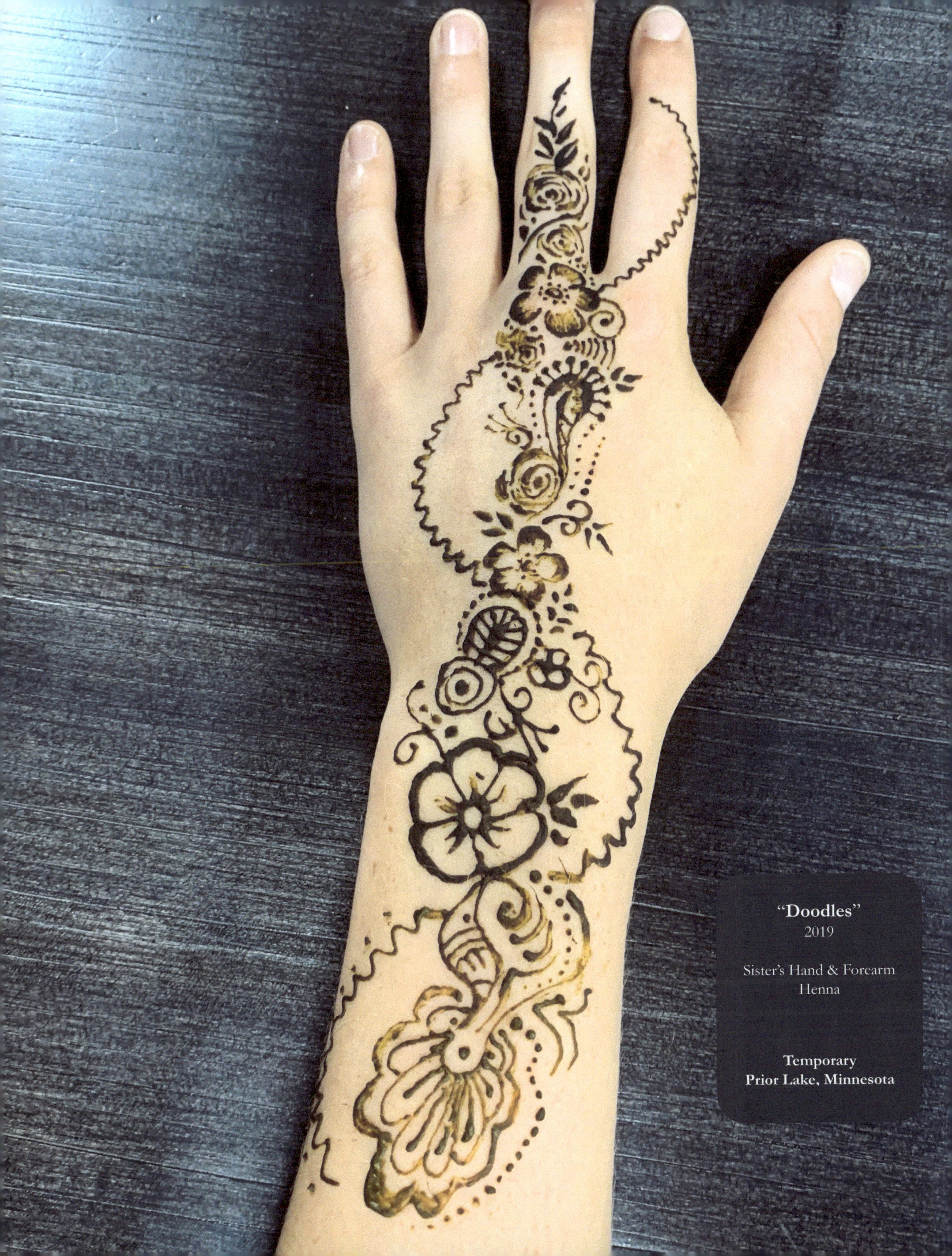

"Doodles"
2019

Sister's Hand & Forearm
Henna

Temporary
Prior Lake, Minnesota

"Pachyderm"
2017

Live Edge, Unfinished Basswood Board
Woodburn
16.0 L × 11.0 W Inches

Commissioned by Private Art Collector
Whitestown, Indiana
Reprinted with Permission.

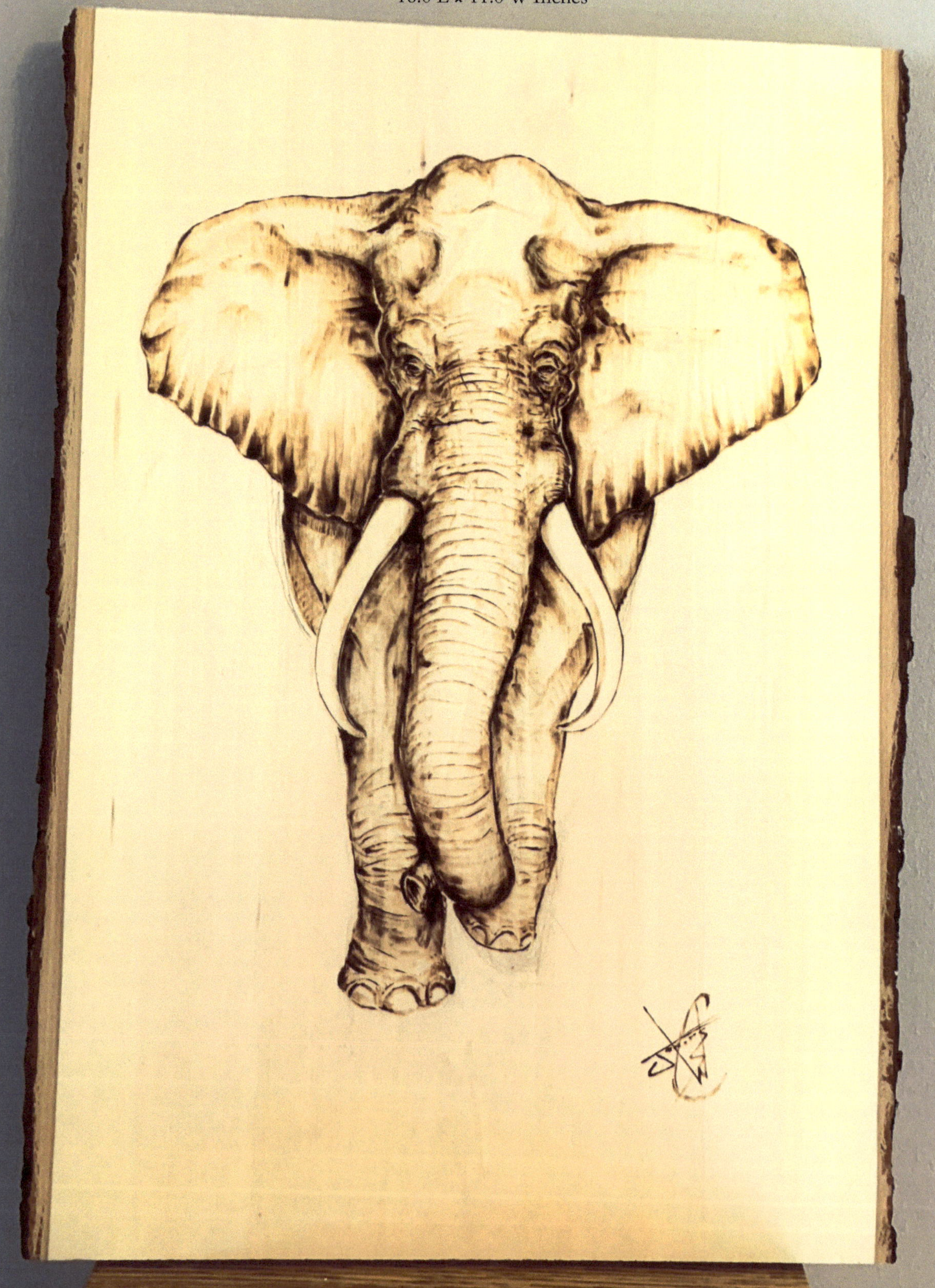

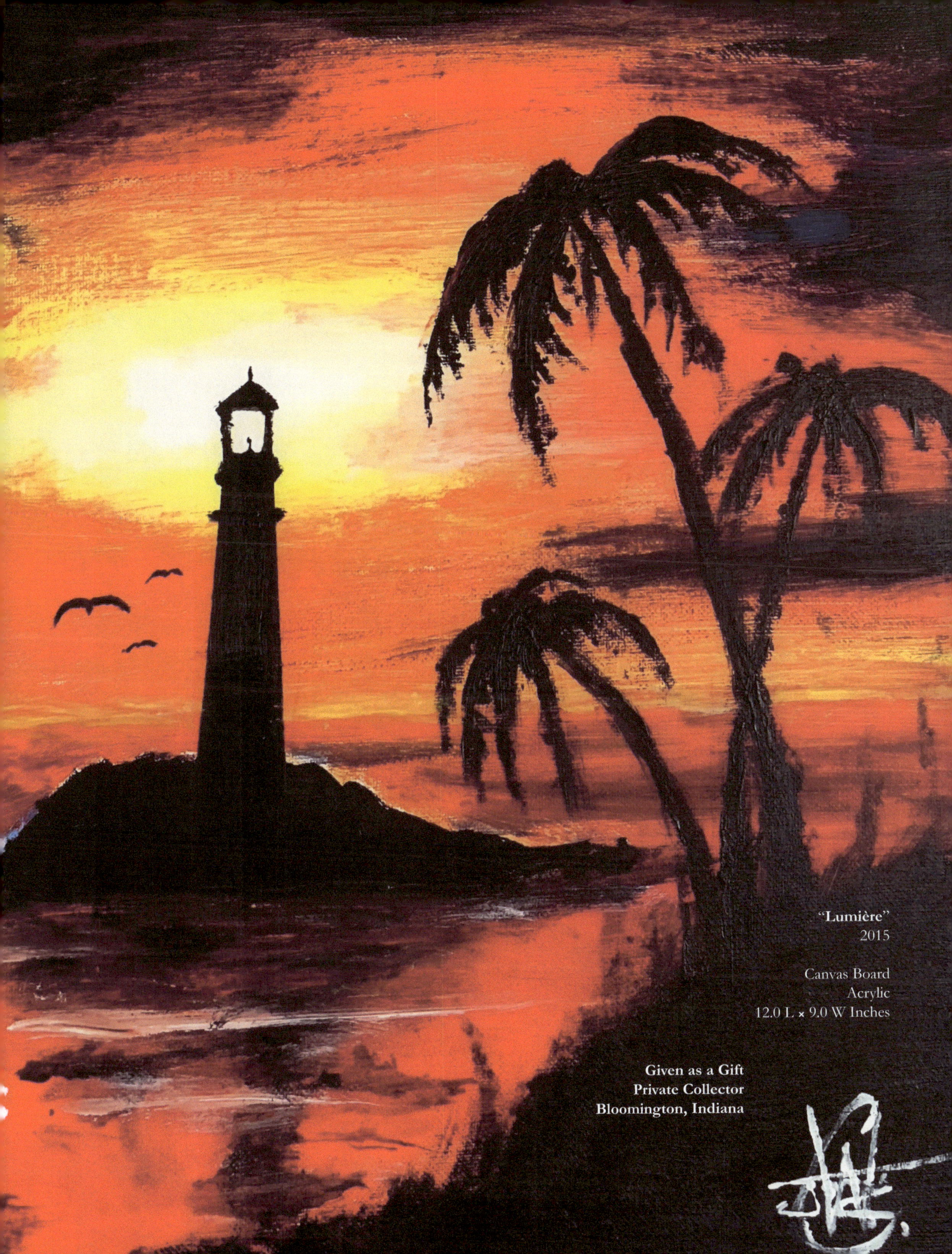

"Lumière"
2015

Canvas Board
Acrylic
12.0 L × 9.0 W Inches

Given as a Gift
Private Collector
Bloomington, Indiana

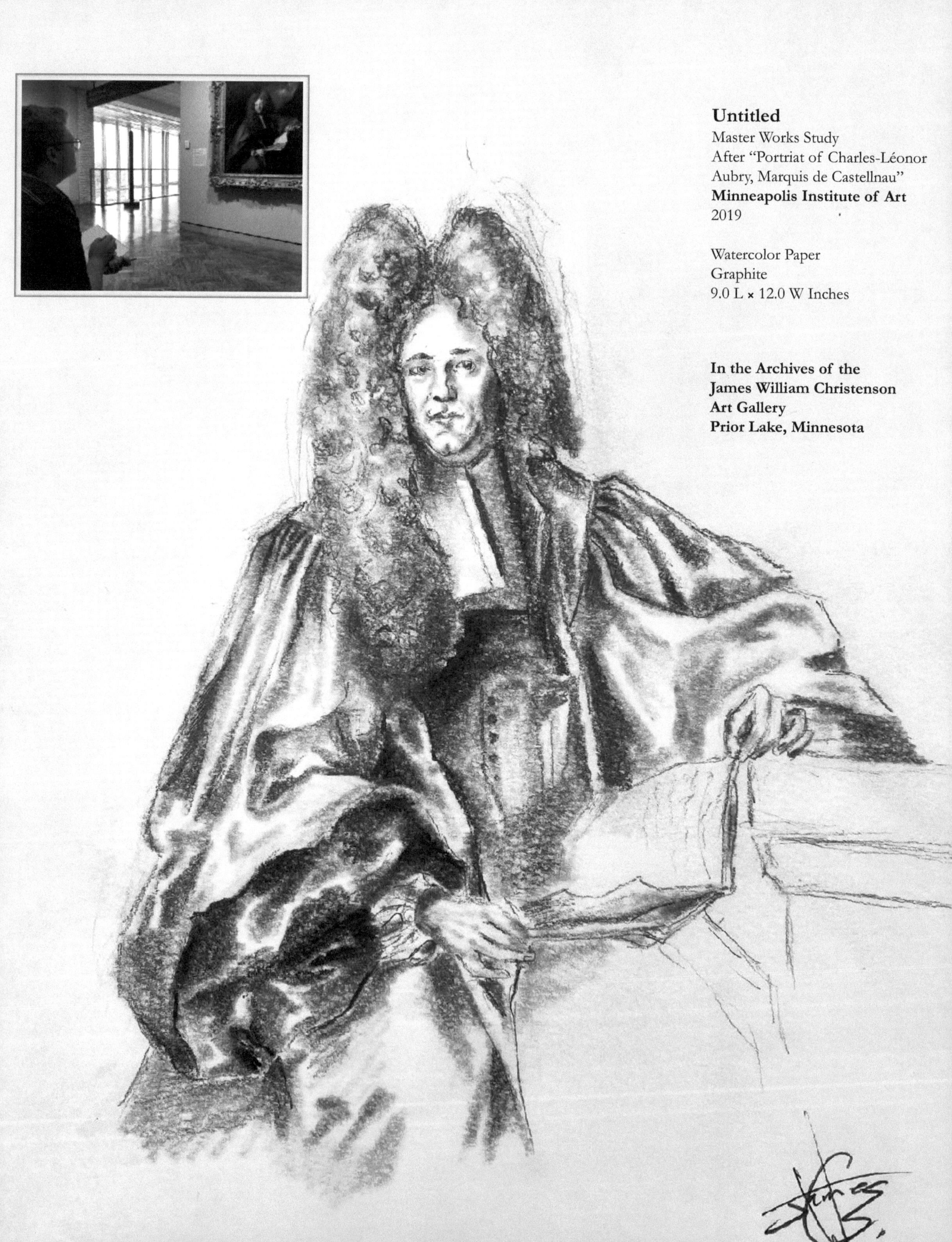

Untitled
Master Works Study
After "Portriat of Charles-Léonor Aubry, Marquis de Castellnau"
Minneapolis Institute of Art
2019

Watercolor Paper
Graphite
9.0 L × 12.0 W Inches

In the Archives of the James William Christenson Art Gallery Prior Lake, Minnesota

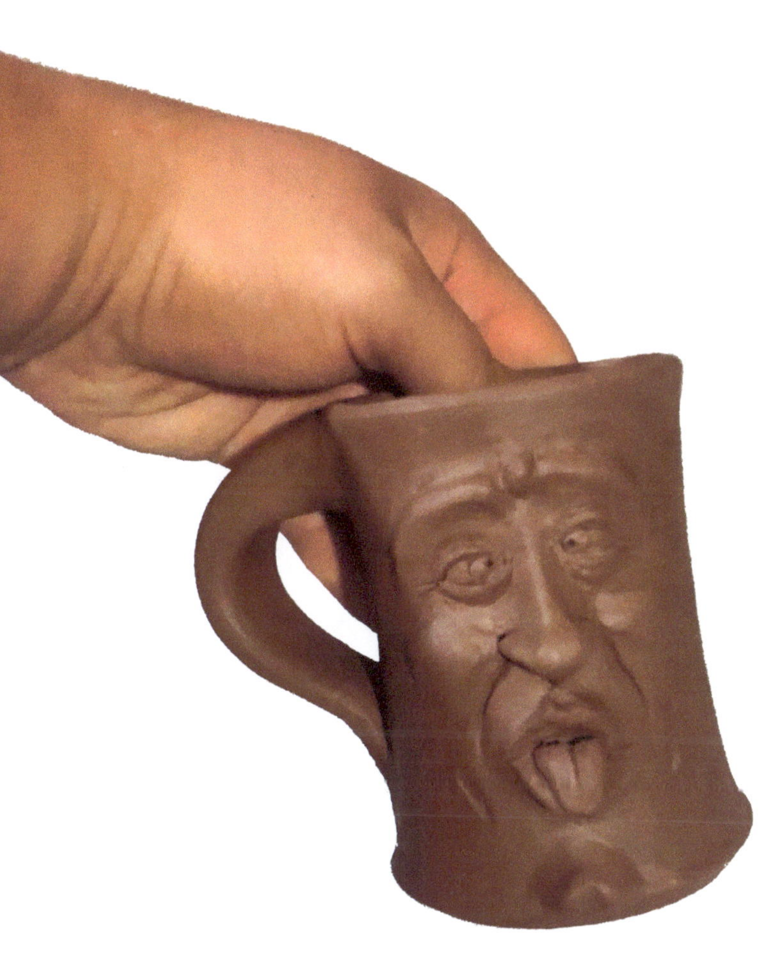

"Ugly Mug"
2019

Terracotta
3.5 L × 5.25 W x 5.5 H Inches

In the Archives of the
James William Christenson Art Gallery
Prior Lake, Minnesota

"Couch Potato"
2018

Potato
Ink
5.25 L × 3.25 W Inches

Perishable
Prior Lake, Minnesota

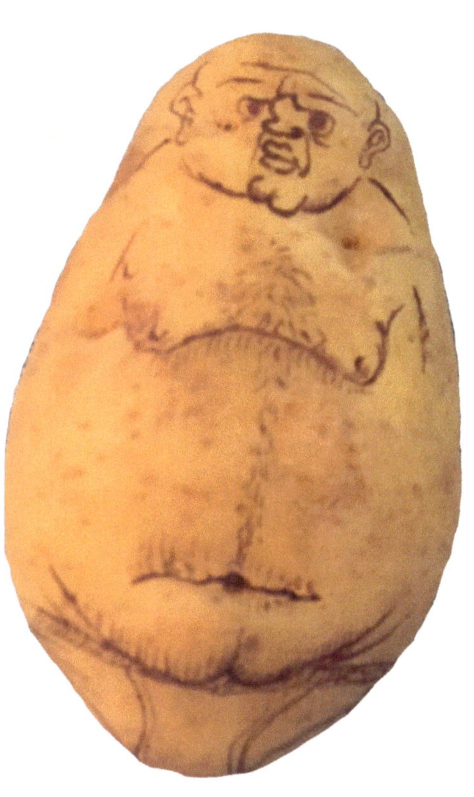

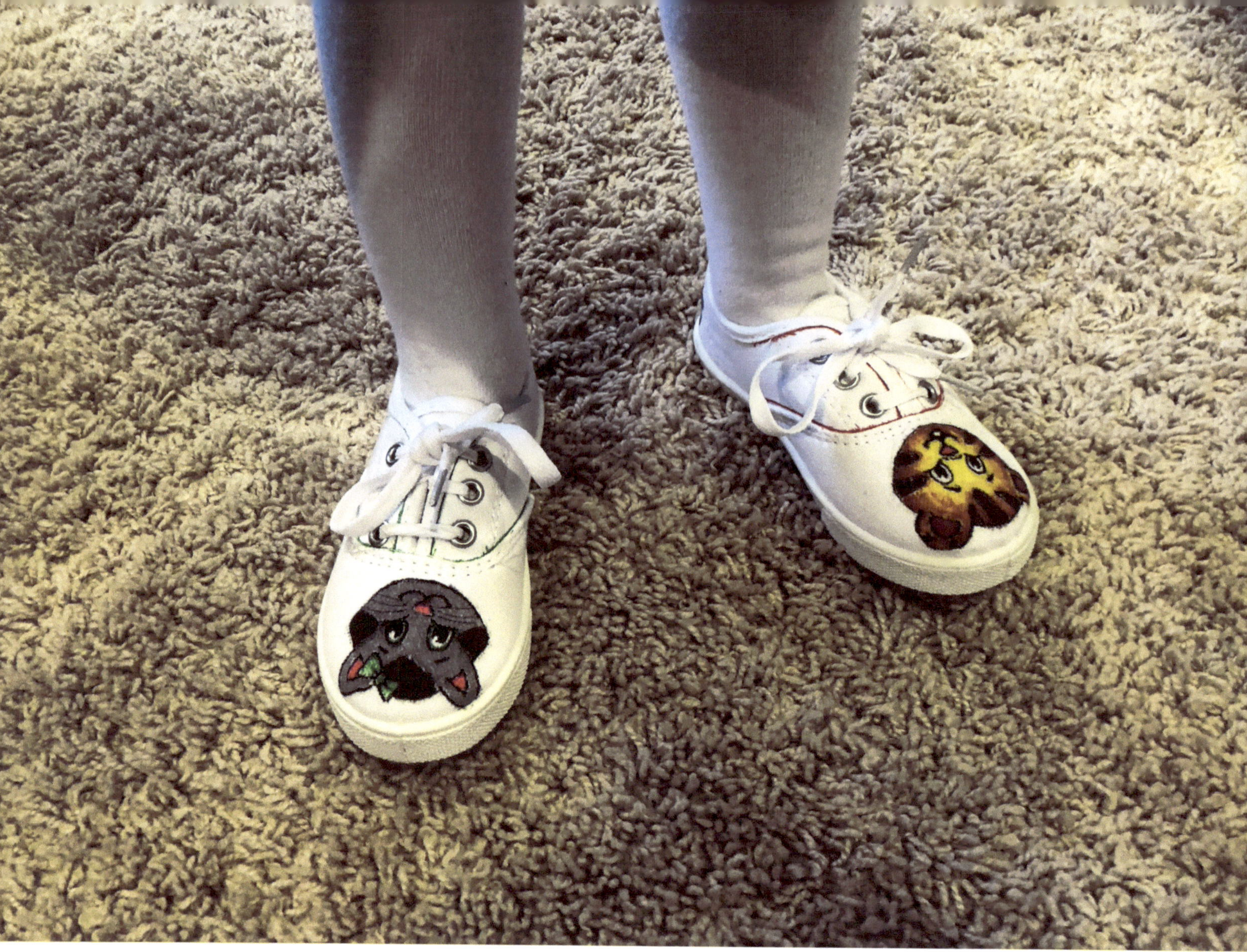

ABOVE

"Ellie's Kicks"
2019

Shoes, Toddler Size 7
Felt Marker

Given as a Gift.
Whitestown, Indiana

FACING PAGE

"Tree Frog"
Batik
2018

Rice Paper
Ink, Wax, Watercolor
12.0 L × 9.0 W Inches

In the Archives of the
James William Christenson Art Gallery
Prior Lake, Minnesota

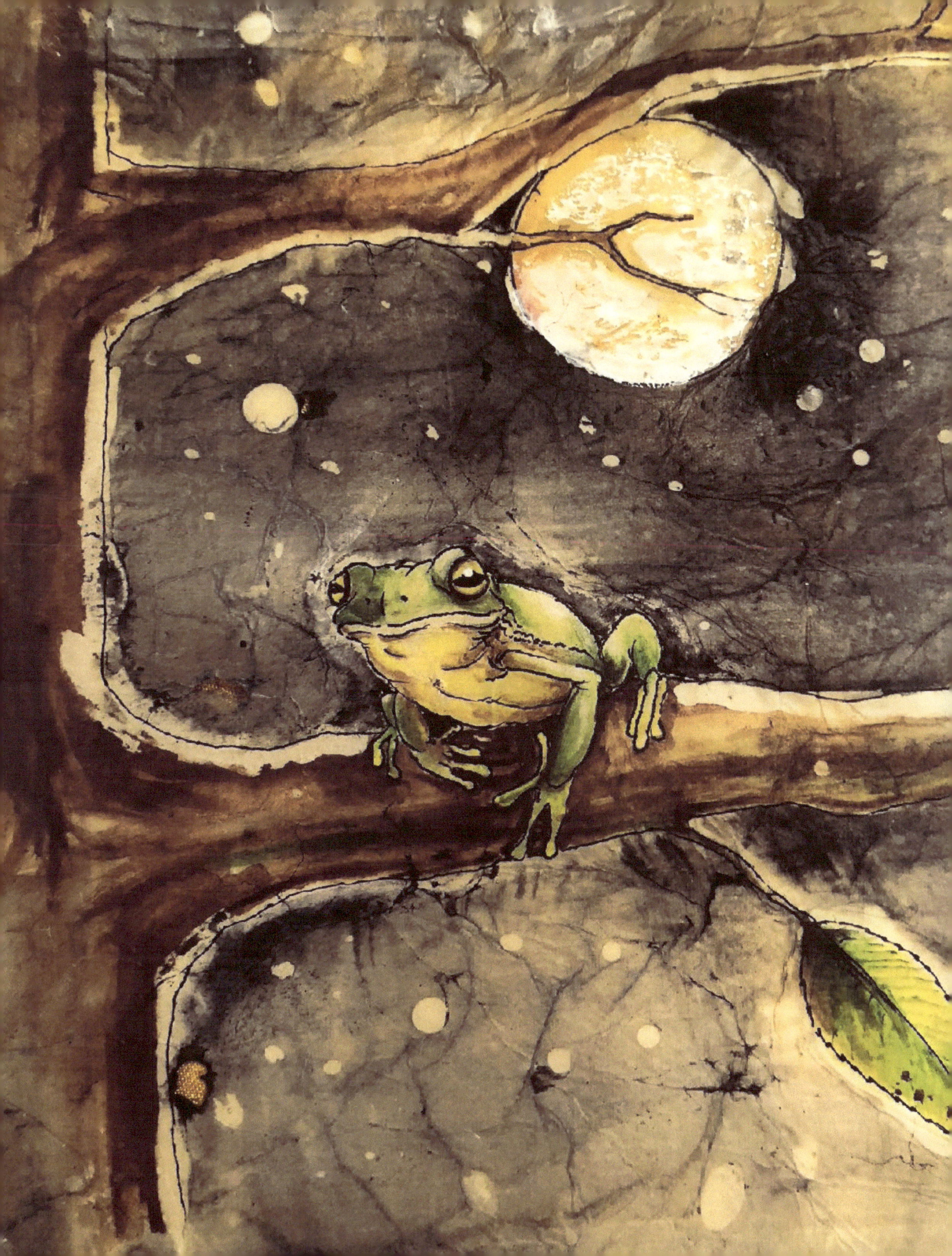

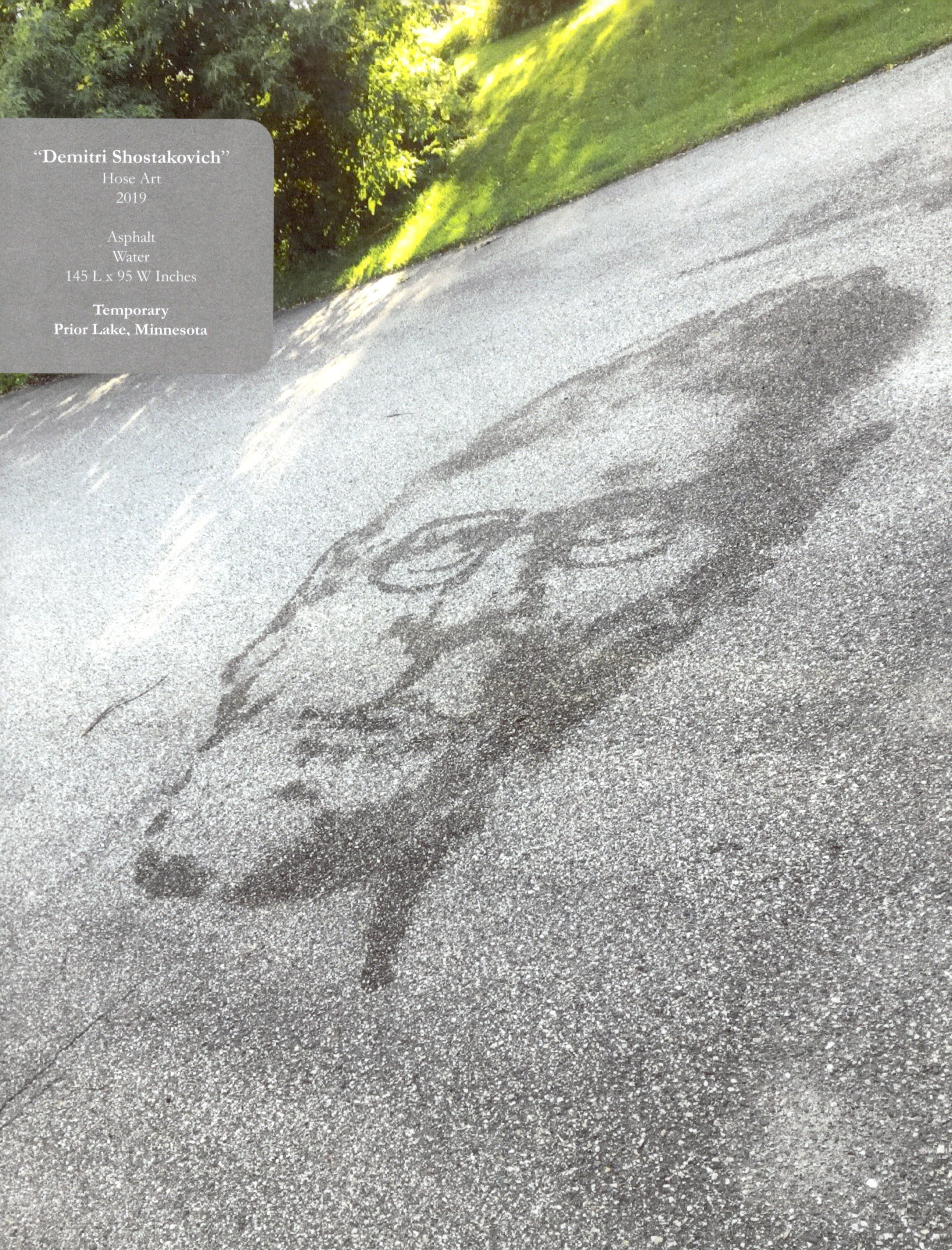

"Demitri Shostakovich"
Hose Art
2019

Asphalt
Water
145 L x 95 W Inches

Temporary
Prior Lake, Minnesota

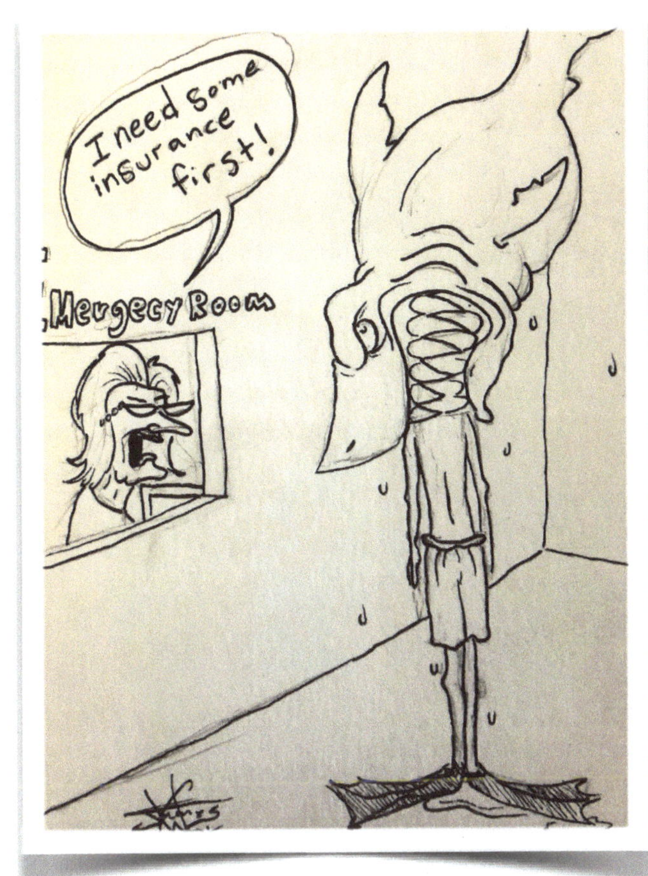

"ER Visits"
Postcard
2019

Watercolor Paper
Graphite, Pen
5.5 L × 4.0 W Inches

In the Archives of the
James William Christenson Art Gallery
Prior Lake, Minnesota

"Math"
Postcard
2020

Watercolor Paper
Graphite, Ink
6.0 L x 4.0 W Inches

Sent as a Gift.
U.S. Army Military Police SPC
Mihail Kogălniceanu, Romania

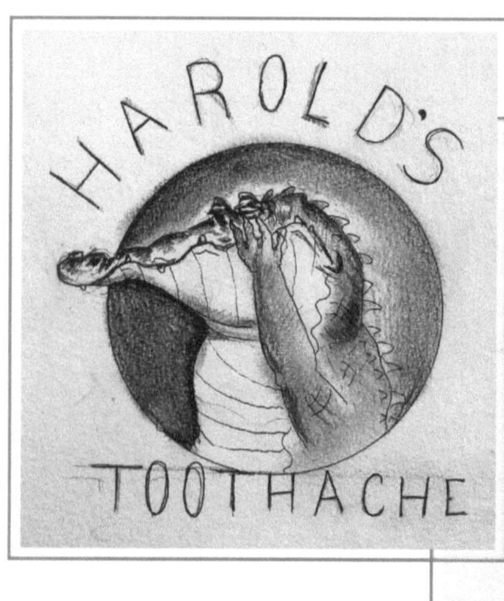

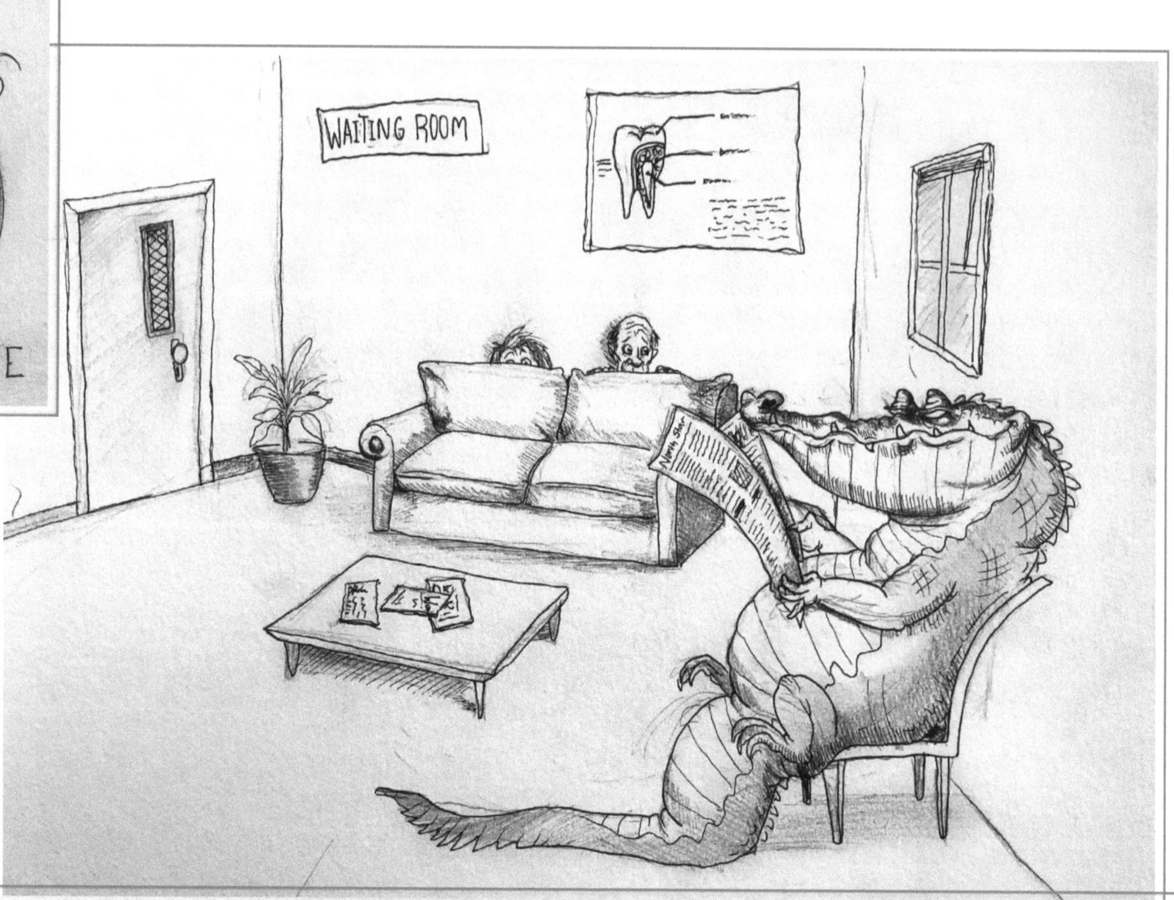

Stories With Uncle Jim
"Harold's Toothache"
2018

Watercolor Paper
Graphite, Ink
9.0 L x 12.0 W Inches

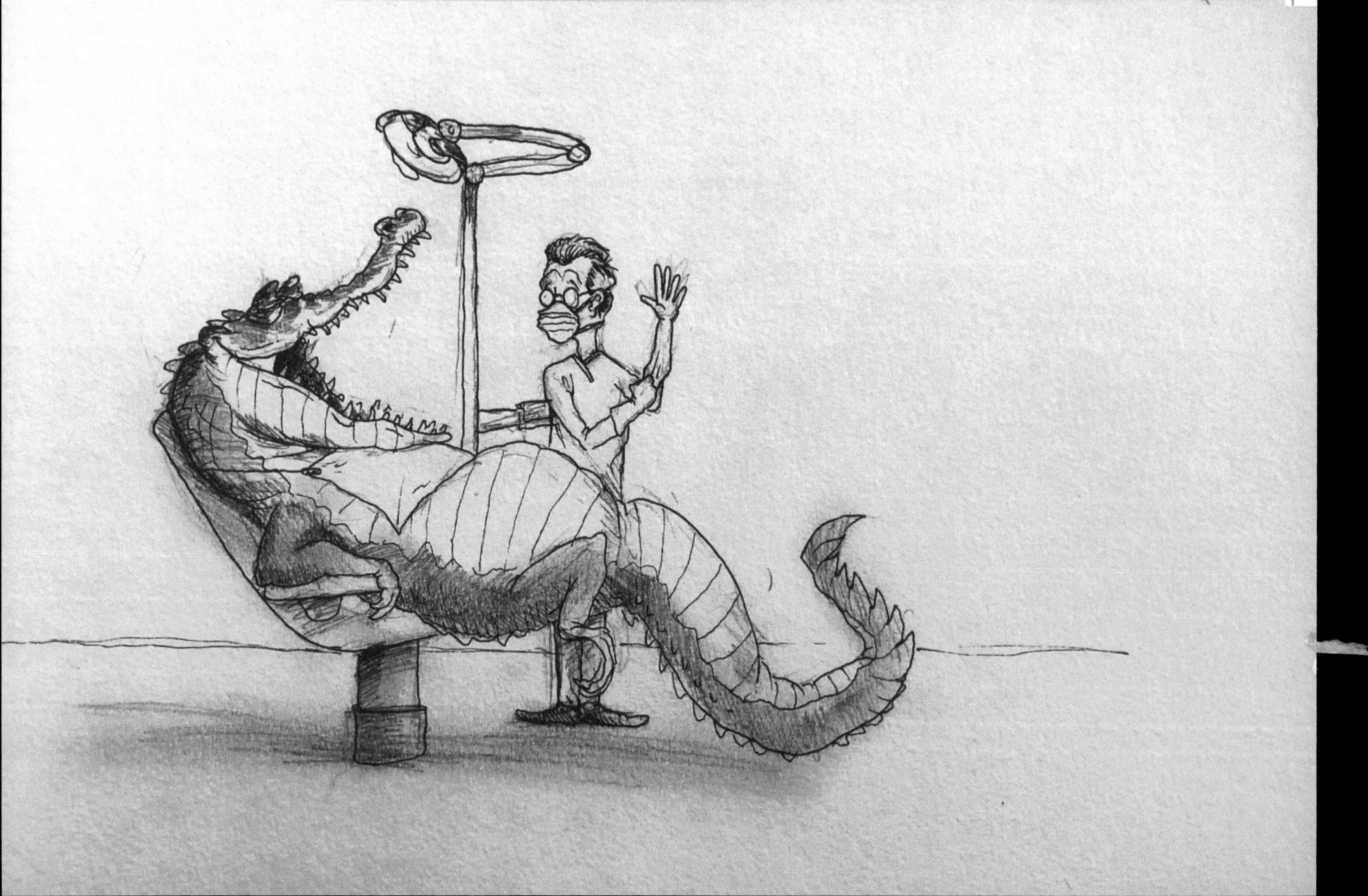

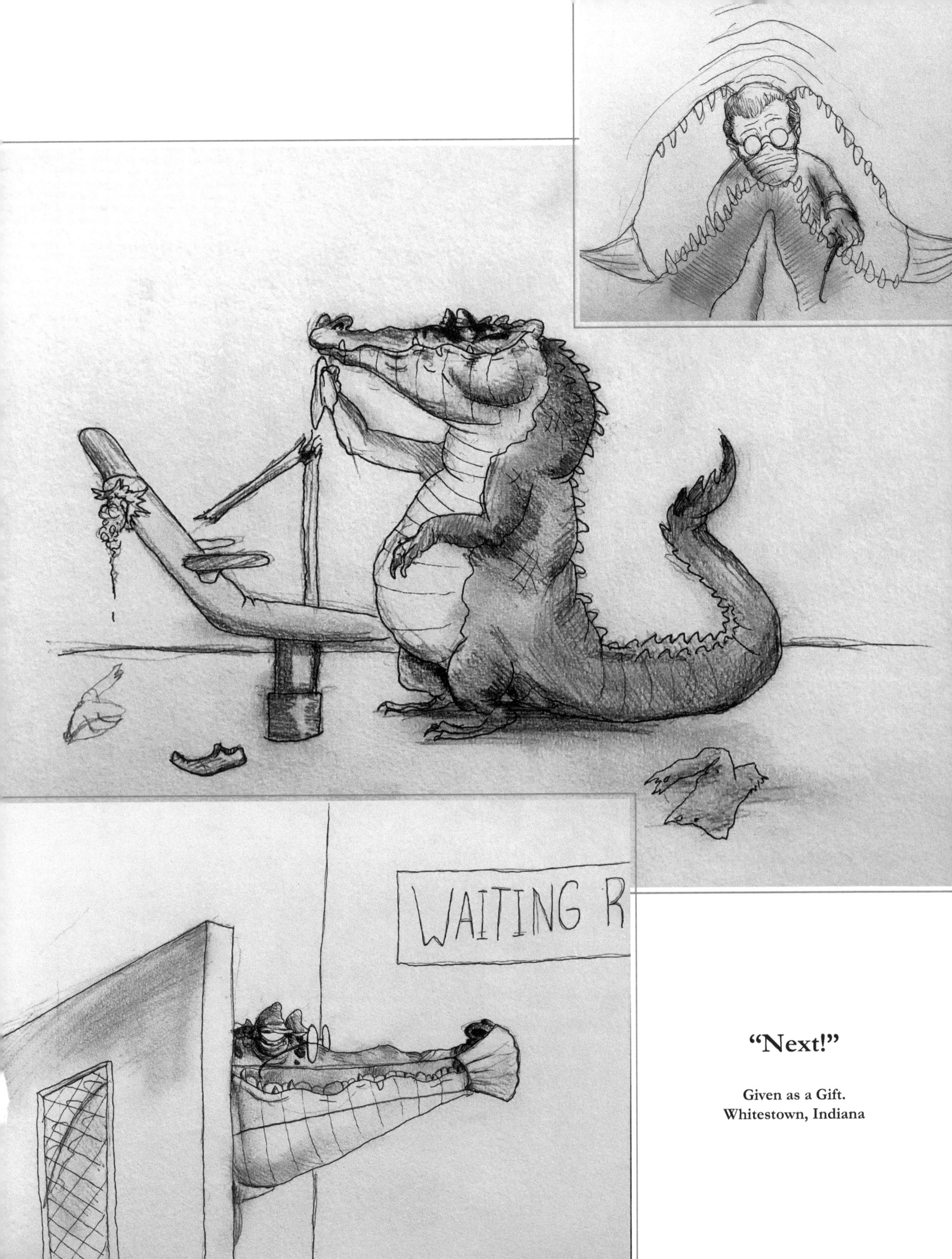

"Next!"

Given as a Gift.
Whitestown, Indiana

“**Katrina Visits Winston**”
2019

Watercolor Paper
Graphite & Pen
9.0 L × 12.0 W Inches

Given as a Gift
Private Art Collection
Ann Arbor, Michigan

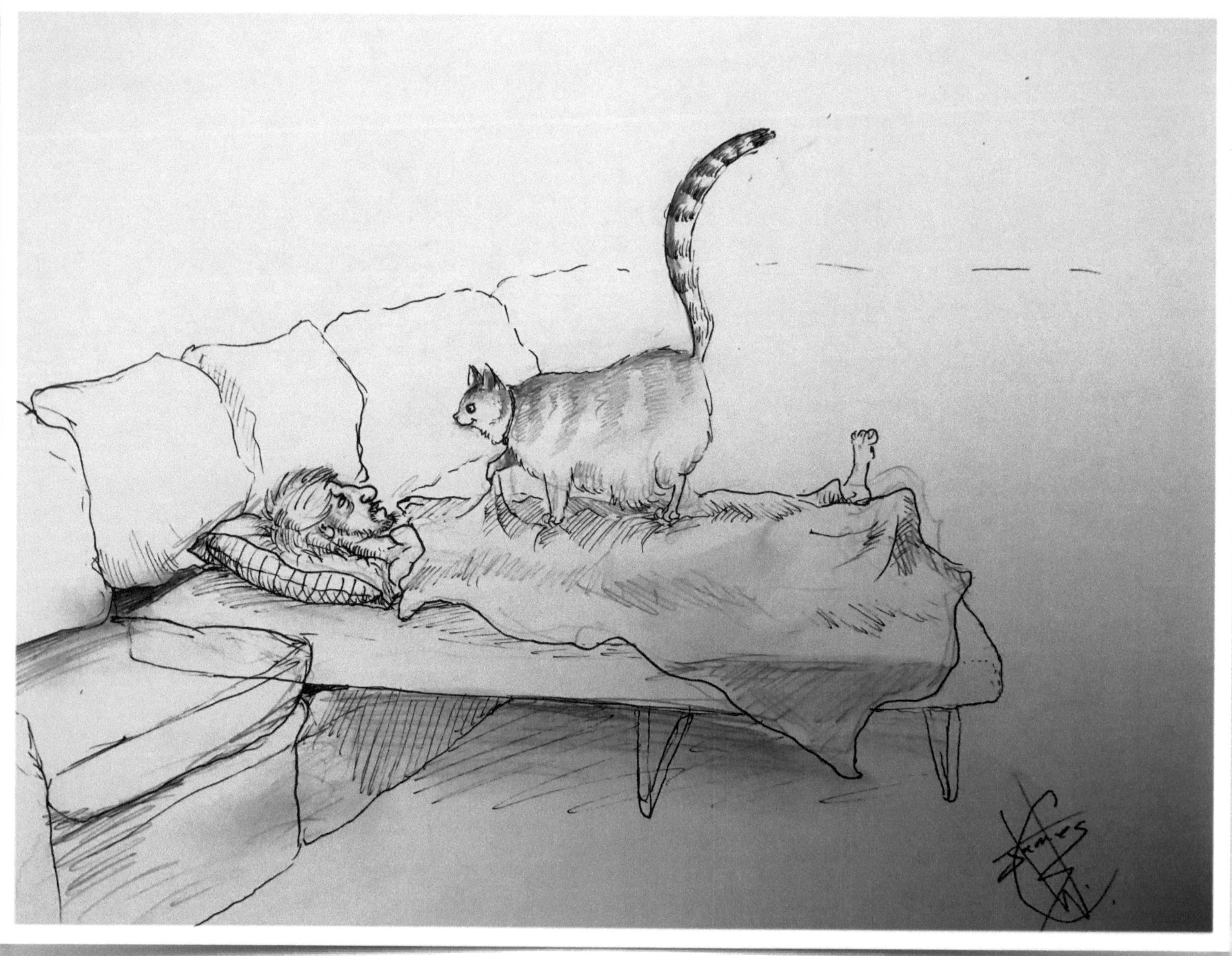

“Gilbert, the Peruvian Delicacy”
2019

Watercolor Paper
Colored Pencil
12.0 L × 9.0 W Inches

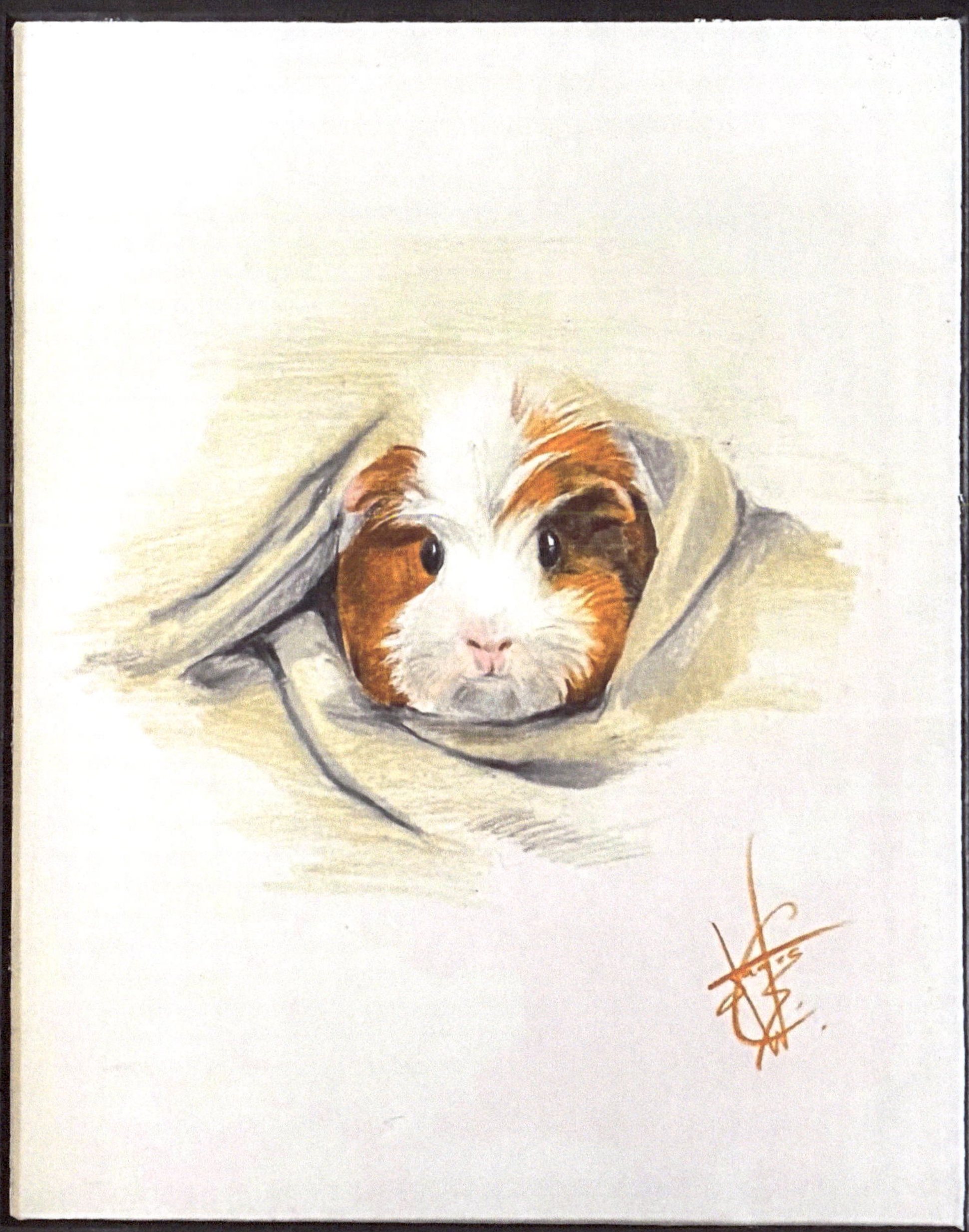

In the Private Art Collection of
Maison Vicaire
Savage, Minnesota
Reprinted with Permission.

Untitled
Sand Art
2019

Beach Sand, Rock
13.75 L x 6.25 W Inches

Temporary
Sand Point Beach
Prior Lake, Minnesota

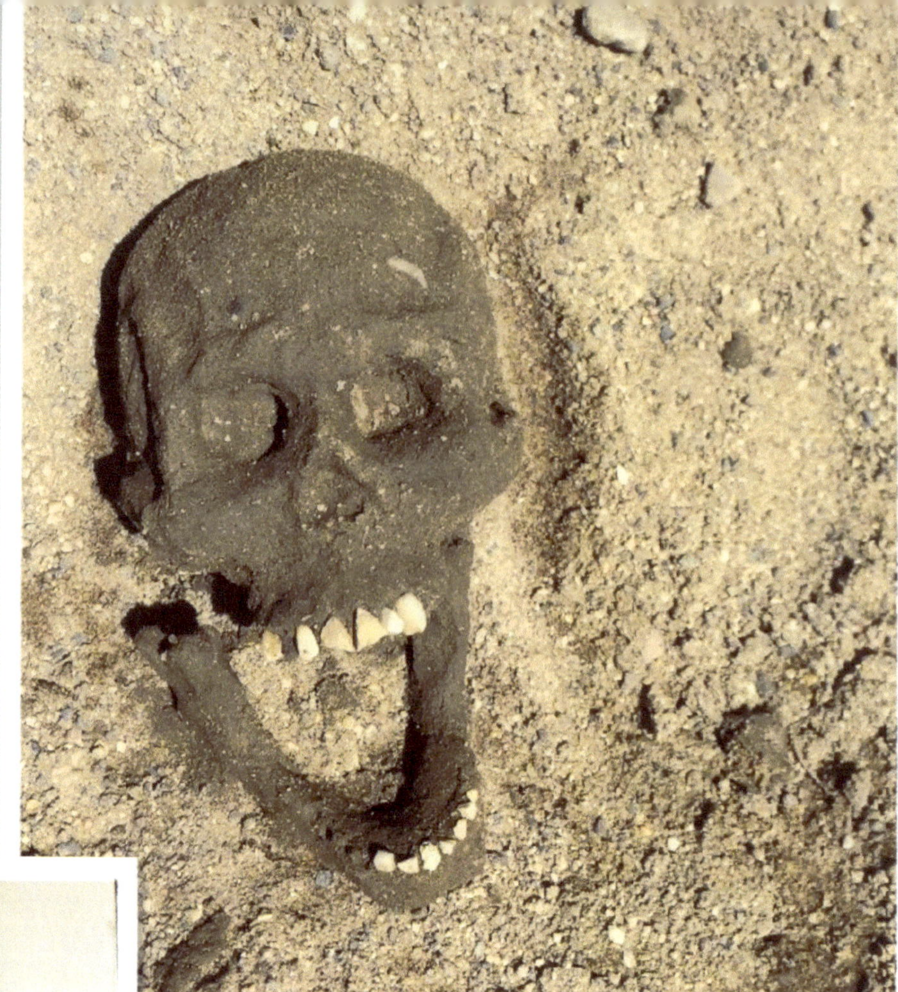

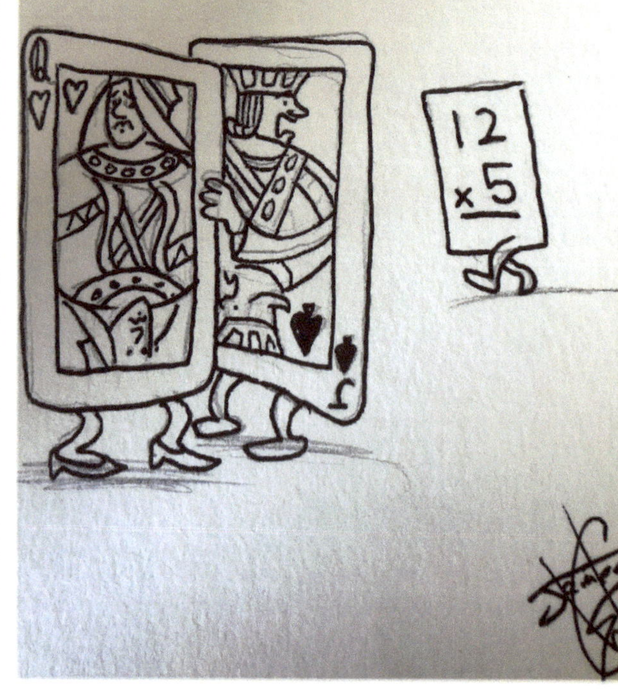

"**Flashcard**"
Postcard
2020

Watercolor Paper
Graphite, Ink
6.0 L x 4.0 W Inches

Sent as a Gift.
U.S. Army Military Police SPC
Mihail Kogălniceanu, Romania

FACING PAGE

"**Jacob's Ladder**"
2020

Photograph
iPhone

Interstate State Park
Taylors Falls, Minnesota

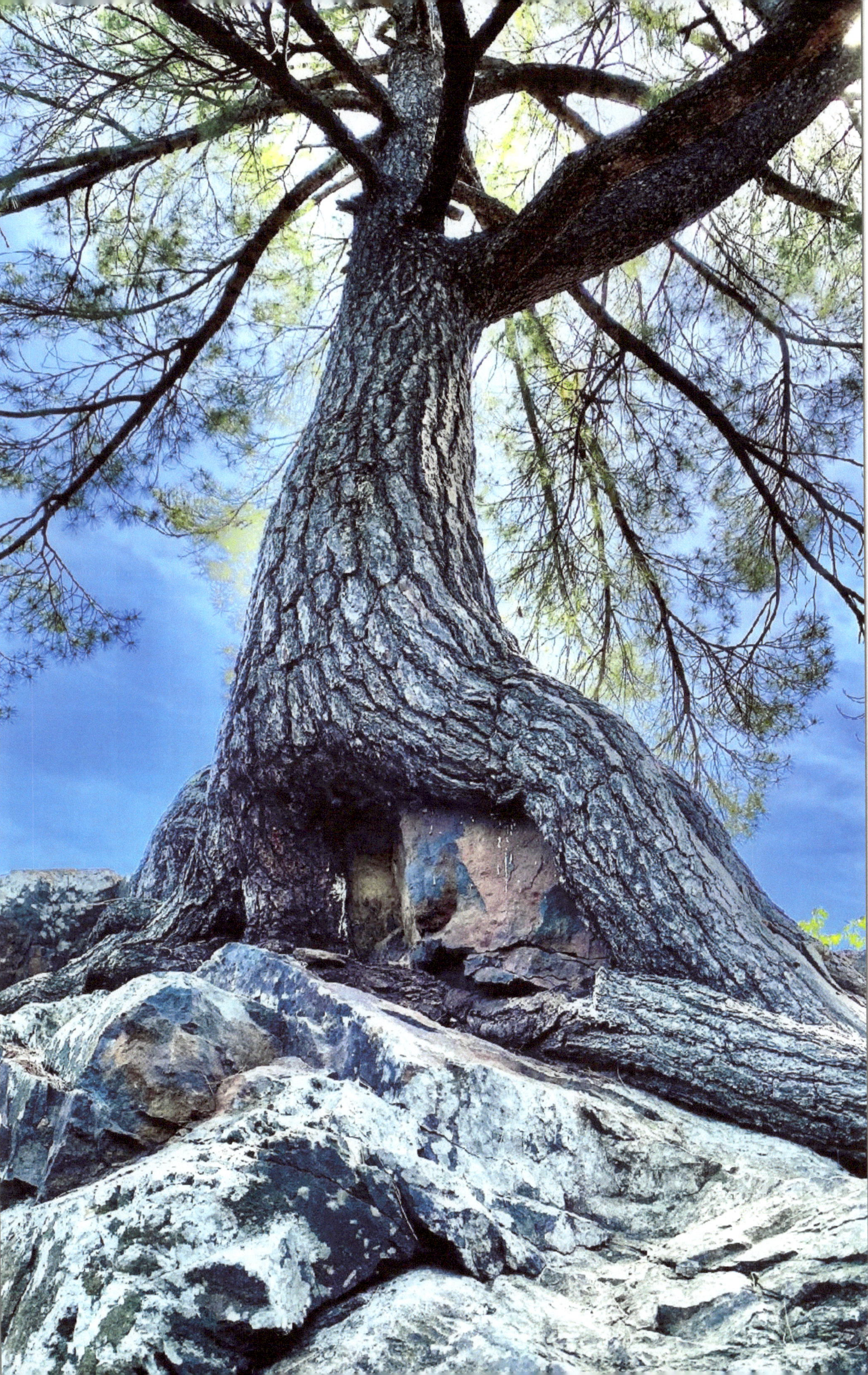

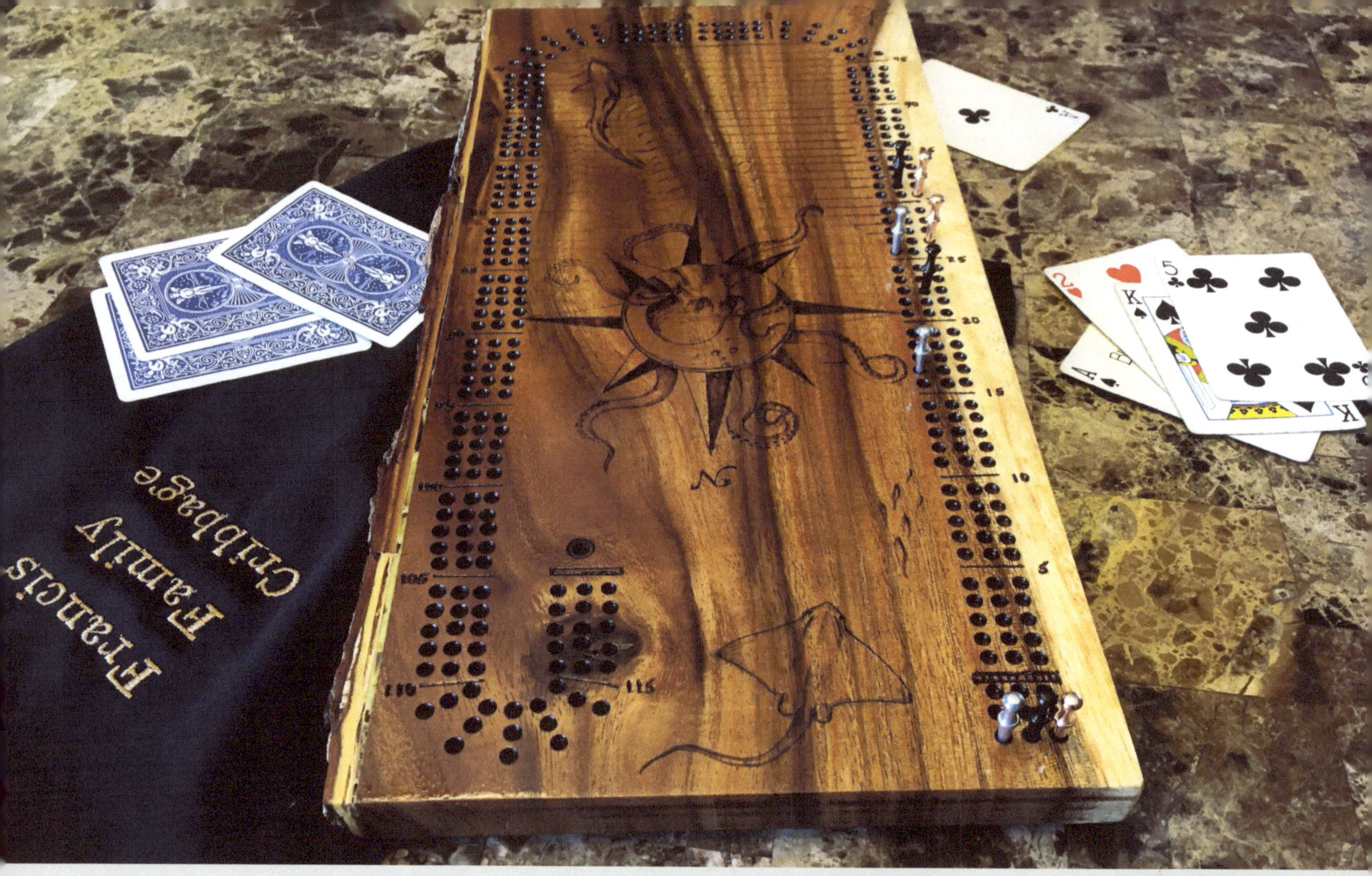
Francis
Family
Cribbage

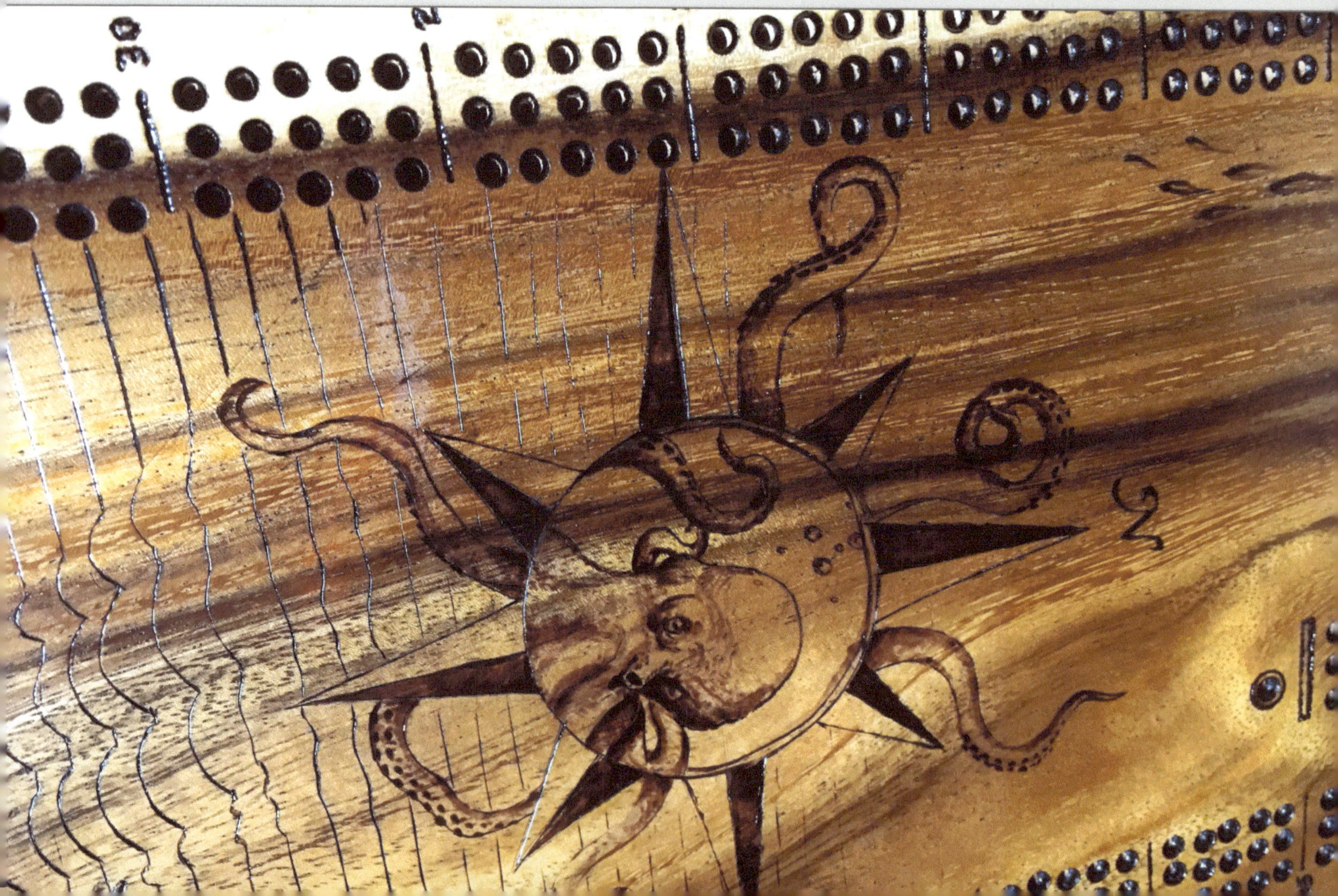

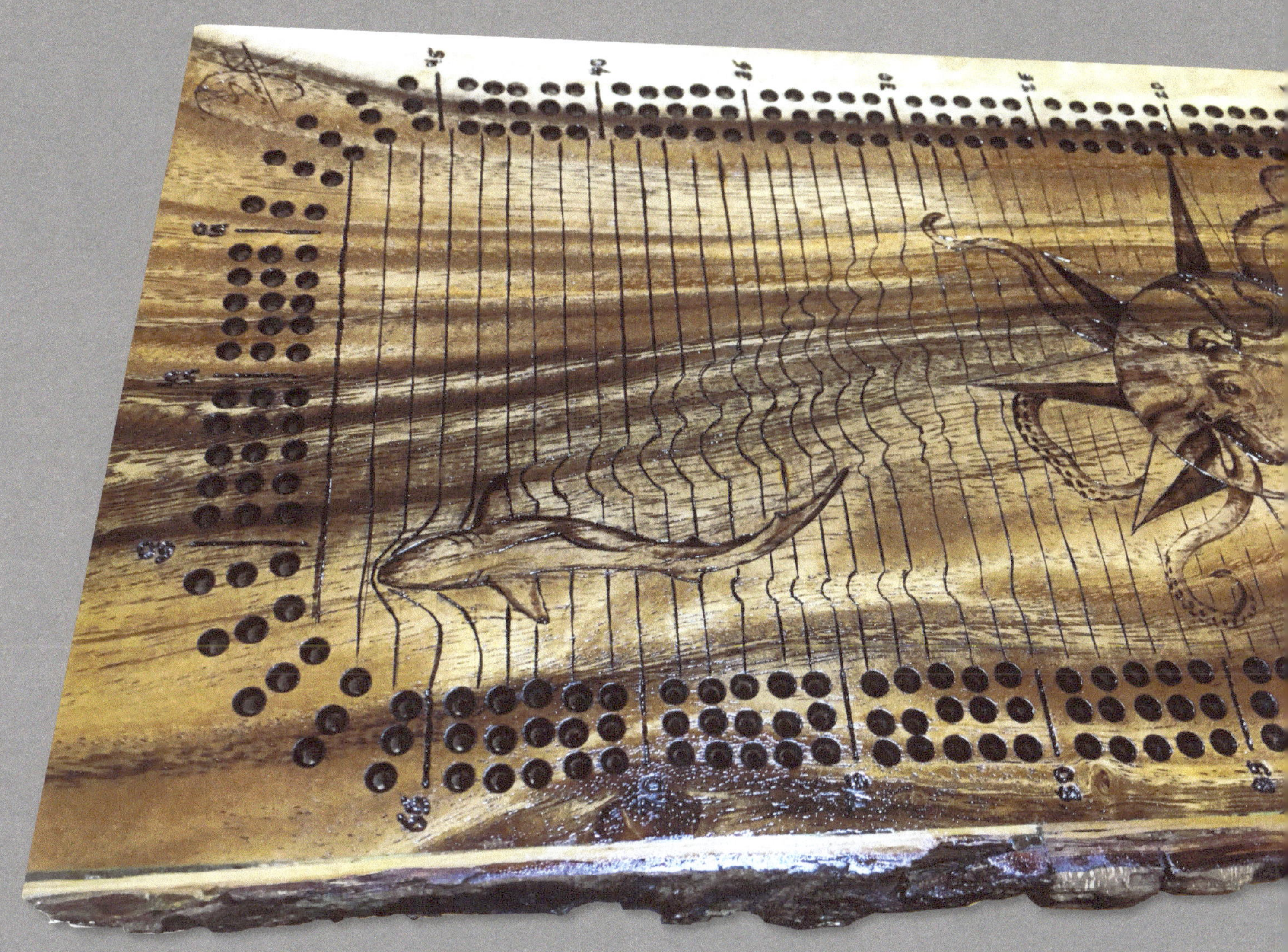

"Mariner's Game"
Cribbage Board
2019

Live Edge Acacia Wood Plank
Woodburn, Lacquer
17.0 L × 8.25 W Inches

Presented as a Gift
Burnsville, Minnesota

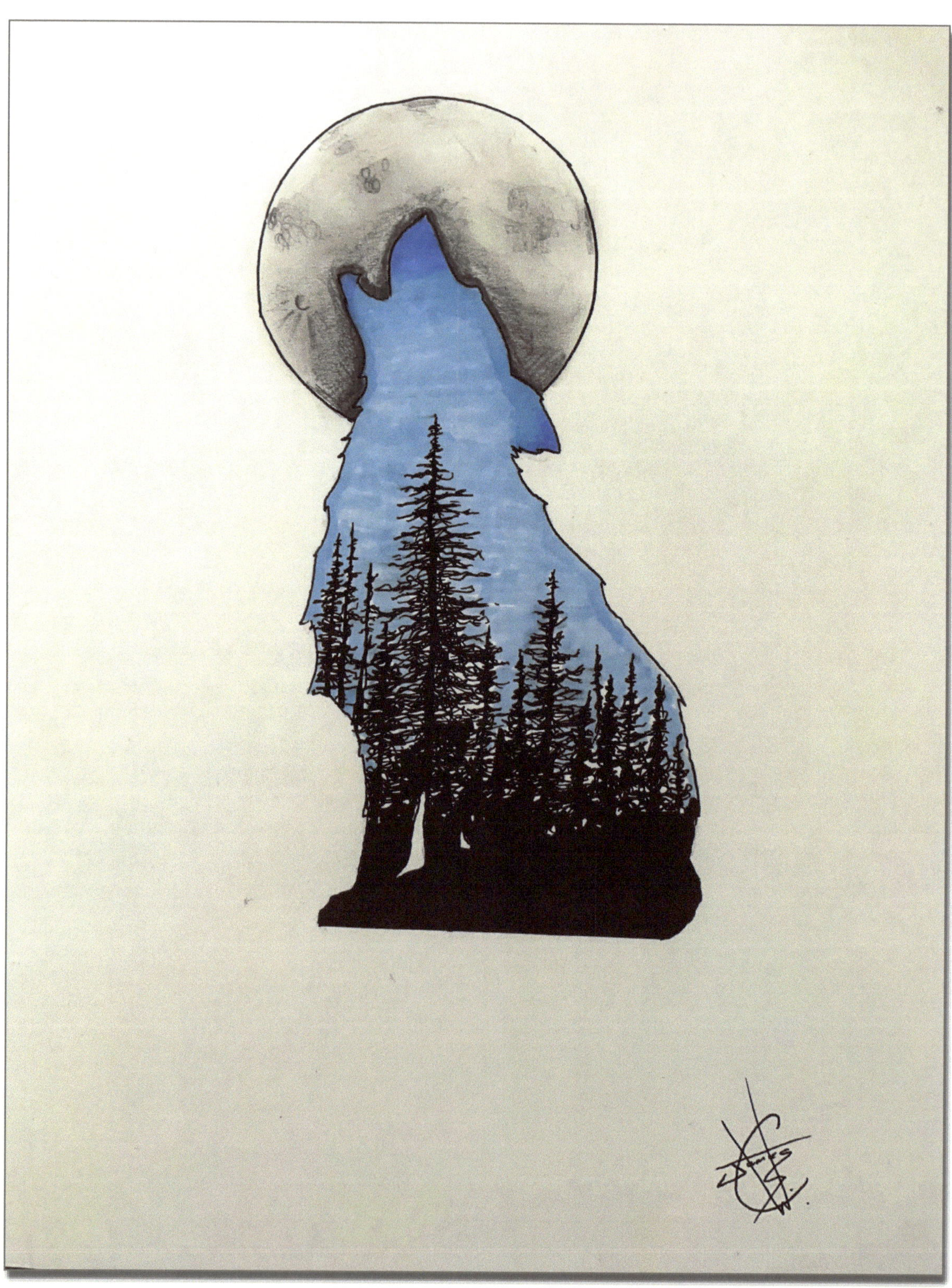

"Lupus"
2019

Watercolor Paper
Graphite, Pen, Marker
12.0 L × 9.0 W Inches

In the Archives of the
James William Christenson Art Gallery
Prior Lake, Minnesota

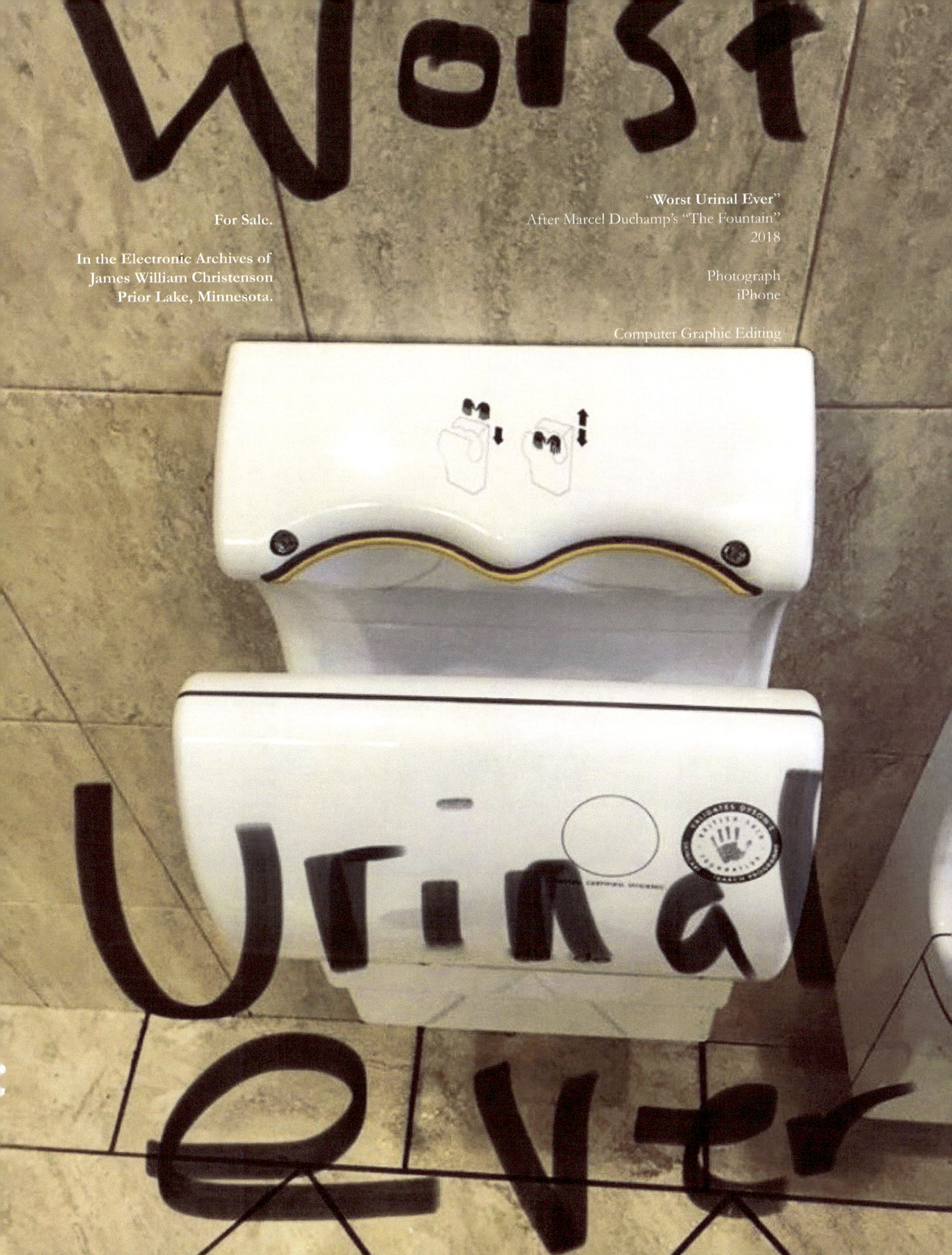

"**Worst Urinal Ever**"
After Marcel Duchamp's "The Fountain"
2018

Photograph
iPhone

Computer Graphic Editing

For Sale.

**In the Electronic Archives of
James William Christenson
Prior Lake, Minnesota.**

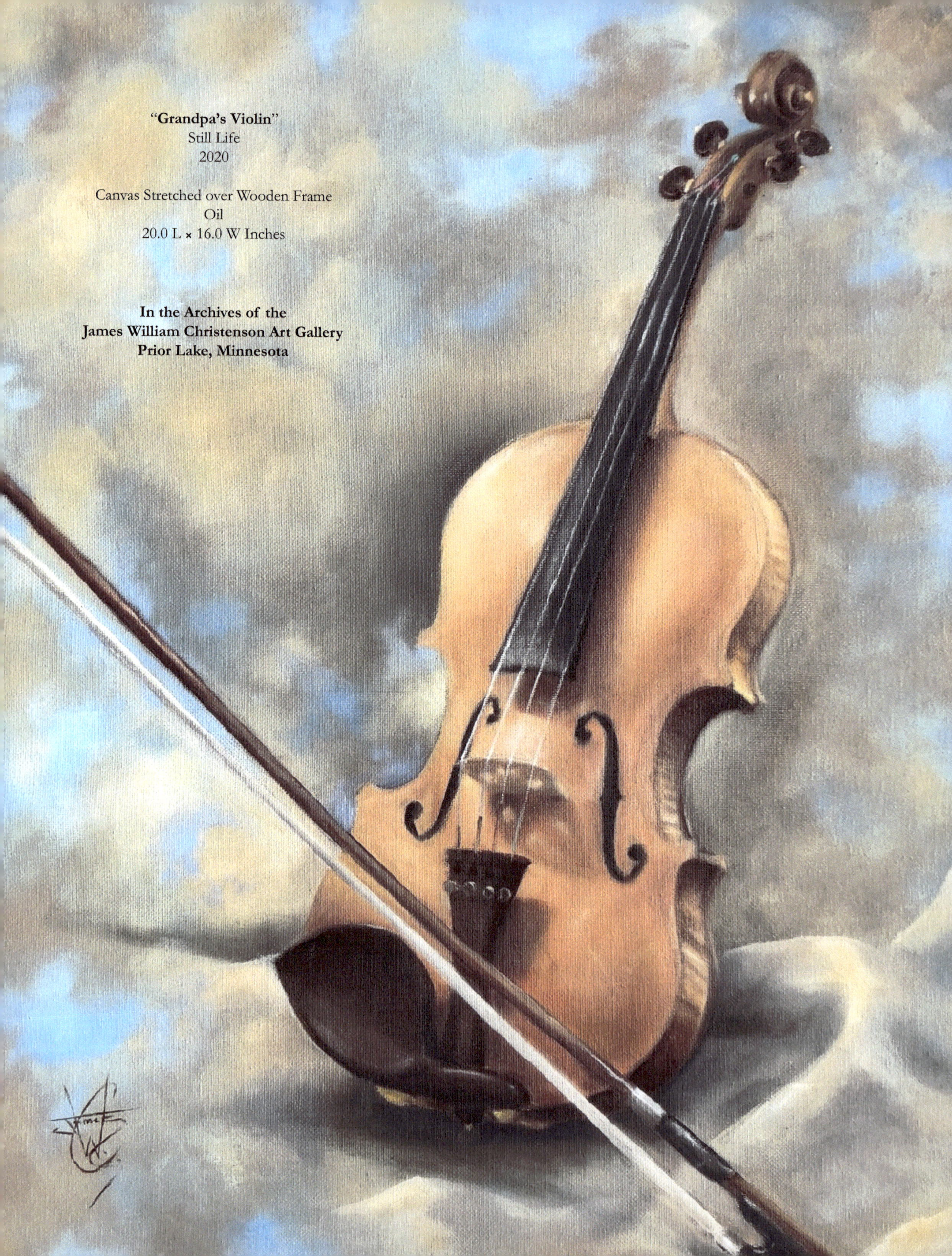

"Grandpa's Violin"
Still Life
2020

Canvas Stretched over Wooden Frame
Oil
20.0 L × 16.0 W Inches

In the Archives of the
James William Christenson Art Gallery
Prior Lake, Minnesota

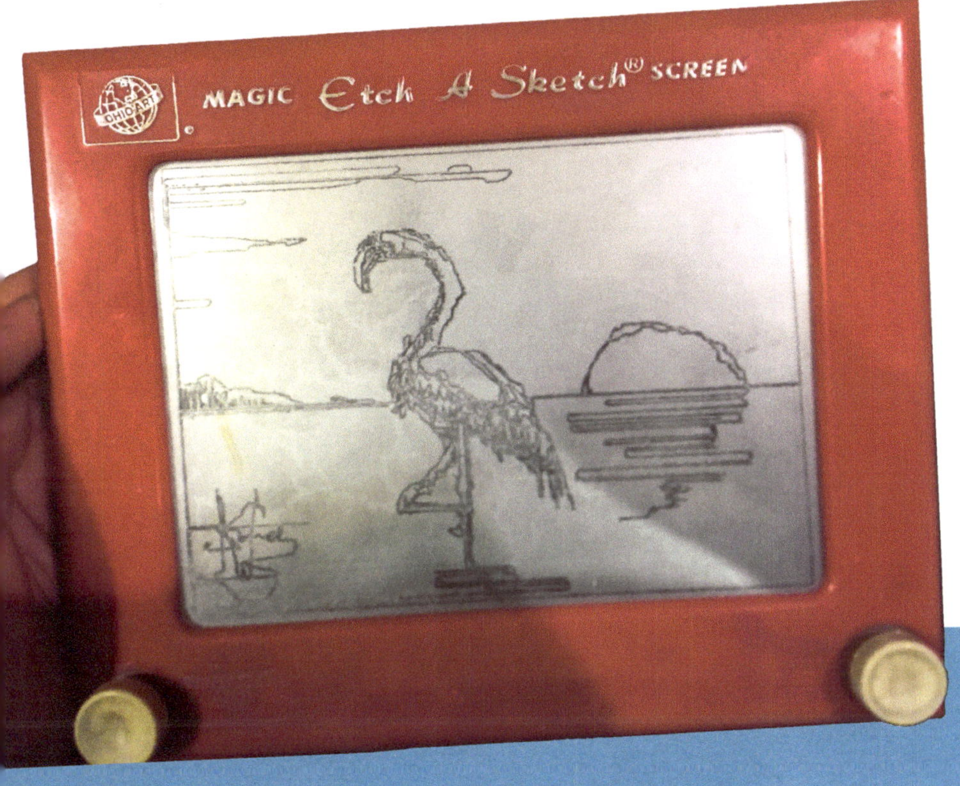

"Margaritaville"
Single Line Drawing
2018

Etch A Sketch®
9.06 L x 8.86 W Inches

Temporary
Zionsville, Indiana

"Ray's Crocs"
Sketch
2019

Paper
Graphite
12.0 L x 9.0 W Inches

Lost
Prior Lake, Minnesota

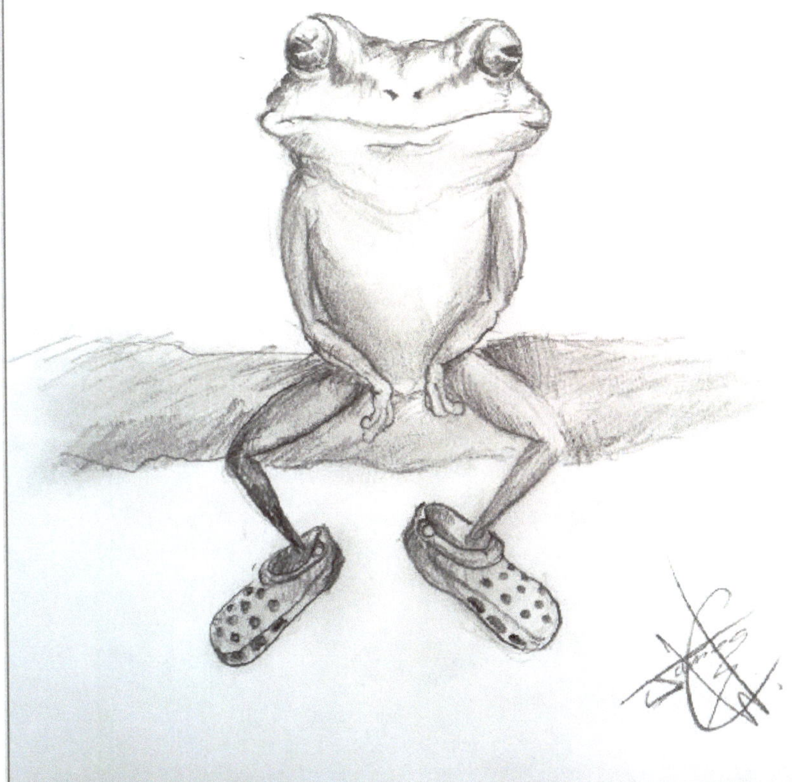

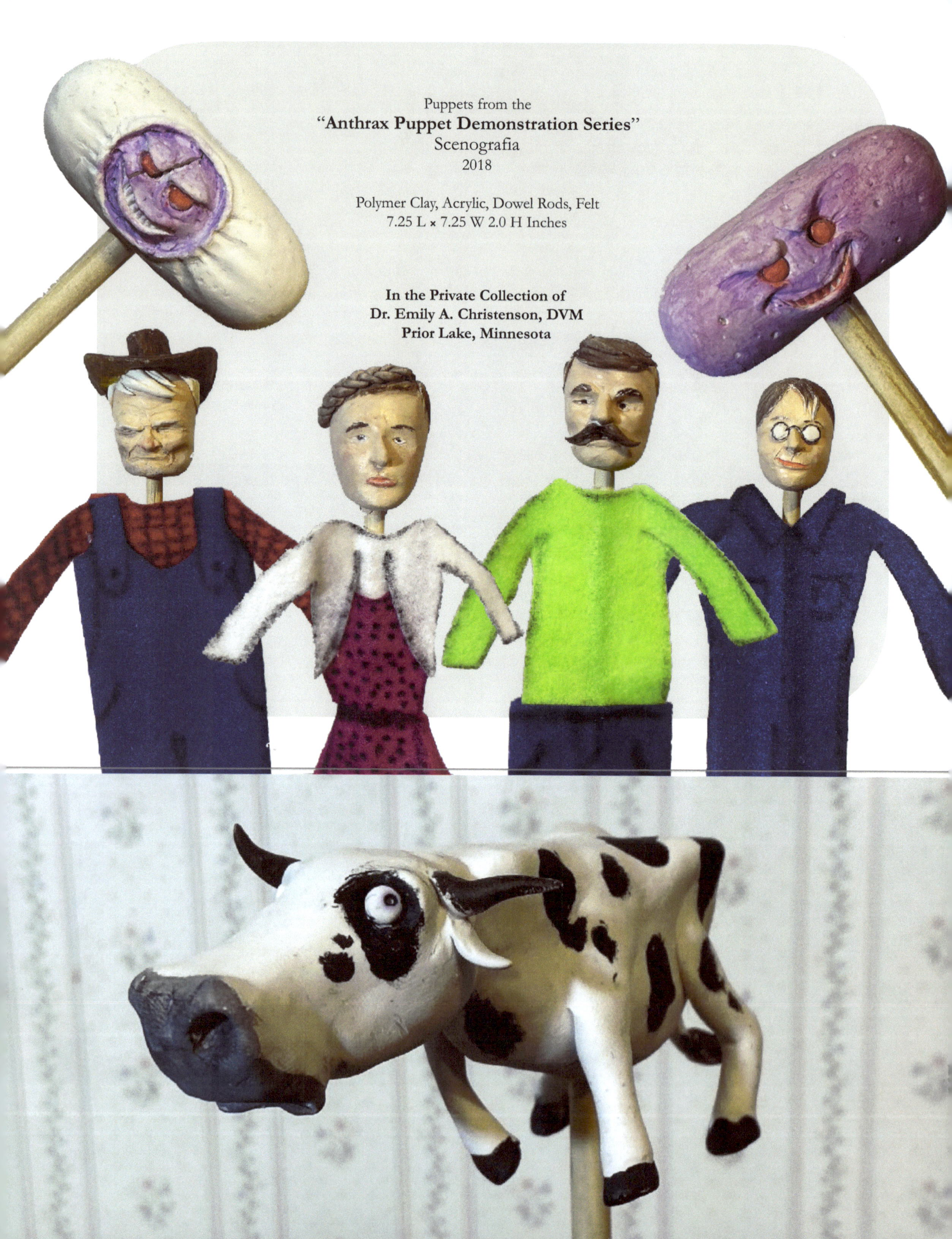
Puppets from the
"Anthrax Puppet Demonstration Series"
Scenografia
2018

Polymer Clay, Acrylic, Dowel Rods, Felt
7.25 L × 7.25 W 2.0 H Inches

In the Private Collection of
Dr. Emily A. Christenson, DVM
Prior Lake, Minnesota

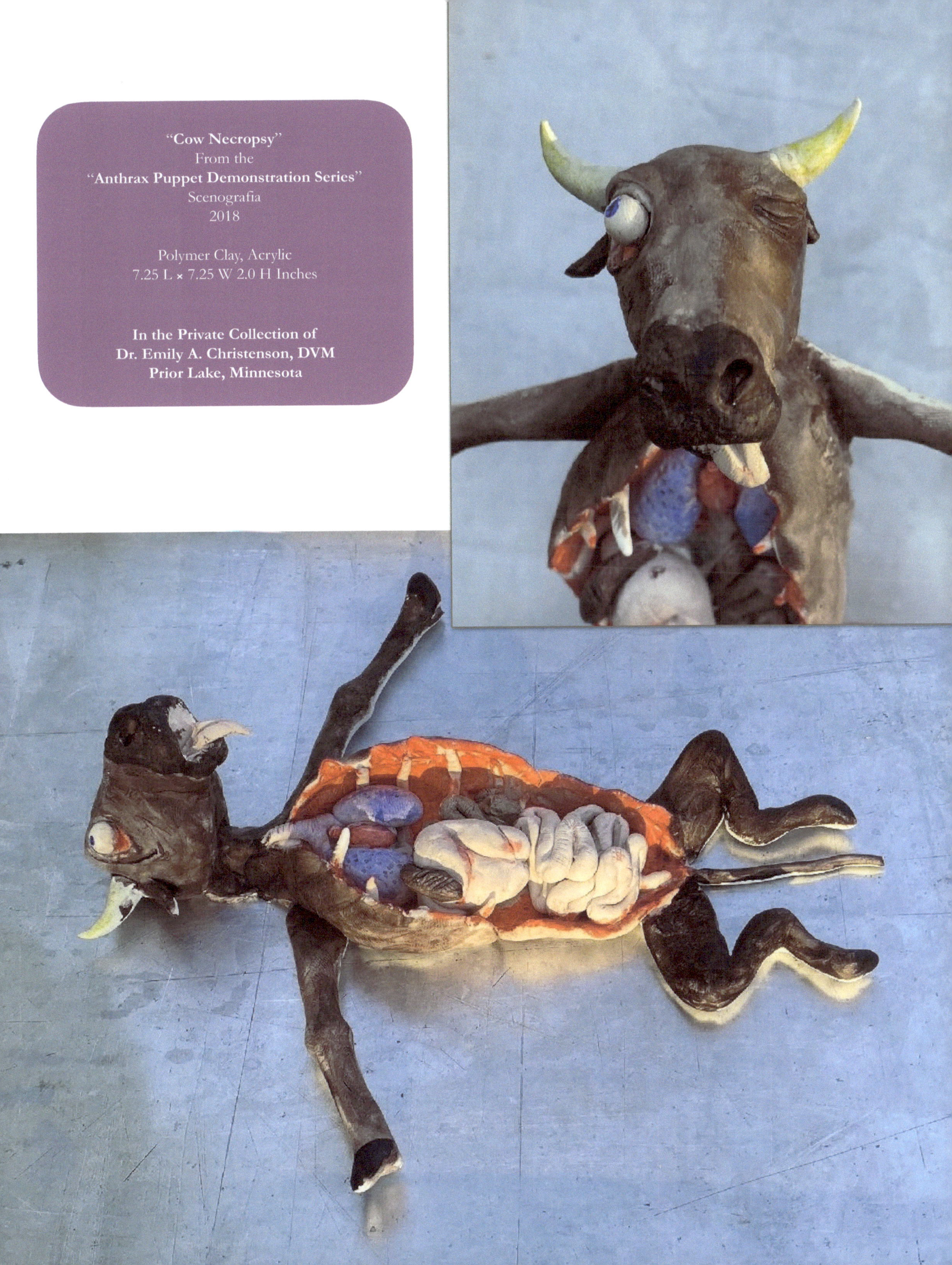

"Cow Necropsy"
From the
"Anthrax Puppet Demonstration Series"
Scenografia
2018

Polymer Clay, Acrylic
7.25 L × 7.25 W 2.0 H Inches

In the Private Collection of
Dr. Emily A. Christenson, DVM
Prior Lake, Minnesota

"Still Life"
2018

Paper
Graphite
12.0 L x 9.0 W Inches

In the Private Collection of
Palazzo Guglielmi
Burnsville, Minnesota
Reprinted with Permission

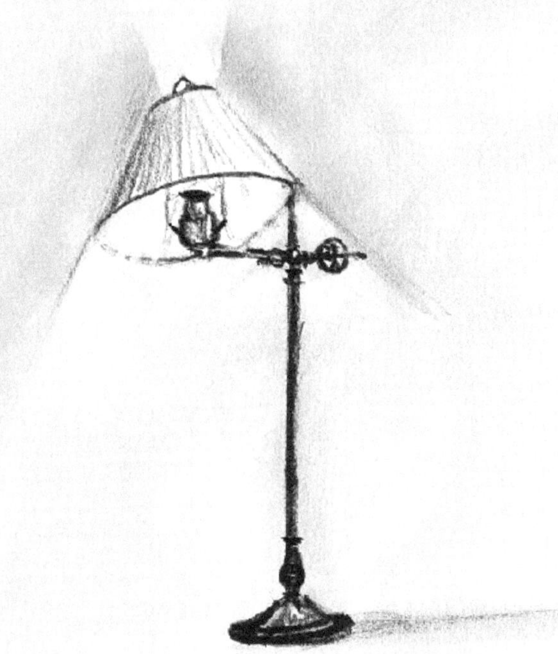

The Lamp Just Sat there...
Like an Inanimate Object.

"Two Loons"
Quick Character Sketch
2020

Paper
Graphite
8.5 L x 5.5 W Inches

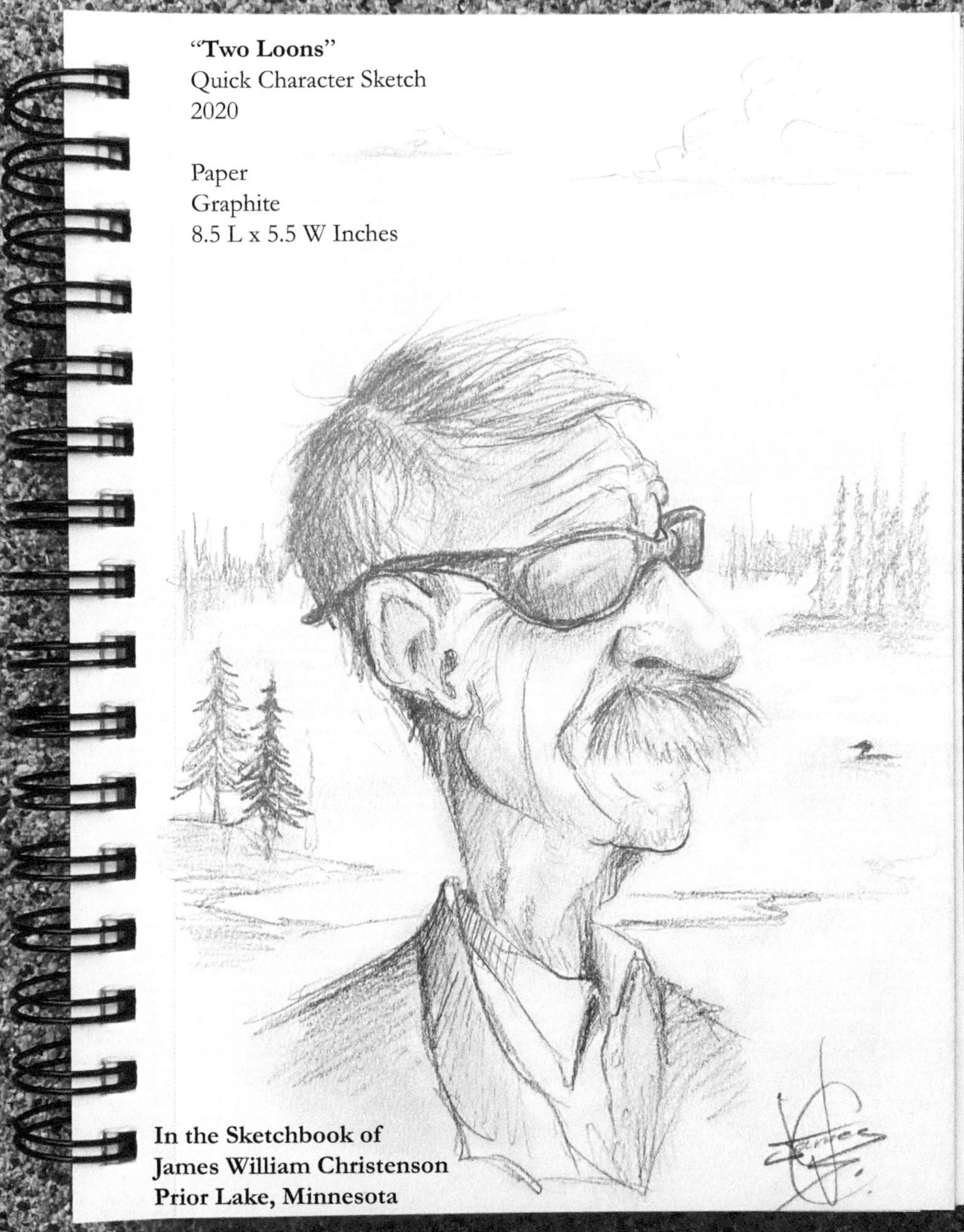

In the Sketchbook of
James William Christenson
Prior Lake, Minnesota

Before You Go

Thank You!

With so many books and different forms of entertainment available these days, it is such an honor and a delight to me that you chose to purchase *Effervescent Road Trip*. It is my sincere hope that you have had a surprisingly fun experience - even if it was a little surreal!

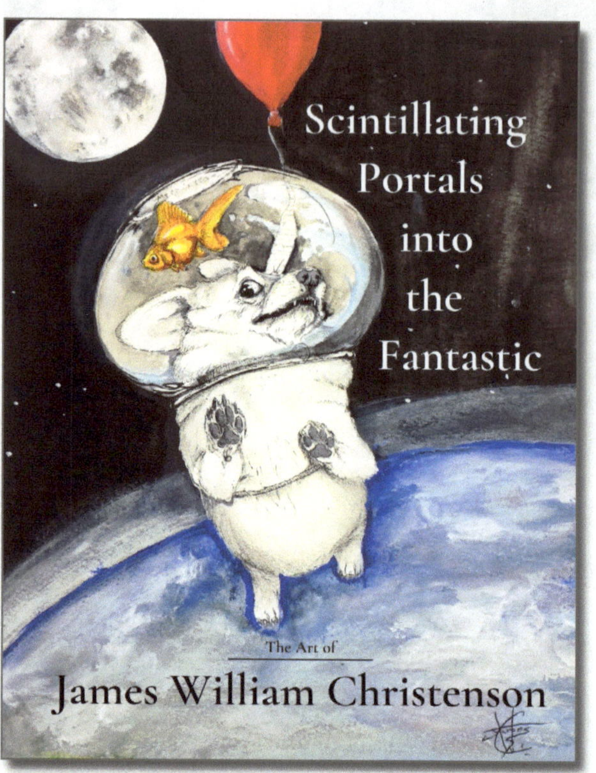

Other Books by James William Christenson

If you enjoyed *Effervescent Road Trip*, you will also enjoy *Scintillating Portals into the Fantastic*! Most pieces of artwork in this collection tell a story in an astonishingly diverse body of work. Nevertheless, there is a commonality: An often understated humor and a deeply ironic juxtaposition can be found in nearly all of his pieces. While certainly interesting in their own right, the real delight with James William's work is sharing it with others and watching their reactions or depth of observation. Multilayered and shared amusement gives deeper experiential depth to Christenson's work. *Scintillating Portals into the Fantastic!* is available today on Amazon.com and at other book sellers around the world.

Please Review!

Finally, if you enjoyed *Effervescent Road Trip*, would you consider leaving feedback on Amazon.com, your local art store, or your bookseller of choice? I would greatly appreciate it! These reviews also make this book more visible to those others who might not otherwise discover it. Everyone seems to request reviews these days, but your thoughts would be more than usually valued and appreciated!

Bonus points to the person with the most clever & fun review! Again, thank you.

All the best,

James William Christenson

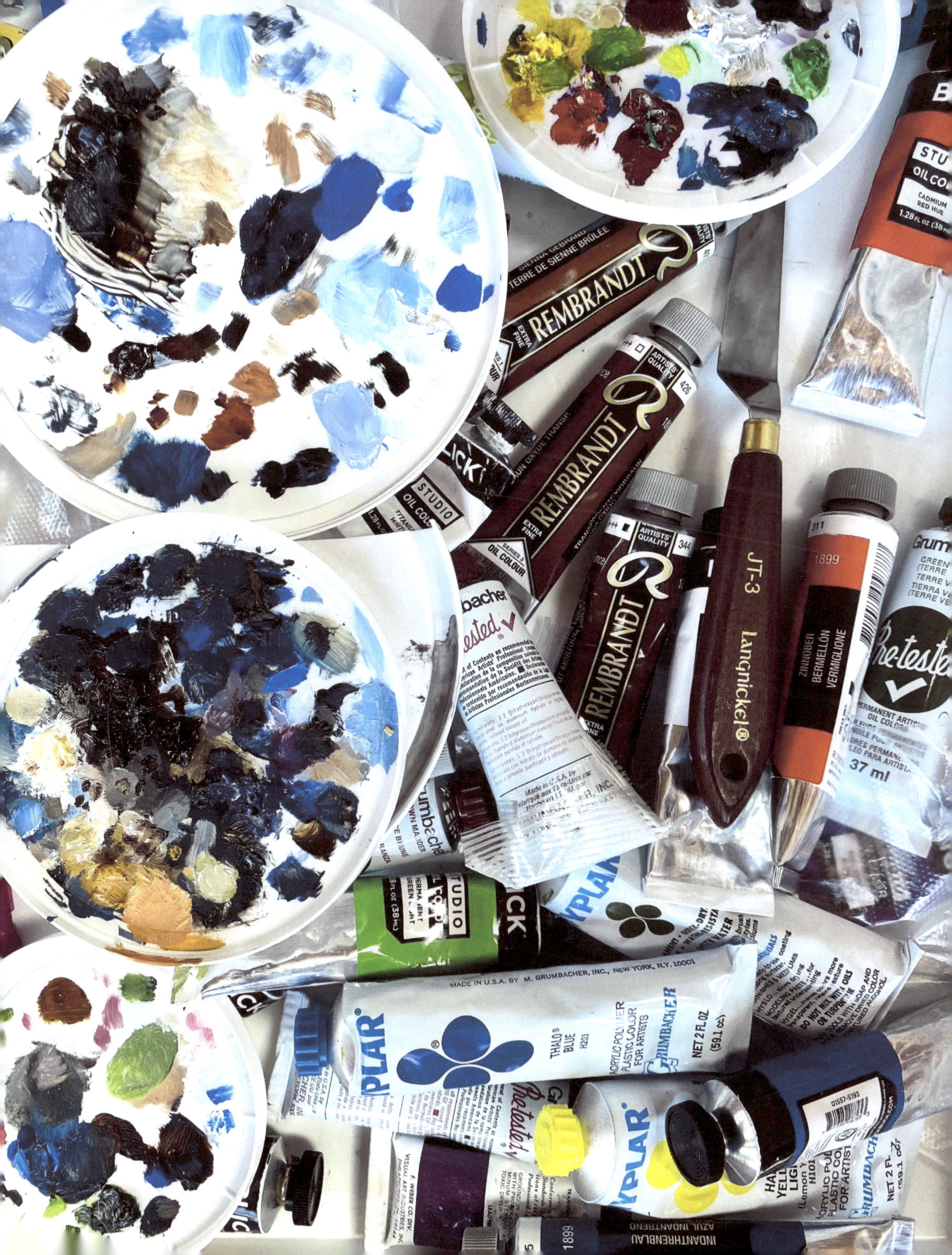
TERRE DE SIENNE BRÛLÉE
REMBRANDT
EXTRA FINE
ARTISTS' QUALITY
426
REMBRANDT
EXTRA FINE
SERIES 3
OIL COLOUR
ARTISTS' QUALITY
344
REMBRANDT
CADMIUM RED HUE
1.28 FL OZ
STUDIO
JT-3
Langnickel®
311
1899
ZINNOBER
BERMELLÓN
VERMIGLIONE
Pre-tested
37 ml
MADE IN U.S.A. BY M. GRUMBACHER, INC., NEW YORK, N.Y. 10001
THALO® BLUE H203
ACRYLIC POLYMER PLASTIC COLOR FOR ARTISTS
GRUMBACHER
NET 2 FL OZ (59.1 cc)
DO NOT MIX WITH OILS
01557-5193
AZUL INDANTRENO
INDANTHRENBLAU

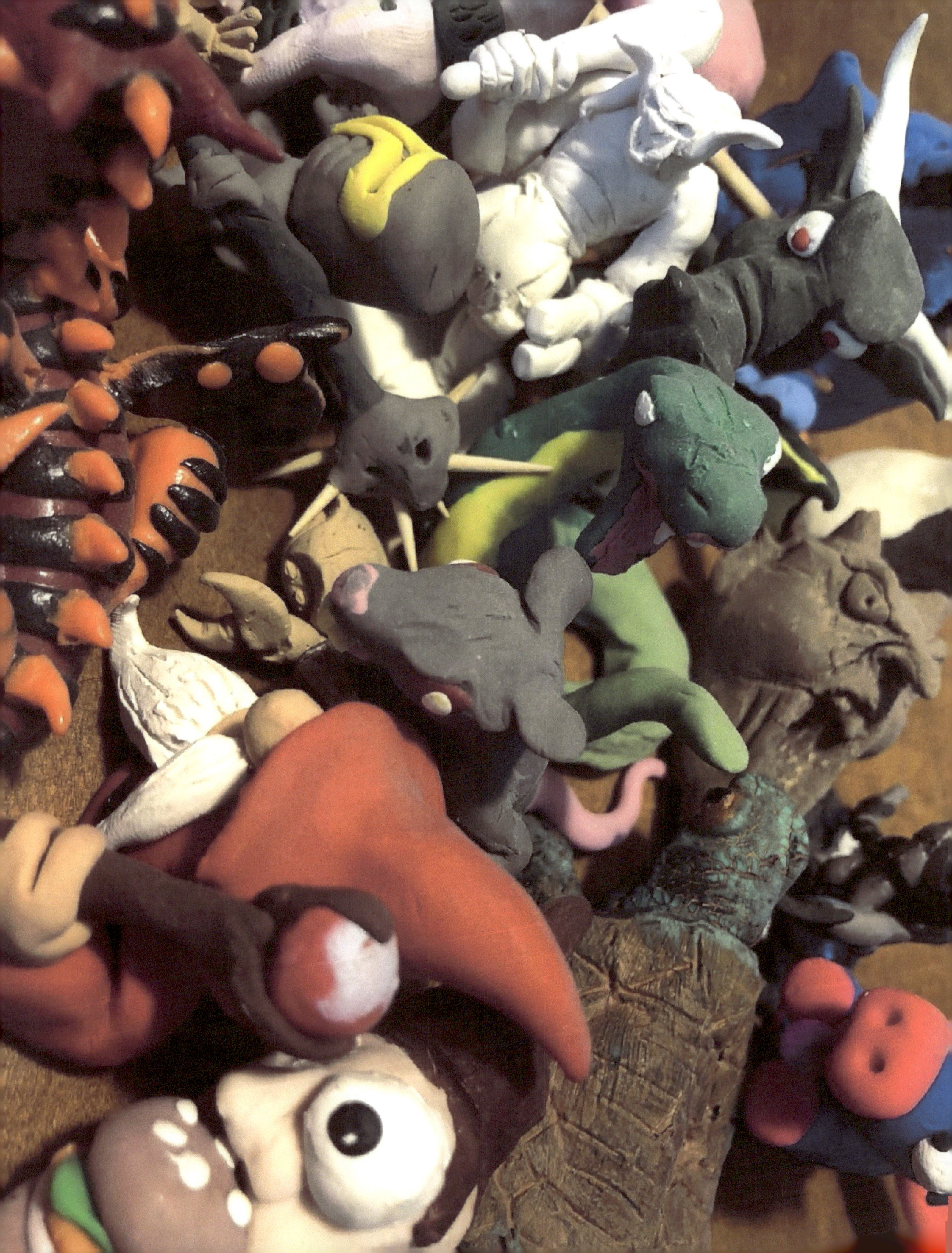

www.ingramcontent.com/pod-product-compliance
Lightning Source LLC
LaVergne TN
LVHW070123110826
845147LV00002B/177

9781732712935